Philosophy of the Teacher

D1352565

WITHDRAWN FROM
THE LIBRARY
UNIVERSITY OF
WINCHESTER

KA 0296243 8

Philosophy of the Teacher

Nigel Tubbs

Blackwell
Publishing

© 2005 by The Journal of the Philosophy of Education Society of Great Britain

First published as a special issue of *the Journal of Philosophy of Education*, 2005

BLACKWELL PUBLISHING
350 Main Street, Malden, MA 02148-5020, USA
9600 Garsington Road, Oxford OX4 2DQ, UK
550 Swanston Street, Carlton, Victoria 3053, Australia

The right of Nigel Tubbs to be identified as the Author of this Work has been asserted in accordance with the UK Copyright, Designs, and Patents Act 1988.

All rights reserved. No part of this publication may be reproduced, stored in a retrieval system, or transmitted, in any form or by any means, electronic, mechanical, photocopying, recording or otherwise, except as permitted by the UK Copyright, Designs, and Patents Act 1988, without the prior permission of the publisher.

First published 2005 by Blackwell Publishing Ltd

Library of Congress Cataloging-in-Publication Data has been applied for

ISBN 1-4051-3886-6

A catalogue record for this title is available from the British Library.

Set in Advent 3B2
by Macmillan India Ltd.
Printed and bound in the UK
by TJ International, Padstow, Cornwall

The publisher's policy is to use permanent paper from mills that operate a sustainable forestry policy, and which has been manufactured from pulp processed using acid-free and elementary chlorine-free practices. Furthermore, the publisher ensures that the text paper and cover board used have met acceptable environmental accreditation standards.

For further information on
Blackwell Publishing, visit our website:
www.blackwellpublishing.com

UNIVERSITY OF WINCHESTER

370.1 TUB | 02962438

Contents

Acknowledgement to the Cover Artist

I am very grateful to Jess Wood for allowing me to put her painting on the cover of *Philosophy of the Teacher*. In its beautiful and tender way, it conveys broken middles between slavery and freedom, transcendence and roots, ancient and modern; and yet, at the same time, puts the teacher between these dualisms and re-presents their difficult relation to each other. This teacher's diaspora is exile from heaven as from earth. Yet with his hand on his heart his teaching is also his prayer. It is to the idea of the teacher as within broken relationships between teacher and student, and between theory and practice, and to the spirit of the teacher working within broken relationships of ancient and modern, reason and faith, and philosophy and education, that this book, and its graceful cover, is offered.

Preface

How, as a serving teacher, can one come to think better about one's practice? How can one understand the strange contradictions with which one is confronted? How address them? How be a better teacher? And how as a teacher educator, or as someone whose research seeks the better to understand the context and the engagement of education, can one think about these questions with greater precision, with deeper insight, in more penetrating ways? These are questions to which Nigel Tubbs' *Philosophy of the Teacher* responds.

The book in effect offers two texts in one. Its central section speaks to the serving teacher about the nature of the experience of teaching, but this is framed within a broader, more theoretical discussion, which analyses and challenges dominant positions in the philosophy of education and examines the cultural conditions within which all this takes place. The result is a rationale for, and account of, an understanding of teaching that reveals tensions in the very experience – tensions that most teachers feel but that rarely figure in theorisations of their work, let alone in familiar prescriptions for better practice.

Nigel Tubbs brings to this project not only the wealth of his own experience in the education of teachers but also profound knowledge of a tradition of philosophy that has always been alert to the complex pressures that teaching and learning exact; his experience of realising these philosophical ideas in practice is reflected in these pages. The result is a challenge to anyone interested in the good of education and the qualities in teachers that this requires.

Paul Standish
Series Editor

Acknowledgements

I would like to express my thanks to Paul Standish for his suggesting how this project might be pursued, and for his generous and graceful way of encouraging critique of and improvements in the text; to Marianna Papastephanou, John Drummond and Ian McPherson for helpful comments on parts of the text; to Julie, for her emotional and editorial support when it was most needed; to Adrian Money who commented on Part II at an early stage; and above all to the students at King Alfred's College, soon to be the University of Winchester, who have helped to shape the form and content of the project with their work on courses in *The Power of the Teacher* and *The Philosophy of the Teacher*.

Dedication:

To Pete, Barbara, Kate and Dan.

Introduction

> [N]o human thinking can escape from contradiction. Contradiction itself, far from always being a criterion of error, is sometimes a sign of truth (Weil, 1988, p. 173).

> Marianne Weber said of her husband Max Weber that he was 'moved, above all, by the fact that on its earthly course an idea always and everywhere operates in opposition to its original meaning and thereby destroys itself' (Bottomore and Nisbet, 1978, p. 362).

It is necessary, to begin with, to say a little about the structure and style of this study of the teacher. Its three parts are very carefully and deliberately demarcated. Originally the whole project consisted only of Part II, *The Experience of the Teacher*. It was to be a short, provocative text designed for existing teachers and student teachers. It limited its objective to making available to them a variety of political and philosophical material that would speak directly to some of the dilemmas and contradictions that teachers face in their practice and in their thinking about that practice. It was structured in particular around the difficult relation between authority and freedom, and played out between the characters of the master and the servant as they appear famously within Hegel's *Phenomenology of Spirit*. This part of the now, newly enlarged volume remains intact. It is still written for teachers and can stand being read without reference to the rest of the book. It is, in effect, a book within a book and its tone is more conversational than Parts I and III. As a result I hope that teacher educators may direct their students to Part II with the confidence that no prior reading or knowledge is required. Part II also encourages teacher educators and other tutors in universities and colleges to see their own dilemmas reflected in the same text.

The book has, however, developed much further than its original rather limited objective. Part II is now sandwiched between a full philosophical assault upon many current perspectives within the philosophy of education and educational theory in general. This critique is launched by invoking the concept of the 'broken middle' against abstract and sceptical forms of reasoning that refuse to recognise the experience of abstraction or scepticism as a substantial philosophical education. In Part I the question of the broken middle is raised in terms of the relationship between education and philosophy, and, in particular, in and around the suppression of education and philosophy as a *culture* of modern abstract experience. Part III offers a speculative (educational and philosophical) interpretation of three philosophers who are most commonly assumed to be opposed to each other in one way or another: Hegel, Nietzsche and Kierkegaard.

The argument presented here is that these three thinkers, in their different ways, understand the culture, the *re-formation*, of philosophy and education by each other within modern social and political relations—or, what amounts to the same thing, within the domination of abstraction. As a result, they are examples of how the modern and broken *experience* of philosophy and education is both educational and philosophical. In Part III, then, the logic and substance of modern experience introduced in Part I, and observed in Part II, is retrieved from within the different ways that Hegel, Nietzsche and Kierkegaard comprehend the formation and re-formation of this experience. Part II becomes here the work of the broken middle—that is, the experience of the broken middle; this is work that is re-presented more abstractly in Parts I and III.

What marks out the work of Hegel, Nietzsche and Kierkegaard in particular against postmodern and post-structuralist interpretations is that, first, they recognise and work within the limits that abstraction, in all its domination, imposes; second, they recognise this domination within the aporia of reasoning that re-presents it; third, they do not posit the overcoming or non-overcoming of such domination; but fourth, they do not disavow their philosophical education within these difficult and contradictory experiences. What is meant by 'contradictory experiences' is crucial here. It might be thought that it refers, for example, to the conflict between two educational perspectives, say, that between R. S. Peters and Lyotard. However, contradiction obtains not just between positions but also within the standpoint of positions, within what we shall call *natural consciousness*. This contradiction is of an altogether different order of philosophical and educational significance. This significance lies in the fact that, on the one hand there is no avoiding the presenting of positions and that, on the other, each such positing suppresses the experience of it that one has, and so in that respect is illusory. In short, Hegel, Nietzsche and Kierkegaard know they must work with the re-presentation of the modern political form of natural consciousness, for that is who they are, and who we are. As we will see, attempts to reconcile, overcome, not-overcome or aestheticise contradictory experiences do not take the domination of our abstract natural consciousness over our philosophical experiences seriously enough and in effect elide current political conditions. This natural consciousness can be educated regarding itself and its deformations; but it cannot be assumed either as having been overcome and replaced by something new, for example, some new ethical relation, nor, in cultural terms, as remaining untouched by its critical work and as merely an empty reproduction. Part II lets these contradictory experiences for the teacher speak for themselves, whilst Parts I and III explore different ways in which natural consciousness both dominates and is dominated. This exploration requires that the latter are written at a more difficult level than Part II and are directed more immediately to an academic audience.[1]

But let me ask finally: who will want a philosophy of the teacher as it is presented here? The answer, I hope, is any teacher who feels, deep down, that there are educational truths in what they are doing that remain unrecognised not only within their schools, colleges or universities, but also within the theoretical perspectives that are designed to serve such work. I know now that, when I was training to be a teacher, I needed a philosophy of the teacher that could speak from within my own difficulties with theory and practice, with control and authority, and with the teacher–student relationship—the kinds of anxieties that, at some time, are common to all teachers. But in educational work on the teacher I found no real philosophy (that is, no real *speculative* philosophy, as I shall come to explain), and in philosophy there was very little interest in education in general or in the teacher in particular. Perhaps this book will find others now who are searching for the same thing, even if, as yet, they do not know it quite in this way.

*

In addressing this book, also, to the academic audience of philosophers of education and educational theorists, I note in advance that educational theory in general, and philosophy of education in particular, have developed a variety of different camps from which intellectual skirmishes are fought with each other. Seldom, however, do I think they stray far enough from these shored positions ever to learn about themselves from within their relation to each other. If a philosophy of the teacher is to be presented, it would, I am sure, be a safer strategy to join one of these camps: perhaps the analytic camp of the founding fathers of the modern incarnation of the philosophy of education; perhaps the post-foundational thinkers who collectively eschew the possibility of the identity of such camps; perhaps the critical pedagogues with their interest in collective emancipation; or perhaps the academic journalists who merely comment on the state of the campaigns.

At the risk of biting the hand that feeds and for reasons that will slowly be revealed, however, the philosophy of the teacher that I am presenting here can join none of these camps. For the philosophy of the teacher as it is pursued here, these alternatives represent at most half-told stories that have more in common with each other than they do with the no-mans land between them, a land that is after all their *casus belli*. It is into this no-man's land that the following account now strays, aware of being shot at by all sides. But, even at this early stage, let it be made clear that the philosophy of the teacher being presented is not a philosophy found growing like grass between the warring factions, in some Deleuzian sense; rather, it is the representation in philosophy and education of the broken relation between them.

There is an altogether different form and content of philosophy to those listed above, one that refuses to acknowledge politely the differences between these perspectives. It is what might be called the speculative tradition. There are reasons why this has had little impact within educational theorising,[2] and some of these will be explored in due course in terms of *culture* and *experience*. It is in this tradition, I shall argue, that a different form of the relation between philosophy and education can be retrieved. In essence, what I want to show is how philosophy and education share a *telos* that does not replace analytic or critical traditions, or postmodern and post-structuralist visions, but actually is the truth of their collective illusions. As such, speculative philosophy is not an alternative to any of the perspectives within education, for it is to be found within their forms of reasoning and in particular the illusions carried therein. This claim, no doubt, already turns many against it, for it seems to offer a kind of meta-critique over and above the whole of educational theorising. This, however, is not the case. What the speculative experience can provide, which other perspectives do not, is a re-presentation of the conditions of the possibility of each of these philosophical representations. Because speculative philosophy knows abstraction, with all its dominant force, to be the pre-condition of any thinking at all, it is more deeply entwined within contingency even than those perspectives that claim contingency or historicism as their starting point. Indeed, there is a dependency here that must be acknowledged. Speculative philosophy arises out of and against the inevitable abstractions of these other perspectives. It is the philosophical experience of their opposition to each other and to themselves.

Yet the speculative reaches even further into the heart of philosophising. The abstract forms of analytical philosophy and the anti-foundationalist forms of post-Enlightenment philosophy do not count within the speculative as genuinely philosophical at all. This is because their ways of working are seen to suppress philosophical experiences by refusing to allow these experiences to become their *own* content, to think about themselves as their own (obviously compromised) condition of possibility. The experience of this suppression is at its clearest when theorising seems to circulate between opposing positions (that is, between different positings), each used to undermine the other, and each giving the appearance that a comprehensive perspective can never be reached. The 'debate' between these camps becomes interminable, each pointing out contradictions in the others' arguments but few making the experience of these oppositions the subject and substance of educational and philosophical enquiry. The experience of this ritual that passes for philosophising has its own substance, and if thinking is ever to do justice to itself and to its own misrecognitions, it is this that needs to be explored in its own right. Therefore, in what follows, the philosophy of the teacher seeks to expose and take seriously this suppression of philosophical experience in some of its many forms. This will not win friends among those who find themselves accused of such suppression and who reside in one of the many camps that seek ways of overcoming the domination of modern abstract consciousness (unaware how they remain complicit with it). But perhaps, in a sense, the philosophy of the teacher can speak directly to their experiences as teachers or students of one kind or another. The overall design of the book aims to achieve this.

NOTES

1. But that is not to say that Parts I and III cannot be read by students and teachers alike. I have over thirteen years worth of essays that show that undergraduates can deal with, indeed often demand, such difficult material.
2. Clearly the Idealist tradition has had an impact in education. However, this has largely been the kind of right-wing Hegelianism that offers only a one-sided approach to Hegel. Equally, Hegelian-inspired left-wing critical theory has been and continues to be a major player in educational theorising. What has not made an impact is speculative reasoning, defined here as the relation between, and the identity and non-identity of, philosophy as education and education as philosophy. For those interested in a more detailed account of this speculative relation and its representation of *philosophy's higher education*, I have explored this in *Philosophy's Higher Education* (Tubbs, 2004). In many ways, the current volume on the philosophy of the teacher is a companion piece to this slightly earlier book, which explains in greater philosophical detail the kind of argument I am making here.

Part I

The Broken Middle of Philosophy, Education and Culture

Chapter 1
Philosophy in Education and Education in Philosophy

THINKING PHILOSOPHICALLY

It is the aim of this opening chapter to retrieve the educational significance of speculative experience from within the contradictions of different forms of educational theorising. This means philosophising with a Janus face, turned towards both its contingency within the conditions of its possibility, and its experience of its freedom in recognising these conditions. I will show below how some perspectives within the philosophy of education and educational theorising adopt only one-sided positions towards this aporetic modern experience of freedom and necessity. The cost of doing so is the suppression of philosophy and education as *relation*. Those who would seek *either* to free us from *or* further to engulf us within the scepticisms of historicism in fact only reinvent ever more ingenious ways to dominate the aporias that define both attempts. It is philosophy—and here philosophy has to mean speculative philosophy—wherein aporia can have educational and formative significance for both sides in the dispute. To introduce the way that the recent work of Gillian Rose underpins this philosophical perspective, I begin by noting that she describes the significance of modern social relations upon modern thinking in the following way:

> I mean to draw attention to a construal (which I could call Hegel *or* Nietzsche) which has expounded the autonomous moral subject as free within the order of representations and unfree within its preconditions and outcomes, and modernity as the working out of that combination (Rose, 1996, p. 57).

To illustrate what is meant by the philosophical experience borne in and by speculative thinking, I will turn at this early stage to Hegel and Kierkegaard, and return in a moment to Rose's notion of 'the broken middle'.

Hegel distinguishes between our natural consciousness and our philosophical consciousness. The former is the consciousness that experiences the world as it appears. The latter is our thinking about those experiences, but it also contains a further opposition within it. There is a consciousness that relates, now, to the relation between natural and philosophical consciousness. This third partner in the work of recognition and misrecognition is *spirit* and it takes different forms at different times in history within different social and political relations. In the sense that philosophical consciousness is known to itself in a way that natural consciousness is not, we can say that, for Hegel, philosophical thinking is our thinking about thinking. But it is important to remember the triadic and not the dualistic nature of this activity. If spirit is not recognised as a representation of the (negative) relation between thought and object, then there is neither philosophy nor education in the relation, and thought is denied its participation in the antithesis by which it is known to itself. Spirit is not the resolution of the relation between natural and philosophical consciousness, it is the form in which their relation appears for us, a form that is characterised by recognition *and* misrecognition. Against readings of spirit in Hegel that argue for spirit as final, as the suppression of others, and as imperialism, Rose counters that spirit in Hegel's *Phenomenology* 'means the drama of misrecognition that ensues at every stage and transition of the work—a ceaseless comedy, according to which our aims and outcomes constantly mismatch each other, and provoke yet another revised aim, action and discordant outcomes' (Rose, 1996, p. 72). Spirit in this sense, as the opposition of theory and practice, has immediate import for the experience of teachers.

Our philosophical consciousness arises, then, in our experience of the surprises and unintended outcomes that reason provides for us. Hegel says that since natural consciousness 'directly takes itself to be real knowledge' (1977, p. 49) then these experiences that oppose it have 'a negative significance for it, and ... count for it rather as the loss of its own self' (ibid.). One might imagine here a teacher who, after a disappointing lesson, comes to question whether or not she really is good enough to be a teacher. Doubts creep in and undermine her belief in herself as able to perform effectively. There is here something distinctly uncomfortable but at the same time educational about such experiences. Left merely as doubt, such thoughts can be insidious and undermining. But within the philosophy of the teacher as it will be explored below, these doubts are formative, for they educate us to realise that comprehension is always 'provisional and preliminary' (Rose, 1996, p. 72). This, says Rose, is 'the meaning of *Bildung*, of formation or education, which is intrinsic to the [Hegelian] phenomenological process' (ibid.). This education is where the truth of the relation between teacher and students becomes also the truth of the teacher who, in relation to herself, is the philosophical teacher. What is significant in this account is that spirit and education as provisional can sit alongside the realisation of the absolute.[1] We must suspend for the moment an examination of the 'difference' that such educative relations can make for the practitioner.

Of course, when things get *too* difficult we often seek consolation by not thinking too much. That, however, will not do for a philosophy of the teacher whose business is precisely the difficulties of learning and education. Besides which, there is one final and dramatic conclusion that

Hegel draws from this education of consciousness about its knowledge of and relation to the 'real' world. If anyone were to try to withdraw from the difficulties presented to them by the negation of certainties, he argues that they would find this impossible. We are always experiencing the world negatively. It is never how it first appears. Our philosophical consciousness always undermines any stability we might fleetingly claim. Hegel states here:

> consciousness suffers this violence [of negation and of philosophy] at its own hands: it spoils its own limited satisfaction. When consciousness feels this violence, its anxiety may well make it retreat from the truth, and strive to hold on to what it is in danger of losing. But it can find no peace. If it wishes to remain in a state of unthinking inertia, then thought troubles its thoughtlessness, and its own unrest disturbs its inertia (p. 51).

Thus we might say that for Hegel education is as inevitable and as unavoidable as experience, the only difference being that our philosophical consciousness is often poorly educated in how to understand itself in relation to natural consciousness *as* learning and *as* education.

Kierkegaard has a slightly different way of exploring the same idea of philosophy as thinking about experience. When we ask a question, he says, we are admitting to not knowing (the truth of) something. He says that by asking about the truth I am also experiencing the absence of truth, or untruth. I am in doubt. Again the educational experience here is a negative one. Doubt is what brings natural consciousness into relation with another aspect of itself, the self-consciousness or awareness that knows that it doubts. Consciousness therefore learns about itself from within this relation. It brings what we know into relation with what we do not know, and into a further relation with the consciousness that knows that it does not know. This consciousness he calls the third partner in a relation between truth and untruth (see Kierkegaard, 1985, p. 169). Like Hegel's notion of spirit, this third partner is our way of knowing the experience of opposition between knowing and not-knowing. It is our learning that we do not know from within difficult experiences and irresolvable dilemmas. In the philosophies of the teacher presented below in Part III, including from Kierkegaard, each, in different ways, shows how teachers can learn from the oppositions that they experience.

These two philosophical ways of thinking about thinking will be implicit within the experiences of the teacher described in terms of master and servant outlined in Part II below. In Part III they will appear more explicitly as ways in which teachers' work can be philosophically comprehended as the experience, the relation, of the master and servant. To anticipate this, we can say here that the teacher who, in a philosophical sense, appears as master represents the certainty of our natural consciousness. He is the enlightened one, the one who is sure enough of the world to induct others into it. The teacher who appears philosophically as servant, on the other hand, represents the negation of the identity of that master and of his understanding of his work. These teachers, in a variety of ways, seek to negate the students' immediate understandings of the world through the doubts that are produced by critical questioning and thinking. In addition, they aim to reveal to the students not only how those understandings are dependent upon the world as it is, but also how they prevent different ideas about how the world might be, or should be, from being taught or even thought about. These teachers aim to serve the critical education of their students by teaching for what some call deconstruction and others see in terms of emancipation. If certainty, or natural consciousness, is the 'identity' of the master and doubt is the 'identity' of the servant, then potentially, together, as the experience of what we will come to see as the broken middle, they are the contradictory or oppositional relation that is the philosophical teacher.

It is necessary to keep in mind that in these two philosophical models what is of central importance to the two consciousnesses is that they are inextricably related to each other in and by thought. For both Hegel and Kierkegaard the *experience* of doubting what we know is *the third partner* in any duality, or the relation of certainty to doubt. It is this experience that the study that follows takes as philosophy proper, and that means as philosophy and education. For Hegel as for Kierkegaard, natural consciousness is always what we know, and philosophical consciousness is the doubt and uncertainty of 'knowing' what we know. But they cannot exist apart from each other. As such, certainty without doubt is blind for it does not know of itself, and doubt without certainty is empty for it has no content of its own. It is only in their relation to each other that natural consciousness and philosophical consciousness produce the work that is our (philosophical) learning and education. It is this relation wherein we will find the philosophy of the teacher.

THE BROKEN MIDDLE

Gillian Rose has sought to retrieve the speculative experience for philosophy against what she believed was the domination of the neo-Kantian tradition.

> Philosophy as I practise it has a different orientation based on a different logic and a different story. From Plato to Marx, I would argue, it is always possible to take the claims and conceptuality of philosophical works (I say 'works' not 'texts': the former implying the labour of the concept inseparable from its formal characteristics as opposed to the latter with its connotations of signifiers, the symbolic and semiotics) *deterministically* or *aporetically*—as fixed, closed structures, colonising being with the garrison of thought; or according to the difficulty which the conceptuality represents by leaving gaps and silences in the mode of representation (Rose, 1996, pp. 7–8).

Around the term 'the broken middle', Rose argues that the latter approach, the aporetic, galvanises 'the difficulty of thinking in the wake of disaster, without generating any fantasy of mending the world' (p. 9). Refusing the consolation of repairing that which appears broken, Rose finds the speculative experience to be where our modern experiences find themselves, not only re-presenting a broken middle, but also determining that re-presentation in and by their own thinking. It is one of the implications of the broken middle that whilst not being able to repair that which we separate without re-presenting that separation, we can nevertheless seek to renew our own understanding of this most ancient way of thinking. Part of this renewal means comprehending how the torn halves of the middle are most often related to each other without reference to the *philosophical* experience of their separation. This is where the appearance of the dualisms of modern and postmodern, theory and practice, subject and object, etc., relate to each other as oppositions but without such dualisms being experienced as the broken middle of education and philosophy. It is as if philosophical experience, when it is characterised by the aporetic, the difficult, has no substance at all, and is to be suppressed, again, in favour of one side of the dualism or the other. This misrecognition and suppression of philosophical education affects philosophy as much as educational theorising.

Kant's separation of the necessary but unknowable transcendental law and the realm of practical ethics have shaped philosophy since his time in very particular ways. His diremption of metaphysics and ethics underpins many subsequent dualisms. How can universal, unknowable, *a priori* metaphysical laws become at one and the same time particular moral actions chosen freely by autonomous persons in civil society? In particular, it becomes the question of theory and practice. Yet this question of theory and practice, of metaphysics and ethics, is not itself experienced by persons from within the broken middle of their relation. Rather, it is experienced, or appears to be experienced, exclusively from the side of the person: how can I be free and yet obey? How can I be autonomous yet also under metaphysical *a priori* necessities? What is of absolute significance here is that it is within the *personal* experience that the problem comes to be judged. The illusion here, borne by all modern reflection, is that the object of experience is not also the experience of the object. By this chiasmus I mean to draw attention to the way that experience works with a concept of the object that has already formed the relation between experience and the object. The representation of that prior political relation, and the repetition of that representation, is the universal that then defines the relation between universal and particular as aporetic. In other words, the universal—we might say here the transcendent—is present in the conditions that rule out its possibility of being known. The recognition of this misrecognition is our education regarding the illusions of the appearance of the universal in relation to the particular. This cannot be separated from the political forms that illusion takes. This contingency forms the substance of speculative enquiry.

This relation to the relation, or the difficulty that is education and philosophy, is the no-man's land where one gets shot at from all sides. For the analytic mind such speculation is not pure reason; for the post-foundationalist mind it is absolutely pure reason. The former retains a purer form of metaphysics; the latter retains a purer form of ethics. Western-style philosophy is currently riven into this division.

In her early work Rose offered critiques of the two paradigms that emerged out of the illusions of the personal perspective.[2] The paradigm of *method* gave priority to the question of the rules of the synthesis of perceptions into objects of enquiry, and their validity, and culminated in Durkheim's social facts *sui generis*. Alternatively, the paradigm of *morality* gave priority to the legitimacy of values, culminating in Weber's sociology of culture. A more recent development, more pertinent to the philosophy of education, and to educational theorising in particular, is the way that the relation of method and morality is played out between the grounding and non-grounding of values. I will explore this in some detail in the following sections of this chapter. Suffice to say at this point that philosophies of education and educational theory have powerful voices within them arguing the case for ethical relations. Such calls are often borne out of frustrations with—some would say failures of—the ability of the metaphysical to sustain clear and objective values. Instead of the illusory and imperialist objectivity of a transcendental ethic, there is a clamour for a 'new ethics' (Rose, 1996, p. 1), one generated without metaphysical presuppositions, and created out of genuine, perhaps face-to-face encounters. On the one hand, the desire behind such new ethics exhibits 'a low tolerance of equivocation' (p. 2), whilst nevertheless claiming elements of the same for the ethic of the encounter. On the other hand, the speed with which ethics permits itself to claim 'the other' for itself as its philosophical object, even in claiming it as totally other, bears witness to the poverty of philosophical experience in educational terms. When ethics begins with the other, philosophy, and its ability to comprehend the social and political formation of the concept of the other, and our own determination in relation to that formation, is deemed to be at an end.

What Rose writes of the warring between the libertarians of free market exchange and the communitarians of 'ethnic and gender pluralities' (p. 5) applies also to the warring camps in education, where battles rage between the individual virtues and moral objectivity of the *phronimos* (in many guises), on the one hand, and the pluralism implicit in the many manifestations of the ethical, on the other.

> These two apparently warring engagements have a lot in common; and they participate in the very archetype which they claim to overthrow ... By maligning all putative universality as 'totalitarian' and seeking to liberate the 'individual' or the 'plurality' from domination, both ... disqualify themselves from any understanding of the actualities of structure and authority, intrinsic to any conceivable social and political constitution and which their opposed stances still leave intact (Rose, 1996, p. 4).

Rose saves her sharpest criticisms for the philosophers who, she says, 'blame philosophy for the ills of civilisation [and] have themselves lost the ability to perceive the difference between thought and being, thought and action' (1995, p. 118). Indeed, Rose finds here a suppression of the relation between education and philosophy that, whilst claiming for itself the high ethical ground of non-foundationalism, has in fact only served to reinforce the illusions inherent in modern social relations. She writes,

> terrified of their own inner insecurity at the border between rationality and conflict, between the new academic political Protestantism and politics as the art of the possible, they proceed as if to terminate philosophy would be to dissolve the difficulty of acknowledging conflict and of staking oneself within it. To destroy philosophy, to abolish or to supersede critical, self-conscious reason, would leave us resourceless to know the difference between fantasy and actuality, to discern the distortion between ideas and their realisation. It would prevent the process of learning, the corrigibility of experience. This ill-will towards philosophy misunderstands the authority of reason, which is not the mirror of the dogma of superstition, but risk. Reason, the critical criterion, is forever without ground (1995, pp. 118–119).

It will be argued in what follows that this speculative working of philosophy offers a philosophy of the teacher that addresses the same kinds of problems as those outlined above, and explores how such philosophy speaks directly to the contradictory experiences of teachers' practice, without taking sides between metaphysics and ethics. Into the interminable quest to find either the metaphysical dogma or the slip into relativism of the opposing camp, or the ingenious ways in which justifications are made by both sides to have avoided such moves, I want in a moment to offer a way of philosophising about the teacher that not only understands the illusions of this opposition, but that also acknowledges that 'it may be the very severance of ethics from metaphysics that undermines the value and effectivity of both metaphysics and ethics' (Rose, 1996, p. 2). What Rose leaves unsaid here is that it is the education that this separation holds for us wherein modernity can be addressed according to the dilemmas that are its substance. The speculative can retrieve the non-foundational experience of thought at the same time as the authority and integrity of reason. We do not need to choose, nor do we need to make teachers choose between metaphysics and ethics, or between abstract and post-foundational or critical educational theory. Rather, they can find themselves in the broken middle of their experience of the relation between them.

However, I recognise that such philosophical critique can often seem only to cloud further what are already reasonably complex philosophical arguments. The question will arise as to what use such critique can be within the practice of education. In the rest of the book I will address this concern by trying to show how difficulty itself, in all forms of educational practice, can be shown to have meaning—deep philosophical and spiritual meaning—for those who experience it. But I want also now to counter the perception that this kind of speculative thinking is not appropriate as educational theory and practice by describing briefly how such models as those of Hegel and Kierkegaard described above have been and continue to be the underpinning of an undergraduate honours degree programme in Education Studies at the University of Winchester, the context of my own work.[3]

PHILOSOPHY AS COURSE STRUCTURE

At Winchester we have developed an undergraduate programme in Education Studies that reworks the structure of the speculative philosophical experience into the model for progression from levels one to three. The programme was validated in 1992 as a field of study within the Combined Honours programme. The team of tutors who initiated the field were mostly involved previously in the professional studies component on the Bachelor of Education primary teacher training course. As the amount of professional studies on such courses was reduced, so tutors looked to other possibilities for their teaching. In line with a number of other Higher Education Institutions, King Alfred's College, as it was then, was widening its undergraduate provision with a modular Combined Honours Programme, and Education Studies joined that programme in 1992 with an initial cohort of seventeen students. It was by no means clear who would apply for Education Studies, nor, to begin with, what their reasons would be for doing so. This uncertainty was reflected in the tutors' own ambivalence regarding the identity of the subject.

The programme that was validated in 1992 was constituted by the disciplines of philosophy, sociology, politics, psychology, history, etc., which seemed to make up the study of education. Education *itself* was not seen to be more than the sum of its parts. In the thirteen years since its inception, this definition of Education Studies has been transformed by a new group of tutors. They have, in several reviews and revalidations since 1994, sought to retrieve a much more ancient and yet equally contemporary notion of education as a subject of study, one that does not rely on the integrity or otherwise of other disciplines for its own coherence and relevance. In essence, we were retrieving this ancient notion of education not only as a form of social, political, cultural and historical critique, but also as a formative experience that can shape and determine, as Plato saw it, both the soul and the city.

It is in seeking to nurture this understanding of education as social and political experience, critique and development that we have concentrated our efforts on trying to ensure that our programme is not just *about* education but is educational *in itself*. In doing so, we have sought to avoid the programme's becoming merely a catalogue of modules that lists different aspects of educational provision but lacks any educational *telos*. All programmes in Higher Education are presumably 'educational', but we felt that it fell to Education Studies to include within its own field of study the question of exactly what 'educational' means here. In so doing we called upon the notion of experience found in Hegel and Kierkegaard, described briefly above,[4] and have set this at the heart of the structure of our learning programme. This means that we neither merely study sites of education provision—classrooms, curricula, methods, policy—nor, also, just the theoretical perspectives that can be applied to them—modern, postmodern, feminist, cultural, political etc. We also examine what is educational for us in our experience of actually doing this work. As such we want to move Education Studies on from the disparate and incoherent understanding of education that is produced by the 'disciplines approach' by examining what is (and is not) educational about such disjointed and fragmented experiences, both of the disciplines themselves and in the lives of our students. This, of course, may suggest to some that the programme rejects recent postmodern critiques of meta-narratives and merely chooses arbitrarily to impose one of its own. Such criticisms are suspended here, but they have been implicit in the discussion above regarding the relationship of philosophy and education, and they will be returned to below in Parts II and III. However, the programme interprets the relationship between narrative and meta-narrative, between synthesis and difference, in an altogether different way from that found, for example, in Lyotard's *The Postmodern Condition* (1984). What we are attempting to do here is to retrieve Education Studies as what might be called *the philosophy of cultural critique*.[5] We believe that studying what is actually *educational* about anything that calls itself education can lead to a coherent identity for the academic study of education. The astonishing corollary of this claim, if it can be sustained, is that Education Studies then becomes the terrain on which the disputed meanings of the experience of 'culture' in other academic subjects is fought out. In addition it becomes an essential element of all academic study and perhaps the basis for determining notions of 'value added' in higher education.

To achieve this philosophy of cultural critique, the structure of the Education Studies programme at Winchester has been designed to embody a threefold model of (1) experience, (2) theory and (3) critique, which unfolds during the three years of undergraduate study. In short, we have based this model of experience, theory and critique on the speculative and educational structure of philosophical experience outlined above. As will be seen below in Part III, while still the headteacher of the Nuremberg *Gymnasium*, Hegel put into practice his own threefold model of philosophical experience, consisting of immediacy, mediation and spirit. In more logical terms these correspond respectively to the stages of the abstract, the dialectical and the speculative. For Hegel, abstractions appear immediately but are immediately mediated in (dialectical) experience by the understanding and are consequently known in experience as always objects *for us*. The final (speculative) stage of this experience is the attempt to know and understand the relation between immediacy and mediation in such a way that the relation is not suppressed by being totally understood or totally misunderstood. Hegel himself in his letters noted that his students very rarely, if ever, achieved the third stage. He also noted that they tended to find the second stage, the dialectical, very difficult, preferring the concrete certainties of abstraction, immediacy and the world of objects.[6] The same challenge is evident in our Education Studies programme, where often the comfort of voice is preferred to the risk of theory, at least to begin with. Most students, however, do eventually take the risk of suspending their disbelief. Level One is designed to enable students to begin the programme without necessary prerequisites in terms of subject content or knowledge. The first half of this initial year introduces students to educational ideas from so-called 'great' educators but also offers students the chance to reflect upon their own educational autobiographies, with a view to applying to those experiences some of the new concepts that they gain in Education Studies and other fields. The intention is not to argue that any experiences in the students' prior education have been right or wrong, successful or ineffective, but to seek to enable them to learn different perspectives and different concepts with which to make sense of their experiences and, where appropriate, to criticise them. Most importantly, in Year One, students are encouraged to develop their own voice, to write about themselves, the world as they perceive it and their educational experiences within it.

Level Two is devoted almost exclusively to introducing students to a range of theoretical perspectives. The aim here is for students to realise that their own understandings of the world and of education can be supplemented, and in some cases replaced, by a reworking of the world through one or more of these theoretical perspectives. The voice that has been encouraged in Year One is now transformed as we ask that students subsume their voice within such theoretical perspectives. This can and does include postmodern perspectives. At this stage the students' own opinions of the theories, although obviously important, are not as significant as the degree to which they understand those theories. Their voice will return, but for now it is being tutored by the work of a wide variety of theoretical perspectives.

Importantly, we do not offer Level Two students theory within the traditional academic disciplines of sociology, history, psychology, etc. Instead, theories and theoretical perspectives are offered from any and all disciplines that we feel can play their part in shaping and contributing to the educational experience of the programme. So, for example, students will be introduced to Marxism, critical theory, critical pedagogy, models of learning, feminism, anti-racism, social and political theory, as well as to issues of epistemology, representation and ontology. These theoretical perspectives are used to explore concepts relating, among others, to gender, 'race', nature, power and the child. What is particularly challenging about the Level Two programme for students and tutors alike, is that we have set ourselves the aim of making the skills of theorising generic to all modules. This means it should not matter whether, as a result of module choices, a student studies 'race' or gender or power because each module should be exploring and practising the same kinds of theorising and the same discipline of understanding. Generic learning outcomes for all modules at Level Two have proved a significant benefit to this way of working.

Levels One and Two together, but the latter in particular, constitute a training in theory—not abstractly, but as a theorising and an experience about 'what is'. Theory is always related to live issues but students are encouraged to suspend what they think about what 'ought' to be, i.e. practical philosophy, until Level Three. This leads to the often- heard lament from students: why can't I give my own opinions? The observation that Pythagoras's students had to remain silent in their learning for the first four years finds little sympathy. Our explanation is that we are trying to enable their opinions on 'what ought to be', i.e. on practice, to be informed by theories of 'what is'. They are then able to use those theories and concepts with which they agree as support for their own ideas and opinions. In this way we hope the students move from opinions based on personal experiences to theoretical perspectives in which, often, the merely personal and arbitrary is lost in the work of understanding. This understanding is then applied to matters of personal and social interest, or, better, theory is then able to be found (or found to be hidden) in what counts as practice. In addition, some students 'take off' specifically as a result of their direct experience of the difficulty of the relationship between theory and practice, particularly in their examination of the social and political formations that the theory/practice relationship repeats. They learn of the unintended consequences that accompany all attempts to mend the world and are often plunged into innovative forms of theorising in which educational theory and Continental philosophy maintain a difficult but fruitful alliance.

Level Three, then, seeks to move students from learning about theory to becoming theoretical in practice. This development marks the return and enhancement of the voice expressed in Year One and suppressed in Year Two. Year Three is characterised by an emphasis on students' critique informed by what is hopefully becoming a difficult relationship to theory. As indicated above, inevitably the experience of aporia is central to this final year. Students learn quickly that the divide between theory and practice repeats itself despite theirs and others' best attempts to re-theorise new and ingenious ways of overcoming the divide. Third-level modules try not only to recognise this repetition and its consequent aporias but to offer philosophical insights into this experience, in particular into its educational significance and import.

I will take this opportunity to quote from two recent dissertations by Level Three students to illustrate the kinds of insights that the programme can enable. The first, from a dissertation on doubt, notes that

> to discover, as Hegel, Kierkegaard and Weil have done, that doubt has a significant truth, is to unlock the potential to glimpse something profound about consciousness. Doubt has truth. Perhaps doubt is truth, and this truth is the truth of the self. It is not knowing the true self, but knowing the self through untruth. For these three philosophers, it is knowing the untruth of the self through the truth of God (Cox O' Rourke, 2002, p. 36).

The second dissertation ends by stating

> the way of hope from the knowledge of Man's finite nature and inability to know all is 'to make a virtue out of the limitation: the boundaries of

legitimate knowledge are endlessly changeable,' (Rose, 1995, p. 129) so we need not fall into nihilism and despair. We experience both sides of the dualisms of community and individual, safety and freedom, knowledge and faith. As finite Man we cannot know both sides of dualisms simultaneously, yet because of the continual protest—the dialectic of reason—there is hope that we will know both sides eternally, truly eternally ... [as] a journey, an education, and a life (Pike, 2004, p. 29).

Both authors have chosen to pursue teaching as a career. Their philosophical experiences have inspired in them both a sense of vocation. The more complex reasons why this might be so will be the subject matter of Parts II and III below.

In answer, then, to the question as to what kind of experience Education Studies is claiming as educational, I am suggesting that in the experience in which (critical) philosophical consciousness contradicts (abstract) natural consciousness and knows itself to be spirit as the relation of their misrecognition, there is a notion of the absolute or the true: namely, the relation of philosophy and education known in and for itself. It asks no more and no less than that students have the courage to risk further experiences, to seek more learning by asking more questions, *and* that they recognise the substance that inheres in such work. The aim of the programme, in the spirit of Hegel (and others), is that students should, in studying education, learn about themselves and about the fundamental significance of education as personal, social, spiritual and political development. Level Three is therefore the year of *philosophical* experience in the sense that students think about the formative significance of their own experiences and about the difficulties that the necessary structure of these experiences imposes upon them from without and from within. The two quotations from the student dissertations should not hide the fact that for them, as for many others, the work is intensely personal.

I am putting forward the case, then, that through a programme structured around such a notion of philosophical experience, students are offered the chance to make their own difficulties the content of their studies without sinking into the merely reflective. It is to embody what Rose referred to above as 'the process of learning [in] the corrigibility of experience' (Rose, 1995, p. 119). The course also stands as testament to the way that instrumentalism and performativity need not dominate the philosophical subject and substance of higher education, as so many within the philosophy of education repeatedly caution.

It is also interesting to note that much of the published work in the philosophy of education and in educational theory is only of limited value on such a degree programme. This is because difficulty is rarely made its own philosophical subject and substance in these traditions. I want, therefore, now to explore in more detail how educational theorising misrecognises (interminably) its own broken middle within the aporias of modern abstract reasoning. In a way similar to Rose's critique of neo-Kantian sociology, educational theory will be shown to fall into one-sided readings of modern contradictions, and to give priority either to the objective, the subjective or to new ethical relations that claim and reject the middle at one and the same time. Each of these positions is rehearsed now. Where priority is given to the objective, there I will argue philosophy dominates education; where priority is given to the subjective, there education is seen to dominate philosophy; and where priority is given to an ethical relation there the relation of philosophy and education is both claimed and eschewed at the same time. I will argue that David Carr's argument for moral objectivity illustrates the domination of philosophy over education; that Nicholas Burbules gives priority to education over philosophy; and that Nel Noddings ethic of care colonises the middle by a notion of duality that is neither philosophical nor educational. These misrecognitions are each, in their own ways, attempts to mend the middle. But, as we will see, to mend the middle is to create new tyrannies and new forms of domination. In Chapter 2 we will begin to explore the social and political determinations that these misrecognitions repeat.

PHILOSOPHY WITHOUT EDUCATION (CARR)

David Carr's work represents the middle posited as moral objectivity. 'Any sensible account of education', he says, 'needs to steer a course between reasonable pluralism and indiscriminate relativism' (Carr, 2003, p. 3). The middle in question concerns the fate of moral objectivity within post-enlightenment thinking. Against the idea that morality is merely a local and contingent phenomenon, perhaps even incommensurable with other local moral discourses, Carr argues that it is still possible for education, in its considerations on theory and practice, to discern 'groundfloor conceptual considerations and distinctions' (ibid.). The mistake, as he sees it, of strictly non-foundational critique is that the latter often falls into 'the old error of dualism' (Carr, 1998, p. 121) when it opposes 'the enlightenment fiction of universal moral reason ... to the conclusion that moral values are merely culturally contingent social constructions' (ibid.). David Cooper, in the same volume, succinctly sums up the dilemma of the post-foundational paradigm: 'Either the philosophical positions appealed to are compatible with our actual ways of judging, enquiring and 'going on', or they are not. If they are, it is hard to see what radical implications for educational practice there could be. If they are not, what reason is there for accepting those positions?' (Carr, 1998, p. 46). Carr's response to this contradiction is to argue for the ground-floor conceptions of common sense and/or intuition. Common sense, he says, provides for the survival of the human species a reasonably accurate correspondence between facts and observations. It is true that 'there may well be occasions on which we are not sure whether a given moral claim is true or false, but this is also true in other realms of human enquiry and does not generally undermine the point that we often know what is right or wrong with some certainty' (Carr, 2003, p. 74, emphasis removed). He adds therefore that it is probably the case that 'our ordinary pre-theoretical intuitions about the nature of theories, values, facts and observations are in good philosophical order' (Carr, 1998, p. 122). When uncertainty enters we can often know 'in our bones' (Carr, 2003, p. 74) what is morally right.

At first glance this might appear as a form of Kantianism. If our bones are where we feel duty then these bones might be the site of desire and freedom uncontaminated by the particular. But Carr denies any such relationship, arguing that Kant suffers from 'a particularly virulent form of Cartesianism' (p. 6). He states:

> for Kant there can be no genuine personhood without the freedom of rational autonomy or self-determination–but, in turn, no such self-determination apart from the rational disinterest and impartiality that characterises the moral law: hence, the real personhood of pure practical reason has to be significantly independent of the world of familiar self-referenced (if not self-interested) drives and motives. For Kant the *real* person is not the empirical self of familiar everyday association, but rather the metaphysical *noumenal* self of transcendent practical rationality (ibid.).

He goes on to say that few would nowadays endorse 'Kant's highly metaphysical view of personal agency as rooted in some non-empirical source of rational legislation' (p. 79).

However this reading suppresses the real significance of Kant's broken middle of practical reason. Carr is wrong when he suggests that the moral person 'has to be significantly independent' of motives. For Kant, the existence of motives *is* the law of freedom in each of us. Indeed, on one reading at least, Kant is far closer to a moral theory of bones than Carr is, for where Kant leaves the middle open as a site of competing motives wherein duty makes itself known—and in which freedom and necessity are contested—Carr sees it only as a separation of freedom from necessity. His bones, therefore, can tell him when he ought to do something, but he can never know this as a contestation of freedom. His bones, sadly, refuse their own moral significance and are not in fact in good moral order. This is because Carr closes down the very site of contestation that his bones are communicating to him. He argues that 'once the Cartesian gulf between thought and world is bridged via the common sense idea that our concepts directly identify real features of an external world ... the way is clear to a more apt view of the relationship of facts to values' (Carr, 1998, p. 123).

However, this suppression of the aporetic in Kant is only one illustration of a more general problem of the argument within Carr's work for moral objectivity. At root, the reason that underpins Carr's desire for moral objectivity—and the fact that it is a desire is of absolute significance here—is, on the one hand, a refusal to accept the consequences of a wholly contingent moral relativism and, on the other hand, an incredulity that morality should be freed from common-sense judgements that are made every day. He states that 'if it is in the interests of (amongst other things) human survival that our theories about the world are in some perfectly ordinary sense true, how might we know them to be true unless there are observations or facts which our theories do or do not succeed in explaining?' (pp. 121–122). We have seen that Carr finds the distinction between fact and value at times to involve a virulent Cartesianism—that is, a distinction between mind and the physical. This distinction means for Carr that nothing that is known empirically could be theory-free, and if nothing is theory-free then, he concludes, 'any explanation of the nature of theory would be circular' (p. 122). Quite so. Here, precisely, is one of those philosophical occasions where we do feel something in our bones, where there is, in a perfectly ordinary sense, an observation of facts that our theories do not succeed in explaining. We observe that justifications are circular and self-defeating. Why should this observation, the common-sense experience of contradiction, be ruled out as a valid observation? On what common-sense grounds can this common-sense experience of difficulty and aporia be assumed to be untrue? Why does the gulf between thought and the world need to be bridged unless it does not fit into some pre-judged notion of what the true *should* be? And is this not precisely the point: to judge difficulty or aporia as leaving morality defenceless against a lack of certainty is already to have to hand a view of exactly what morality looks like when it is certain. The problem with Carr's response to the aporia of moral reasoning is that it is one-sided. It grants priority to his 'pure' desire for objectivity over and against the experience of this desire.

I will illustrate this in two ways. First, by prioritising pure desire over its experience Carr ironically and presumably inadvertently gives precedence to the *a priori* over the *a posteriori*, which is the kind of transcendental move that he chastised Kant for making. In having to hand a definition of morality as other than circular and self-refuting Carr has lifted morality free from its determination in motives or in experience. The tables are truly turned here. Not only does Carr reinstate the objectivity of morality as uncircular and, therefore, freed from any contamination in and by the experience of aporia, but, quite the contrary, Kant clearly brings out the aporetic nature of his categorical imperative in his essay 'On the Common Saying: This may be True in Theory but it Doesn't Apply in Practice' (1793). In this essay he states that 'no one can have certain awareness of having fulfilled his duty completely unselfishly' (Kant, 1991, p. 69). This is 'too much to ask for' (ibid.). Perhaps, he says, 'no recognised and respected duty has ever been carried out by anyone without some selfishness or interference from other motives; perhaps no one will ever succeed in doing so, however hard he tries' (ibid.).

Kant's notion of the categorical imperative has suffered, in the philosophy of education as in philosophy in general, from the assumption that it is a heteronomous and external imposition of conduct. Nothing could be further from the case. The fact that the categorical imperative appears external is precisely because the modern *zoon politikon* is grounded in abstract notions of freedom. In fact, Kant's categorical imperative is present when we know there is a choice to be made between what we ought to do and what we want to do. The significance of the categorical imperative is that it makes itself known negatively or in its absence, and it makes itself known precisely through the thing that stands in its way, motives. Motives then are fundamentally ambivalent in a philosophical sense. What we want is always accompanied in our bones by what we ought to want. The categorical imperative is present when there is a choice to be made because the choice cannot be made. Motives, says Kant, are 'the absolute *law* itself, and the will's receptivity to it as an absolute compulsion is known as moral feeling. This feeling is therefore not the cause but the effect of the will's determinant and we should not have the least awareness of it within ourselves if such compulsion were not already present in us' (p. 68). Put simply, morality in the first instance is not the decision we make: it is the very existence of the dilemma itself. And against all readings of Kant, including Nietzsche's, that complained of the smell of cruelty[7] in the categorical imperative, or that see it as the imposition of an external formula or *logos*, the provisional nature of moral action is built into the ambivalence of freedom and the very existence of morality in the first place.

So, whereas in Kant the clash of motives is the ground, as it were, of freedom, for Carr the refusal of morality as within the self-refuting circle of its being known, or theory, leaves his own notion of morality in danger of being purely metaphysical. If Carr is truly concerned to do justice to the common sense concepts that 'directly identify *real* features of an existing world' (Carr, 1998, p. 123) then he should accept the aporetic nature of moral reasoning as just such a concept. His own work on morality exists in the space opened up by the aporia and is dependent upon it. Eschewing this most fundamental dependency for a preconceived notion of moral objectivity is not to do justice to morality. It is a prejudice that runs counter even to his own notion of ground-floor distinctions that must arise out of ordinary experience. The question really is, how can philosophical sense be made of this experience without importing concepts from outside which are granted hermeneutic privilege? I suspect Carr knows in his bones that he owes everything to the existence of aporia despite never giving his master due regard.

There is a second and equally significant critique of Carr's common-sense moral objectivity and his assertion of its independence from the circular. If I am right that Carr's bones feel contradiction whilst at the same time suppressing that feeling, then Carr is in denial of a dialectic in his own reasoning about fact and value. The circle that he claims freedom from for moral objectivity in fact, always, reclaims him to itself. Our common sense tells us that when values are facts, facts are also values. This is not hard to intuit but is much, much harder to comprehend. A dialectic applies here that is the totality of the circle. Values are facts because, with good reason(ing), we believe them to be true; I think Carr is arguing something similar to this. But holding them as true, even by the 'grain of truth of empiricism' (ibid.), does not mean that they hold true universally. It is hard to imagine a more common sense observation about the world than this. Yet, as we saw, it is precisely this observation and its dialectical significance that Carr rules as illegitimate and sees as a dualism requiring to be bridged. The dialectic is a much stronger observation than are Carr's claims for moral objectivity between pluralism and relativism. To live within the circle is to know Adorno and Horkheimer's formulation for the dialectic of enlightenment. In this case values are already facts; facts revert to values.[8] It is within this dialectic that all morality is to be found. The dilemma is its condition of possibility.

By refusing the dialectic that he feels in his bones Carr is doing more than just overcoming our common-sense experience of contradiction. He is granting priority to abstract epistemology over speculative epistemology. The latter speaks for itself and requires no interventions; we all know that morality—doing the right thing—is difficult. The former, however, has to be asserted against our experience and smuggled in under the guise of healing or bridging the rift between fact and value. There is negation in Carr's reasoning, for negation is morality. To judge this negation false is to do so in relation to a merely posited notion of morality. Posing as the remedy to the sickness, it is, as Nietzsche would say, only part of the sickness—another symptom of the negation that it denies.

EDUCATION WITHOUT PHILOSOPHY (BURBULES)

A different but equally one-sided approach to aporetic thinking in educational theory is being forged in particular by Nicholas Burbules. A 1997 publication, *Teaching and its Predicaments*, contains in particular one article that tries to explore the educational potential and significance of aporia in teaching and in education in general. In their Introduction to the book, Burbules and David Hansen define a predicament as 'a problematic state of affairs that admits of no easy resolution' (Burbules and Hansen, 1997, p. 1). The purpose of their book, they add, is 'to illuminate new ways of perceiving those dilemmas, to make them more manageable, less debilitating, and perhaps even a source of interest and enquiry on the part of teachers, prospective teachers, and others who care about the practice' (p. 2). In his own article, Burbules takes as his starting point what he calls 'the idea of a dilemma—not just a difficult choice between two options, not just a balancing act between alternatives . . . but a recognition of a deep, intractable contradiction between competing aims and values' (p. 66). Where Carr sidesteps the epistemology of aporia, Burbules recognises this epistemology and describes it as in some important ways 'tragic'. Against the utopian, Burbules puts contradiction at the very heart of teaching.

> The tragic perspective, I suggest, argues *for* a strong sense of hope in education, but one tempered by an awareness of the contradictory character of what we might count as 'success', an understanding that gains can always be seen also as losses, and an appreciation that certain educational goals and purposes can be obtained only at the cost of others (p. 65).

He says that he intends here 'a positive, constructive way to think about teaching and what it can and cannot accomplish' (p. 66).

Where Carr refused the circle of doubt and knowledge, Burbules recognises the circle and the tragic nature of its dual perspectives as 'helping us accept the inevitability of doubt and disappointment' (ibid.) at the same time as freeing us 'to take those moments of failure as occasions for new learning' (ibid.). This appears then to have overcome the weakness of Carr's abstract and at root uneducational version of morality by placing doubt at the centre of the theory and practice of teaching. This, I suggest, will resonate far more with teachers in all educational sectors than Carr's more abstract approach. The advantage, as I see it, is that Burbules recognises the common-sense observation of contradiction that is the actual experience of morality, whereas Carr, as we noted above, in the name of common sense, rules such common sense as invalid. Burbules finds the substance of conflict between ideals and actions to be something worth thinking about. This is to take the dialectic (p. 71) seriously in a way that Carr does not.

He draws attention to five such conflicts or struggles that he says, 'carry a sense of force and immediacy' (p. 66). These are authority, progress, canonical texts, diversity and success. Each shares for Burbules the characteristic of struggle and contestability. What Burbules says of the first of these echoes, at least to begin with, one of the major themes of the study that follows in Parts II and III below. For this reason I will quote at length what he says about authority.

> Authority is inherent in any teaching-learning relation; it cannot be abrogated or denied even when one wishes to minimise its significance. But authority carries certain costs: It can foster dependency; it implies certain privileges of position that interfere with egalitarian social commitments; it becomes too easily taken for granted in the minds of both student and teacher. Encouraging students to question authority, even inviting challenges to one's own authority as a teacher, can foster valuable learning—but only a person in authority can do that. In one sense, the very purpose of authority in teaching is to make itself ultimately superfluous (because the students themselves become independent learners and knowledge creators). Balancing such tensions is a skill of good teaching. But the terms of success are not entirely within one's control. Institutional customs arrogate dimensions of privilege to teachers that conflict with our attempt to manage authority gracefully ... At a still deeper level, we who have chosen teaching as a career must acknowledge in ourselves the desires that motivate us. However modest we might endeavour to be, the influence that comes with authority and the pride of seeing our plans and intentions (sometimes) come to fruition are seductive pulls back into the temptation to exercise our authority—though only for the 'best' of purposes, of course (p. 67).

This is a perfect summary of the beginning of the philosophy of the teacher as it will be presented later. The struggle here is clearly laid before us; it is a struggle between teaching and learning. To teach, I must accept the asymmetrical nature of the teacher/student relationship. To learn, the student must do the same. How then is the teacher to understand this dilemma that is her authority? This will be returned to in detail later in the book.

The other struggles that Burbules lists are each in their own way related to this issue of authority. If education means progress, then this judgement must reflect the authority of the one who knows over the one who is yet to learn. If education means insertion into culture via canonical texts, then these texts must be claiming the authority to represent one culture over others. If education aims at diversity it must recognise within itself that its authority is largely granted for initiation into conformity and homogeneity. Lastly, any definition of what is to count as success in education must rest upon an authority that excludes competing definitions.

Burbules cites a number of ways in which responses to dilemma seek its resolution. These vary from one-sided prejudices, to compromises or middle grounds, to reconciliation of the oppositions into a new third way, to the denial of the opposition itself, and finally to seeing the extremes of the dilemma as incommensurable. Against any approaches that might synthesise or compromise these difficulties, Burbules argues that instead one should keep the dialectic tension alive for the creativity that this tension can provide. He says he is against any 'middle ground' (p. 71) because the unresolved tension of oppositions offers the sense of 'open boundaries, [and] of unfinished business' (ibid.). Where Carr finds dualism to be an error, Burbules argues for looking at the world 'through a dual lens' (ibid.) without any reconciliation. It provides a tragic yet productive experience. The tragic requires no one path, no one method or subject of study; it recognises that in giving teachers may also be taking away; and it offers an acceptance of uncertainty. Yet it is productive because in contradiction we learn to be open to new possibilities that, in turn, must destabilise and undermine any complacency that teachers have allowed themselves within their privileged positions of authority. In turn, the tragic fosters non-teleological, i.e., exploratory, teacher–student relationships. 'This attitude,' says Burbules, 'respects deep complexity ... [and] the sense of a perpetually open question, always susceptible to new perspectives, new pathways, new discoveries. This suggests a transient and provisional sense of knowledge and understanding' (p. 73).

Burbules adds four further implications of the tragic perspective. It recognises aporia as 'a rich fertile moment of educational potential' (ibid.); it helps teacher and student to think differently; it casts justified suspicion on any one method in favour of 'a deep pluralism of approaches and perspectives' (p. 74); and it negates any sense of self-sufficiency or independence.

What kind of reason, then, or epistemology does Burbules find within this dialectic of aporia? In a different article he argues the case for a postmodern defence of 'reasonable doubt' (Kohli, 1995, p. 82). By this he means to enquire whether 'reason' is to be abandoned altogether as too imperialistic or reconstructed 'along less formal, transcendental, and universal premises' (ibid.), what he calls 'reasonableness' (p. 84). He lists four virtues of such reasonableness: a striving for a concept of objectivity that is non-dogmatic and open to debate; acceptance of being fallible and taking risks that 'run the possibility of error' (p. 93); pragmatism that reflects tolerance and incompleteness; and finally judiciousness wherein is to be found reasonableness in judgement. This last, says Burbules, is 'the key quality to being able to hold competing considerations in balance, accepting tensions and uncertainties as the conditions of serious reflection' (p. 96).

He defends himself against the view that such virtue is merely the *amour propre* of civil society.[9] Such virtues are shared, he says, by different people in many cultures with otherwise completely different value systems. Nevertheless, they are not 'universals' (p. 97); they are generalisable 'in the sense that others might be persuasively brought to recognise them' (ibid.). Whereas universalism asserts qualities over people whether they hold them or not, generalisation offers a weak universalism based upon agreement.

Burbules concludes that reasonableness has 'an essential educational element' (p. 98) because in dialogue learning occurs

> through encountering new, challenging, and often conflicting ideas; through making mistakes and trying to learn from them; through persisting through levels of difficulty and discouragement to something new and worthwhile ... [which] in turn depends upon a range of communicative and other relations the learner forms with other people (p. 99).

I want to make two points in response to this. The first is that where Carr offers philosophy without educational experience, Burbules offers education without philosophical experience. Burbules begins with doubt and aporia, and suggests that they have a fundamentally educative character. But he does not allow this educational experience to know of itself, or to be substantial in any way. Therein he suppresses any philosophy of education, taken here to mean a science of experience as the relation between education and philosophy. In Burbules the dialectic of opposing values is granted status as an aporia and as part of the educational process. But the question Burbules must answer here in relation to philosophy is: how does he know this to be educational? What criteria are being employed here such that education can be recognised? It would appear that for Burbules education resides in making mistakes and having to change our minds or moderate our views in the light of experience. Yet this criterion is never itself made the content that must be risked. The 'reasonableness' of pluralism is raised above the risk that it might be a mistake precisely within the nature of aporia upon which it is based. As such, the definition of education rests upon a presupposition that leaves it immune from the struggle for objectivity in and for itself. This presupposition is fuelled by Burbules' inclusion of Hegel within the list of ways that dilemmas are reconciled. This is the most common and mistaken reading of Hegel in philosophy of education and in educational theory. In seeing Hegelian synthesis as 'another resolution' (Burbules and Hansen, 1997, p. 71) he denies himself the philosophical resources needed both to retain the elements of opposition (which he argues for) and to recognise what is learned from within their contradictory experience. In turn, he rules out spirit as the relation of philosophy and education in which the oppositions have their educational significance for us.

Hegel, then, when read speculatively and according to the logic of education that underpins his whole project, can provide what Burbules seeks but eschews. Instead of seeing Hegelian philosophy as reconciliation, let us see it instead as the consciousness of a mistake known to itself as that mistake. This, as we saw above, is what the notion of spirit means for Hegel. If the recognition of a mistake is not itself recognised as a philosophical experience of consciousness by consciousness, then the education that lies in aporia has no educational or philosophical significance at all. This is the fate of the dialectic in Burbules. Its recognition as the formative process of thinking, its own re-presentation of re-presentation is always suppressed by the more pragmatic view that representation cannot sustain its own truth.

The cost of education becoming such pragmatism is that our philosophical experiences have no educational value or significance in themselves. In Burbules we are not allowed to know that we do not know; we are only allowed to fetishise our not being sure as activity with result. This is fetishism of a higher order than that of commodities, for this is the fetishism of culture *per se*. I will explore this idea again in the following chapter, but what I mean by this is that Burbules defence of reasonableness has traduced reason into a mere rationalism detached from its being known in and as philosophy. This detachment releases education from itself—from its work on itself and from the result of that work—so that now education appears to have a life of its own. Ironically, it is the very attempt not to predefine education that objectifies it. The illusion here is that education can become generalisable. But this illusion is the result of the separation of education from its own experience in and as philosophy. In Burbules the mistake is granted a life of its own away from spirit and as such away from the philosophical education that inheres within formation and re-formation. Burbules has achieved the very opposite of what he intended. Seeking objectivity in the virtue of reasonableness, he has fetishised reasonableness in and as its separation from the only place that it can know (the mistake of) its objectivity. As a fetish, reasonableness is absolutely un-reasonableness, yet as a fetish it appears to enjoy a life of its own. Reason's diaspora is not as this fetish; its home, the home of its diaspora, its broken middle, is its re-presentation, or (speculative) philosophy.

ETHICS (NODDINGS)

Nel Noddings has written an influential study of the relationship in teaching between the 'one-caring' and the 'cared-for'. For those unfamiliar with Noddings' ethical ideal of caring, I will offer a short summary. At root, her thesis is that human existence is universally characterised by the need to be cared-for and to be the one-caring. The fundamental human characteristic therefore is 'relatedness' (Noddings, 2003, p. 49). The truth of this relatedness is care. From this grounding Noddings offers several key features of the structure or 'the logic' (p. 67) of the 'concept of caring' (ibid.). Caring is a natural capacity associated most closely with mothering. It is not a moral principle and can, therefore, preserve the uniqueness of human encounters. The appropriate mode of consciousness for caring is neither rational abstraction not merely emotion. It is rather the reflective consciousness of the 'subjective aspect of experience' (p. 132) in which we are 'aware of ourselves feeling' (ibid.). Against existential anguish where the obligation to relate may be incompatible with a view of existence as solitary, Noddings argues for joy as the recognition, the knowing, of 'the actual or possible caring in relation' (p. 134). This pleasure is the motive wherein the categorical imperative makes itself known; not now as heterogeneous moral principle, but as the fulfilment in relation of each person.

Noddings is critical of Kant. His 'I must' (or the *Sollen*) is present, she says, as duty, whereas the 'I must' of caring is present in love and is not, therefore, an imposition from outside. Where Kant's *Sollen* is principled, Noddings' *Sollen* is sentiment. I have argued above that this reading of Kant suppresses the aporetic nature of the categorical imperative. It is certainly worth adding here that such a view overlooks both the reasons why Kant felt the need to write a third *Critique*, and the nature of reflective judgements he describes there.[10] Nevertheless it is not with Kant that I want to explore Noddings' project here.

The subjective and affective 'I must' that Noddings offers has the significance of being 'the Good'. When one self is in a caring relation to another, this is 'the natural state that we inevitably identify as good. This goodness is felt, and it guides our thinking implicitly' (p. 49). The relation between this actual self and the ideal ethical self, which is itself known in the relation to another, is where caring is fulfilled and becomes our guide for moral action. We should act in such a way as always to enhance this ethical ideal. As we will see in a minute, Noddings' failure to recognise the tripartite structure of this experience has important implications overall for the project.

There is a logic, too, within the concept of care in regard to the participants whose ethical relation is that of care. 'A caring relation requires the engrossing and motivational displacement of the one-caring, and it requires the recognition and spontaneous response of the cared-for' (p. 78). The latter may be an infant who responds to its mother's care, or a student who responds creatively to a task set by a teacher. The only universal here is the maintenance of the caring relation, although how this is to be done can be determined only within each different situation that arises. There is, however, always an idea of reciprocity in the ideal concept of care. 'Caring involves two parties: the one-caring and the cared-for. It is complete when it is fulfilled in both' (p. 68). Caring, then, is 'dependent on the other' (p. 69) who is close at hand. As such, there is a pragmatism to the care relationship. Noddings argues that 'we are not obliged to summon the "I must" if there is no possibility of completion in the other. I am not obliged to care for starving children in Africa, because there is no way for this caring to be completed in the other . . . we limit our obligation by examining the possibility of completion' (p. 86). As such, the one-caring 'acknowledges her finitude with both sadness and relief. She cannot do everything . . .' (p. 112).

We can note here that Noddings finds the ethical ideal in two related moral sentiments: 'the natural sympathy human beings feel for each other and the longing to maintain, recapture or enhance our most caring and tender moments' (p. 104). These two sentiments are the basis of morality and are the end of the ethical ideal of care in seeking to realise and maintain itself. She concludes that 'to receive and to be received, to care and be cared-for: these are the basic realities of human being and its basic aims' (p. 173).

In regard to the teacher–student relationship care is admittedly one-sided. The one-caring, the teacher, can influence the student, in Buber's sense, by presenting the effective world to him.[11] This means the teacher must not shy away from teaching what the teacher judges to be important, but with the proviso that the student be kept aware that 'he is more important, more valuable, than the subject' (p. 174). However, Noddings also remarks that in doing so, the teacher's power is 'awesome' (p. 176). This power is ethical when practising Buber's notion of inclusion such that 'the teacher receives the student and becomes in effect a duality' (p. 177). She receives and adapts the student's own feelings but the student should not also practise inclusion. As we will see later, in Chapter 5, such mutuality for Buber is acceptable for friends but not between teacher and student. There is a cooperation in the teacher–student relation characterised by care—otherwise the teacher would give but not receive. What the teacher does receive from the non-inclusive student is cooperation with the task set. The natural reward of teaching 'is always found in the responsiveness of the student' (p. 182).

Of necessity this is only a brief summary of the ethic of care. I want now to offer three related critiques—political, spiritual and philosophical—of Noddings' model.

First, her ethic of care is, ironically, a morality of persons in civil society. Implicit in Noddings' model is a formal reciprocity between the two who, ideally, become one duality. But the two who are equal are equal in terms of property rights, or as persons. They are equal as masters who have suppressed the philosophical relation of dependence, or again, philosophically, the aspect of themselves as servants.[12] Noddings might argue here that such a political critique is the view of the masculine in the market place rather than the feminine, perhaps the mother at home and in a caring relationship to her child. Noddings is concerned to make 'the voice of the mother heard in both ethics and education' (p. 182). Rousseau provides an interesting challenge to Noddings. His view of human nature is embedded the idea of *amour de soi*, that is, as self-love, and in sympathy for the sufferings of others. Much of Noddings' ethics of care is contained here. Rousseau's natural man must care for himself and will care for others. However, his care for self carries no imperative to care for others who are not suffering. Indeed, they will be of no interest to him. Noddings tries to emulate Rousseau's reasoning here by making the imperative of care both selfish and mutual. Care is selfish because it aims at the joy of its ideal existence. It is practical because each act of such selfishness requires care for the other. 'Caring is, thus, both self-serving and other-serving' (p. 99).

But Rousseau's Emile only learns this second lesson in civil society when it comes to the need to trade. What is given and received here is self-love in the form of objects that can be traded. Self-love can only offer itself in the unequal mutuality of the market place. It is significant, therefore, that the spheres in which the ethic of care can apply are fundamentally unequal. The mother receives reward for her giving care to the child in the 'spontaneous delight and happy growth before her eyes that the caring has been received' (p. 181). But like the student's relation to the teacher, this care lacks the very criterion upon which the ethic of care has been based, namely, that it is complete 'when it is fulfilled in both' (p. 68). Noddings' ethic of care does not survive the transition of the relation of the one-caring and the cared-for into the civil sphere precisely because there it is forced to suppress its inequality. Care in parenting and schooling is power, and is recognised as such in the one-sidedness of those relationships. Care in civil society is the power of market relations, but is misrecognised as equality in the formal mutuality between persons.

How do we know that care is present but unfulfilled in civil society? The answer is because its application, its practice, is contradictory and produces oppositions in our experience between universal and particular. It is here then that we have to look for our second critique of the ethic of care.

To be effective in the political sphere care is required to work against its formal assimilation into the market. To work against this corruption into particular interests it has first to recognise its fate within the opposition of universal and particular. It is a fate recognised but elided by Noddings. She comments that 'individuality is defined in a set of relations' (p. 51). This, of course, is true, but it is not by relations of our own choosing. Even the category of one individual person who meets or encounters another is defined in and by modern bourgeois property relations. The nature of the encounter is pre-determined. If it looks natural, that appearance is a key feature of its pre-determination. We saw above how Noddings chooses pragmatism over politics when she required care to be face-to-face. She acknowledges that a universal of caring is not possible because of its inevitable incompletion, and notes that if it were to be completed in some way it could only be achieved by abandoning the proximal caring that faces one. This contradiction between caring for the one and caring for the all is the fate of care in modernity. Indeed, it is the modern experience of care. Derrida, in *The Gift of Death* (1995), notes that care develops into an economy of calculation where the care for one is already the sacrifice of another, or tens of millions of others. The inequality of care is played out but masked by 'the smooth functioning' (Derrida, 1995, p. 86) of society's 'economic, political and legal affairs' (ibid.) wherein it enables 'the sacrifice of others to avoid being sacrificed oneself' (ibid.). Noddings may argue that if care were the basis of human relations this would not happen. The point, however, is that care for oneself and for others is the basis of human relations, and this is what happens.

The second point to be made here, then, concerns spirit. Noddings eschews the metaphysical or the transcendental as having any role to play in the ethical relations of care. On the one hand, they represent abstractions that take the side of moral principles against the concrete cases of care in face-to-face relations. Against this, Noddings says 'women have been especially fortunate in their opportunities to celebrate the repetitions of ordinary life and thus achieve a balance between being and doing' (Noddings, 2003, p. 130). She takes this argument further. 'What ethical need has woman for God?' (p. 98), she asks, when 'all the love and goodness commanded by such a God can be generated from the love and goodness found in the warmest and best human relations' (p. 97). However, the metaphysical is suppressed by Noddings in the dualism that she finds at the heart of caring. 'Caring', we remember, 'involves two parties: the one-caring and the one cared-for' (p. 68). When care is fulfilled each becomes a duality of self and other, and is experienced as joy 'focussed somewhere beyond both, in the relation or in a recognition of relatedness' (p. 138). In other words, Noddings needs the third partner in the work in order to claim that the duality of care, the 'good' itself, is known and recognised, yet refuses this third partner any actuality. To suppress the third partner, as Noddings does at all points in her book, is to assert a duality that is not-known, and this is the contradiction wherein the transcendental resides, unnoticed and unrecognised as the philosophical education of the broken middle.

Although we can show here that Noddings misrecognises spirit in the Hegelian sense of the broken middle, i.e. as the contradictory experience of the I and the We, there is a different and third way to make this critique, one much more in line with the thrust of this opening chapter. What is extraordinary about Noddings' caring relation is that it does not care enough about itself to become a philosophical education about relation. Yet there are occasions in Noddings when the relation of care is experienced. Noddings makes it very clear that care can be recognised and known as the good, and can be evaluated as 'better than, superior to, other forms of relatedness' (p. 83). There is, therefore, a philosophical experience that differentiates relation from itself. Our natural motive towards care is known as the *Sollen*, and 'arises directly and prior to consideration of what it is that I might do' (p. 82). However, Noddings notes that this feeling often comes in the form of a conflict where the *Sollen* opposes my desires. It is where the *Sollen* 'may be lost in a clamour of resistance' (ibid.). In these circumstances, says Noddings, 'a second sentiment is required' (ibid.) where, despite my feelings towards the other,

I reconfirm my commitment to my ideal ethical self. In the first instance our caring is natural; in the second instance it is ethical. The latter contains a choice; 'we may accept what we feel, or we may reject it' (p. 83). In other words, we have here a relation between the natural feeling of obligation to another and the ethical decision to confirm an obligation to the other.

For Noddings, the ethical is not a principle, it is an ideal, and as such it can motivate us internally toward the external rather than come from outside and be imposed on the inner. But it is this relation between nature and ethics, inner and outer, freedom and necessity, which Noddings does not care enough about. These are well-rehearsed antinomies. It does not matter that Noddings argues that the ethical is only a reflective mode of the natural relation of care. The point is that care itself becomes an object of that reflection. Noddings is clear that 'the source of my obligation is the value I place on the relatedness of caring' (p. 84). Why, then, is a value not placed upon the relation of thinking to the relation of care? Why is no value placed upon the relation of the relation of freedom to nature? Why does Noddings disallow a philosophical experience of resistance and opposition between universal and particular, one that would subsist in the question of how much we care about the concept of caring? It is in our philosophical experience that the model of reciprocity is not itself, but our self-consciousness is never granted the opportunity to be the one-caring about relation and the relation that is cared-for. It may be of no interest to Noddings to pursue such thoughts; she may see them as male abstractions from concrete female realities. But this is to suppress the experience of relation that is, by her own logic, part of how we come to know the ethical. Noddings releases herself from philosophical experience by claiming that all moral decisions can be judged on the extent to which they develop care, either naturally or ethically. But she has nothing to say to the person who experiences care as an aporia. In the political sphere, as we saw above, the ethical is also unethical. This dilemma offers a philosophical education to those who care enough about 'the logic of [the] concept of caring' (p. 67) to sustain a relation to the relation, or to the way caring makes itself known ethically.

It is, then, in philosophy as the care of care that the relation contains and repeats the educational import that Noddings seeks for it. She admits to a 'dialectic between thinking and feeling' (p. 186) but not to the third partner for whom their relation is formative. Indeed, this third partner, the work and result of philosophical and natural experience, is suppressed by Noddings in two ways. First, she argues that the dialectic will perform 'a continuing spiral' (ibid.) through thought and feeling. But spirals, although attractive in terms of progress or development, are illusory in terms of experience. Spirals try to repeat educational movement but in fact, lacking re-cognition of their mis-recognition, they are never known at all. The spiral never learns of itself (as aporia) for it is never allowed its own return. Spirals in curricula or education in general are not a model of education that can be known philosophically except as a misrepresentation of the relation between education and philosophy.

Second, she posits the third partner as beyond dualism. Caring, as we saw a moment ago, involves two parties: 'the one-caring and the one cared-for. It is complete when it is fulfilled in both' (p. 68). Where she does acknowledge joy as the recognition of relatedness (ethics) or in the relation itself (nature), she nevertheless asserts that this thought/feeling is 'somewhere beyond both' (p. 138) in 'a world of relation' (p. 140). Here the how and where of the relation of care is posited as a beyond, and as another new ethics that resolves the aporia of the ethical. It becomes, therefore, a further domination of the knowing of relation in philosophy and education. If care is relation, then one must care for relation in all its forms, including that in which the claim of the truth of care is asserted.

The significance of this can now be brought out in Noddings' working of the teacher–student relationship where, I hold, it fails to realise a philosophy of the teacher. We noted earlier that Noddings acknowledged the awesome power of the teacher. But this power is not itself ever made the subject of the teacher's experience or, more centrally, of her doubts. Rather, the power of the teacher is mediated by the response of the student. As the teacher selects aspects of the effective world to present to the student, so the teacher's judgements are deemed appropriate or inappropriate by their reception in and by the student. 'The special gift of the teacher, then, is to receive the student, to look at the subject matter with him ... The teacher works with the student. He becomes her apprentice and gradually assumes greater responsibility in the tasks they undertake' (pp. 177–178). The teacher nurtures the ethical ideal in establishing the relation of the one-caring and the one cared-for, and works cooperatively with the student 'in his struggle toward competence in that world' (p. 178).

The students' struggles are acknowledged here but not the teacher's. Who is to care for the teacher in her struggle effectively to select the world for the student? Who is to receive the dilemmas of the teacher as one-caring? Who is to confirm her? Noddings is clear that when the relation of one-caring is received by the student then the teacher will be confirmed. But, in what follows in this book, we will be approaching the philosophy of the teacher from the opposite direction. Who will confirm the teacher in her dilemmas and her failures, and in the struggle to care that, from the students' point of view, is so often received as domination? It is here that the merely dualistic model in Noddings deserts teachers in their hours of need. 'If the cared-for perceives the attitude [of caring] and denies it, then he is in an internal state of untruth' (p. 181). Quite so, and even more the case that the teachers are often perceived 'as the enemy' (ibid.). The philosophy of the teacher begins here, in the dilemma that issues from the unequal and asymmetrical relation between teacher and student. It retrieves the inequality of the relation as of philosophical and educational significance: philosophical because the relation is the experience of the teacher as negative; and educational because the relation is also the experience of the teacher as learner. This is an experience that the teacher, in relation to the student as also in relation to herself, is participating in as her own formative work. Here, then, in the philosophy of the teacher as it will be revealed in what follows, it is the teacher who is now in relation to the teacher/student relation. This is her philosophical education. It does not rest in a duality of mutual care. It negates all such identities by placing them, as objects, into relation with thought. As such, the struggles of the teacher reveal an import to her work and identity long before any talk of mutuality becomes possible. Mutuality is revealed not to be the truth of the teacher/student relation. If care for the other is our natural motivation to teach, the philosophy of the teacher begins with the negation, the doubt, the reality of that relation. It is also the negation therein of the ideal of the ethical. In the philosophy of the teacher the ethical, too, is brought into knowing as the relation of the relation. The ethical also collapses. Surely, a teacher might ask, we cannot afford to lose the vision and the hope that the ideal of the ethical carries. Perhaps, but even more urgently teaching cannot afford the luxury of releasing the ethical from its determination in and by modern social relations. Only when the ethical is experienced as participating within its own antithesis can it be comprehended as spirit, or as philosophy and education. The education of others requires teachers to commit to their own philosophical education, and to work within the contradictions it creates for them.

NOTES

1. This coexistence is explored below in Chapter 6.
2. Rose argues in particular that sociology took upon itself the task of healing the rift between ethics and law (Rose, 1981, Chapter 1).
3. This has also been described in Tubbs and Grimes, 2001.
4. In a longer account of these developments, Janice Grimes and I have made reference to the study of Kant on the course. I have omitted reference to him here to ensure continuity in the argument being presented.
5. I will have more to say on this in the following chapter.
6. See Tubbs, 1996 and 1997.
7. See Nietzsche, (1968), p. 501, or *Genealogy of Morals*, Essay II, section 6.
8. This re-works that famous formulation of the dialectic of enlightenment, that myth is already enlightenment and enlightenment reverts to myth; see Adorno and Horkheimer, 1979, p. xvi.
9. Rousseau describes *amour-propre* as a love of esteem in public opinion, a desire that perpetuates itself in the dissimulation of a 'uniform and deceitful veil of politeness' (Rousseau, 1973, pp 6). Burbules, therefore, does not want to see reasonableness as merely the dissimulation of civil society, but as a truer and more generalisable type of human quality.
10. I have explored the relation of the third *Critique* to the other *Critiques* in Tubbs, 2004, Chapter 1.
11. Buber's work is the subject of a more detailed account below in Chapter 5.
12. It is in terms of this relation of master and servant that the philosophy of the teacher will be expounded below.

Chapter 2
The Culture of Philosophical Experience

CULTURE

In the first chapter we have explored ways in which speculative experience is suppressed within various perspectives within the philosophy of education and educational theory. When the speculative experience is comprehended as the broken relation of education and philosophy, not only is the one-sided nature of these perspectives exposed, but also their broken relation is realised philosophically, that is, as an experience of aporia in and for itself. Within this investigation in Chapter 1, we saw the different ways in which this experience is misrecognised, but we also, in brief, described the ways in which philosophy in Hegel, Kierkegaard and Rose re-cognises this misrecognition. This recognition cannot be interpreted as an overcoming of the oppositions that are the substance of its experience. Recognition is tied to misrecognition, and is the relation of philosophy to existing social relations, not its overcoming of them.[1] To be engaged in and by the speculative is to learn to live with, yet in important ways also apart from, the social relations that currently pre-determine both our experience and the thought of our experience. It is to an examination of these relations and pre-determinations that this chapter turns its attention.

These social and political relations are already present, then, in the forms that philosophy of education and educational theorising take. As we saw above, when, for example, moral philosophy posits objectivity or validity as having priority over the dialectic, or negation, or mediation, then it posits itself as a consciousness of the object, but not, also, as a consciousness of itself as object. This is an oft-made critique of such work from within both the emancipatory tradition, which sees it as paying no heed to the universality of modern commodification, as well as for more post-foundationalist outlooks, which see its *logos* implicated in and by a Western epistemological and rational imperialism. Equally, however, when these critical or deconstructive outlooks give priority to non-objectivity, be it as *praxis* or pluralism, this, in turn, refuses political experience a grounding in itself and threatens to make it otiose as thinking that lacks objective educational import.

Social relations, specifically universal private property relations, are carried within both of these groups of perspectives and their critiques of each other. This is experienced by us in the repetition of such critiques where each accuses the other of varying degrees of universality or particularity. Our experience of their opposition, and the repetitions of the aporias of those oppositions, is our experience of the social and political relations that they repeat but do not acknowledge. This is not the education they intend for us, but it is an experience that we have to learn to take seriously (in all its comic forms) if we are to learn how to learn about the modern experience.

We have called this political and philosophical experience the broken middle. Without such a notion, there is no actual significance to our political experiences. The broken middle remains unrecognised in each of the examples explored in Chapter 1, yet they are based on attitudes towards the middle. Moral philosophy in Carr and dialectical (or dialogical) philosophy in Burbules both sought to find the middle way between the universal (reason or thought) and the particular or the local (being). Ethical theory in Noddings also occupies the middle via the duality of care. None of these desires for unity, however, analyses the conditions of possibility upon which the desires are dependent. Why is it the middle that is required? Why is every experience of the middle reduced to a dualism and an opposition between universal and particular? Why is modern experience in all its forms—moral, postmodern, poststructuralist, emancipatory, nihilistic—aporetic? Why do post-foundationalist perspectives have to demand, indeed to assert, that one must look beneath the dualisms that they repeat—for example, between the instrumental and aesthetic in education—for the more sophisticated, more subtle meanings that they intend? Why does modern reason eternally refuse itself a ground, a home? To address these questions the perspectives listed here, and especially as they are employed within educational theorising, are required to confront the illusions that are present in each formulation of the question to be answered. One could here take a Heideggerian line, a hermeneutic line, and argue for a notion of Being-there that has ontological priority over representation. Such an approach is rejected here, for reasons explored below in Chapter 5 and in a footnote to Chapter 6. Instead I intend to pursue the question of illusion, of social and political determination, through some of the work of Max Horkheimer, Theodor Adorno and Walter Benjamin.

Working with aporia means working with the illusions that are present by appearing to be absent in modern experience. In Carr, in Burbules and in Noddings, illusion is present as forms of natural law theorising. Illusion here is not in the object that is either open or closed. Rather illusion is present in the relation of thought and the object to its being known, or as we remarked above, in the thinking of thinking, the relation of the relation. It is illusion, therefore, that determines both the form of modern experience and the aporetic nature of its critique. It is illusion that ensures that we realise the opposition of universal and particular, and that ensures that this knowing repeats the same opposition. It is from within illusion, then, that illusion is known, and that social and political relations can be recognised in our thinking but also recognised as unable to establish new relations. The 'difference' that such recognition makes is the whole question not only of the philosophy of the teacher but also of the *telos* of philosophy in modernity and in its broken relation to education. The brokenness is the question as to what difference education makes. It is, therefore, already a political question pregnant with illusion. To ask the question is to repeat the social and political conditions that construe the question; to learn how to learn from it is to retrieve a notion of the absolute as social critique, or as the education of thought by thought, or, lastly, as the difference that philosophy and education make.

If we are to realise such a philosophy of the teacher, then, we have to find ways of exploring this issue of how social and political relations are carried within the experiences of teachers. I intend to present these experiences in Part II. As a prolegomena I want to address two complementary accounts of why it is that modern societies are so successful in determining thinking in the ways just described. What is it about modernity that abstracts education from itself in our experiences? I want to answer such questions in two ways. First, I will explore how representation—taken here to refer to the way our thoughts are made known to us—hides within itself the ways in which representation is both constructed within particular social formations and realises that construction. We have already come across this idea as the illusion that experience carries but does not acknowledge. Second, I will argue that the real defect—misrecognition is better here—with representation or with modern experience, is that it has no idea of itself as a 'culture'. Culture here has a specific educational meaning and import within speculative philosophy. It refers to the way in which an idea or an experience, in being known, re-forms itself in this being known. Ideas without such a notion of culture or re-formation tend towards dogma because they are asserted without philosophical or educative significance. Applied to the perspectives explored above in Chapter 1, this enables us to say that the philosophies of Carr, Burbules and Noddings lacked a philosophical comprehension of culture. Each, in different ways, suppressed the experience of aporia as culture, and each, in turn, refused the experience its subjectivity and its substance in and as philosophy. It is this re-formation of ideas in being known and in being practised that is the culture of the dualism of theory and practice (as of other dualisms). It is a truism that the philosophy of education and educational theory are haunted by the duality, the bifurcation, of theory and practice. Ideas in practice always have unintended consequences, and practice made theoretical often appears to lose its uniqueness to the desire for abstraction. However, to recognise the culture of theory and practice is to comprehend the broken middle of their relation as both necessary and educative. The difficulty of their relation can then be seen not as the endless repetition of the dead end of their endless repetition; rather it can be comprehended as the experience of aporia as both form and content. It is the case that speculative experience retrieves the truth of culture itself, and is the site whereupon the culture, the re-formation, inherent in experience can be known without new modes of suppression or domination.

What we will now explore, on the one hand, are two of the ways in which critical theory has tried to reveal the illusions carried with representation and the ways that this is manifested in the domination by abstract reason of philosophy and the notion of culture. On the other hand, but equally important, we will look briefly at the fate of the epistemology of culture within modernity and its relation to the separation of philosophy and education. This work is necessary in order to explore the ways in which teachers work within a modern régime of representation that opposes particular forms of education and releases others. This régime lies well hidden behind the ordinary experience of teachers and students alike, but dominates them. Most significant perhaps is its appearance as the idea of the end of philosophy, where 'end' refers to the termination of philosophy as a political or philosophically educational experience. Such claims in fact represent the total abstraction of experience from culture. If teachers cannot see how they are re-formed in their struggles with theory and practice, then not only are they destined to repeat the abstraction of culture, they are also denied the means to learn from these difficulties. In short, denied of the notion of education as culture, as their formation and re-formation, they are denied themselves as an object of philosophical thinking. As we will now see, the political stakes of such denial are very high indeed, for the suppression of the relation of formation and re-formation can and perhaps does leave the way open for forms of totalitarianism. The philosophy of the teacher aims to retrieve the culture of the teacher, not least in response to the appearance of their work as increasingly apolitical.

The following sections, then, trace the arguments concerning representation and culture made by Adorno and Horkheimer and by Benjamin largely in the first half of the twentieth century. This explains their preoccupation with the technology of the time and its impact on culture. But their work is still significant for it testifies to the ways in which experience is formed in and by modernity. The logic of their arguments concerning the structure of experience is still valid, not least for understanding the (lack of a) culture of teaching.

ADORNO AND HORKHEIMER

In Adorno's collaborations with Horkheimer and in his single authored work, the idea that culture has become detached from its educational and re-formative import in and for modern consciousness is a major theme. However, I will concentrate on the *Dialectic of Enlightenment* published in 1947, and shorter essays by Adorno written both before and after the *Dialectic*.

In their essay on the culture industry Adorno and Horkheimer demonstrate not only 'the regression of enlightenment to ideology' (Adorno and Horkheimer, 1979, p. xvi) but also how the 'technological rationale is the rationale of domination itself' (p. 121). The dialectical sophistication of their argument is not to be found merely in the mantra that the culture industry determines individual consciousness. There *are* times, of course, when Adorno and Horkheimer reflect on the total reification under the 'totality of the culture industry' (p. 136). For example they note that 'the whole world is made to pass through the filter of the culture industry' (p. 126); that 'real life is becoming indistinguishable from the movies' (ibid.); that the culture industry has 'moulded men as a type unfailingly reproduced in every product' (p. 127) and has, therefore, inaugurated 'total harmony' (p. 134). They tell us that 'no independent thinking must be expected from the audience: the product prescribes every reaction' (p. 137).

In general terms, though, they identify three determinate results that can be ascribed to the culture industry, each contributing to both the conformity of thinking to the rationality of the technological and to the resignation of thinking that such conformity is inevitable and inescapable. First, they point out that both thought and the very way things are in class-based societies are reduced to conformity and equivalence. Films, or rather movie stars, show success is possible. Yet in this very representation of success the audience, as a mass, is reminded in a surreptitious but forceful way, of the fact that they cannot succeed. The singular, the one, exemplifies the sameness of everyone else. 'Ironically, man as a member of a species has been made a reality by the culture industry. Now any person signifies only those attributes by which he can replace everybody else: he is interchangeable, a copy. As an individual he is completely expendable and utterly insignificant' (pp. 145–146). Here, being brought nearer to the stars that one can identify with also vastly increases the distance that one feels from them. Stars do not, by definition, represent those who have not made it.

Second, the culture industry is iatrogenic, producing conditions it pretends to overcome. In general terms amusement, which is sold as a rest from work, is in fact 'the prolongation of work' (p. 137). In his essay *Free Time*, Adorno notes that where people are led to think that they act freely, i.e., in their free time, such actions are 'shaped by the very same forces which they are seeking to escape in their hours without work' (Adorno, 1991, p. 162). This idea is reinforced by Adorno and Horkheimer, in that 'mechanization has such power over a man's leisure and happiness, and so profoundly determines the manufacture of amusement goods, that his experiences are inevitably after-images of the work process itself' (Adorno and Horkheimer, 1979, p. 137). Here they are clearly showing the relation between the ways in which individuals think and the forms of representation that dominate culture. The representation is taken into thought and becomes the form and the content of thought. Furthermore, they argue that laughter and fun, rather than providing happiness, in fact corrupt it by being employed 'at the expense of everyone else' (p. 141). They argue here that the readiness of the audience to laugh as an audience is 'a parody of humanity' because it represents the liberation of laughter 'from any scruple when the social occasion arises' (ibid.). Behind this laughter is not happiness but only 'the echo of power as something inescapable' (p. 140). All aspects of the amusement industry are pornographic in the sense that like pornography they deny fulfilment to the desires they arouse; 'the diner must be satisfied with the menu' (p. 139).

Third, Adorno also draws attention to the way the pseudo-happiness of conformity is represented in and by music. The division between 'serious' music and 'light' music is symptomatic of the separation of thought from being, and of the intellectual from 'real life'. In each case the latter absolves the former from 'the thought of the whole' (1991, p. 29). Famously, Adorno described their relationship as 'torn halves of an integral freedom, to which, however, they do not add up' (Adorno, 1999, p. 130). Elsewhere he notes that the 'unity of the two spheres of music is thus that of an unresolved contradiction' (1991, p. 30).

In these three ways then, through equivalence, reproduction and conformity, Adorno and Horkheimer show how thought comes to represent the ways in which culture is represented to thought. Clearly for our discussions on the relation between representation and culture these arguments are significant. They amount to saying that culture in modern bourgeois society has, in its technological form, become so abstracted from consciousness that it now represents abstraction *as* culture. As such, consciousness is robbed of the concept by which critical thinking can comprehend itself. The element of learning, of re-formation, is claimed now by a notion of (modern, abstract, instrumental) culture that is separated from its educational significance. There is, in short, no way left for critique to be meaningful.

The melancholy of this perspective is well-known, particularly in Adorno's work. However, the gloom deepens further when Adorno explores the representation of music. He notes a development, here, in the nature of the fetishism of commodities. Whereas in the original formulation fetishism required the concrete production of the object in order to realise its homogeneity with all objects in exchange value, now cultural goods seem to be exempt from the need for exchange and thus from any actual attachment to the object itself. Representation here is freed from the object it represents. Without an object all objects are (only) representation, and as such are the same object for all. This increases the power of culture as conformity in that equivalence is now granted an aesthetic reality. When representation can replace objects with feelings, then the whole world is cast adrift from its being known; or, as Adorno puts it, mass culture, as the representation of a completely reified world, can worship the ticket to the game more than the game itself. This abstraction of exchange value even from the object is now the fetishism of pure exchange; not exchange in and of itself, but its aesthetic, made possible by the standardisation of both object and consumer.

For the teacher, here, we might say that, since representation has become all culture, all forms of thinking that might recognise re-formation in and of themselves—in other words, all critical thinking—become impossible. Since all thoughts are now representations that are the same in terms of their 'value', the idea of thinking as culture, as re-formation, has itself been re-formed as having no relation. In the absence of relation, indeed, where representation claims to be relation, the broken middle of experience, of culture, is otiose. It signifies nothing. It rules out a philosophy of the teacher. It 'corresponds to the behaviour of the prisoner who loves his cell because he has been left nothing else' (p. 35).

This is brought out again in Adorno's critique of the culture industry functioning as the ideology of ideology. There are three aspects to this. First, it is the politicisation of the dialectic between image and reality. On the one hand, 'reality becomes its own ideology through the spell cast by its faithful duplication' (p. 55). On the other hand, 'if the real becomes an image insofar as in its particularity it becomes as equivalent to the whole as one Ford car is to all the others of the same range, then the image... turns into immediate reality' (ibid.). This relation of image and reality has dissolved the recognition of illusion and is now a total relation where each is all of the other. Representation here is the nullity of the distinction between appearance and what is, or is the 'liquidation of its opposition' (p. 56).

Second, this liquidation both creates and feeds its own needs. Every product is always already a representation of the needs of empirical reality, or of the various empirical categories of the consumer. Thus determined, the consumer 'cannot digest anything not already pre-digested' (p. 58). The culture industry is the ideology of 'baby-food' (ibid.)—that is, it is directed towards the needs that it creates precisely in the appearance of trying to satisfy those needs. The ideology of ideology here is the dialectic of nihilism: a feeling of a desire that is fuelled by the feeding and that it is thus never able to satisfy. This dialectic of nihilism is not just another technological domination of nature; it is the 'pure domination of nature' (p. 61) in that it is emancipated from all ends, all objects, save its own fulfilling and self-denying reproduction. Objects pass 'impotently by' (p. 62). 'Nothing happens any more' (pp. 62–63).

Adorno also remarks that 'the liquidation of conflict in mass culture is not merely an arbitrary matter of manipulation' (p. 65). The real beauty of the culture industry, its sublime excess even of its own manipulation, is that it co-opts individuals to collaborate in the pleasure of their desertion by the universal and their consequent destruction. 'Conformity has replaced consciousness' (p. 90) not merely in some vulgar over-deterministic way. On the contrary, the masses come to 'desire a deception that is nonetheless transparent to them' (p. 89). It is not just in the sense of a distraction from objectivity that the masses 'choose', within the ideology of ideology, to opt for ideology; 'they insist on the very ideology which enslaves them' (Adorno and Horkheimer, 1979, p. 134). They know 'as soon as the film begins ... how it will end, and who will be rewarded, punished or forgotten' (p. 125). The formula replaces the thinking that would be required genuinely to experience, to think about, the event as a whole. But it is the formula, in which 'the whole and the parts are alike[,] there is no antithesis and no connection' (p. 126), that precisely defines the viewer as within the mass.

Before turning our attention to Benjamin, it is important to illustrate clearly the political implications here of representation and its colonising of culture. For Adorno it is the totality of such representation that casts the most significant shadow. Against the possibility of critical thinking, where a relation to the object can realise a re-forming of the relation, the totality of representation as technological culture leaves or creates no such productive gaps between thought and being. Not only does culture now become mass production of conformity and equivalence, even time itself is suppressed. Lacking a relation to an event, time never passes, for there is nothing against which change, movement and development—*education*—can register. Time, says Adorno, like critique, is in stasis because the culture machine 'rotates on the same spot' (p. 134).

From these observations, Adorno concludes that culture, in its modern, abstract, technological and undialectical form, is if not the production of Fascism itself then certainly a very significant aid to its development. When the possibility of critical thinking, of re-formation, and the possibility of establishing a relation between the particular and the universal, the whole, are subsumed within a culture of abstract representation, then domination characterises both society at large and the (im)possibility of its being thought and known. Thus, Adorno concludes, 'the new fetish is the flawlessly functioning, metallically brilliant apparatus as such, in which all the cogwheels mesh so perfectly that not the slightest hole remains open for the meaning of the whole' (Adorno, 1991, p. 39). Curiosity, the ground of resistance, falls victim to the ideology of ideology and is socialised by the mass production of information. Fascism is aided negatively by a lack of resistance and also positively by the way that thinking not only comes to terms with reality but also perpetuates it.

Given Adorno's political experiences through the 1930s and 1940s, his concern with the conditions of the possibility of Fascism are not surprising. But his work carries deep significance for the new century. It is precisely where we think that the danger of a slide into fascistic forms of domination and rule are least problematic that, from Adorno's point of view, those forms are at their most effective and opaque. The teacher who, to coin a phrase, says 'there is no problem here' may well not recognise or know how to recognise the elision of political experience that her statement represents.

WALTER BENJAMIN

The critique of culture and representation is exemplified in two of Benjamin's most famous pieces: *The Origin of German Tragic Drama (Trauerspiel)* (1985), written between May 1924 and April 1925, and the shorter essay *The Work of Art in the Age of Mechanical Reproduction* (1992), written between 1936 and 1969.[2] Both works, among other things, offer critiques of 'representation' or, in a Kantian sense, of the way that intuitions are shaped and ordered in the mind by concepts. Both works acknowledge that philosophical critique 'must continually confront the question of representation' (Benjamin, 1985, p. 27). This confrontation of philosophy and representation in Benjamin's *Trauerspiel* is, at first glance, centred around ideas and styles that seem to have little relevance today.

Trauerspiel is the mourning play or play of lamentation that originated in the Counter-Reformation in Germany as in several other countries in the seventeenth century. Rose explains here that Benjamin is arguing in this text that baroque *Trauerspiel* represents nature according to 'the predominant myth of the time' (Rose, 1978, p. 38). She states that

> *Trauerspiel* means a 'melancholy' or 'mourning' play; 'funereal pageant' would be a less literal rendering. The myth comprises the history of the significance which the society of the time has given to nature, and, as a myth, presents that significance as eternal. In seventeenth-century German drama, historical events are the subject of the plays which are thus apparently secular. However, Benjamin shows that the historical life of the time is presented through the contemporary theological situation and that the emblems of ruin, relics, death-heads, have an allegorical or religious significance (ibid.).

We will unpack the importance of allegorical representation in a moment. The relevance of the text for understanding modernity and the relation of representation and culture we are exploring may not at first be apparent. However, as Simon Jarvis has recently argued, 'Benjamin's critique of allegory implies nothing less than a critique of modernity itself' (Jarvis, 1998, p. 10). He justifies this claim in terms that will be immediately recognisable from the preceding study of Adorno. The relationship, says Jarvis, 'between signifier and signified in allegory is arbitrary' (ibid.). Thus, and quoting Benjamin directly from the *Trauerspiel*, 'any person, any object, any relationship can mean absolutely anything else' (ibid.; Benjamin, 1985, p. 175). It is this theme of equivalence in representation that ties Benjamin's study directly to that of Adorno presented above. What melancholy is to Adorno, the nihilism of representation is for Benjamin.

We must now try to extract from Benjamin's *Trauerspiel* the significance of allegory for our own critique of the relation between culture and representation. According to Rose, the Counter-Reformation represents in Benjamin's work 'the unintended psychological and political consequences of Protestant *Innerlichkeit* (inwardness) and worldly asceticism' (Rose, 1993, p. 180).[3] As Luther's doctrine moved the presence of God from the idolatry of good works to the suffering of personal sin such that 'works contribute nothing to justification' (Luther, 1989, p. 47), so the experience of God was one of desertion.[4] The representation of this experience, its form and content, is the mourning play in which desertion by God becomes the myth of the world's suffering. This, says Benjamin, is 'the heart of the allegorical way of seeing, of the baroque, secular explanation of history as the Passion of the world; its importance resides solely in the stations of its decline' (1985, p. 166).[5] As such, through the Counter-Reformation of both Protestantism and Catholicism, the inward anxiety of salvation is related to the ruin of an external world to produce inward asceticism and outward political ruthlessness. This bifurcation of the one theological situation is represented in the duality of human hopelessness and the decay of the world. But it is here that we begin to see the role of representation not as a representation of the metaphysical import of such events, but as the way in which the medium becomes the message. Culture, stripped of its relationship to an object in which education or re-formation can be realised, becomes instead the form and the content of experience itself. 'Anything can be made to stand for anything else only because nothing is absolute' (Jarvis, 1998, p. 10). Thus, culture here is myth without enlightenment.

The allegory of baroque *Trauerspiel* represents theological crisis in the two different faces of power—internally the martyr to events and externally the intriguer who can use the emergency to justify his own political ruthlessness. It is in the figure of the Monarch, or the Prince, that the height of human power, deserted by God, most clearly exemplifies 'the humble state of his humanity' (Benjamin, 1985, p. 70). Indeed, 'the German *Trauerspiel* is taken up entirely with the hopelessness of the earthly condition' (p. 81). The Baroque ethic, then, is not just the representation of the content of the fallen world; as myth it is itself the form of the separation between earth and heaven, or between creature and divine redemption. Allegory both represents the aestheticisation of a world without salvation and encloses this experience within itself. The consequence, says Jarvis, is that without a perspective outside of this aesthetic representation of the absolute, 'the context cannot be interpreted' (1998, p. 10). In our terms, for the philosophy of the teacher, it is wherein philosophical experience ceases to be educational. Hence, in representing fallen nature as politics without salvation (and here we can begin to see links with Adorno's concerns with Fascism), allegory lends itself to political ruthlessness and violence. In the merely civil society of the Baroque ethic, power must protect itself in myth, secure that there is no revelation, no enlightenment, which will restore its critical dialectic. Mythical representation of the universal in ornamentation not only suppresses critique; most significantly it both fixes the world as without metaphysics and grants to itself emergency powers to restore (and repeatedly fail to restore) the universal. This representation of state and religion is 'the spirit of fascism, or, what fascism means' (Rose, 1993, p. 196)—namely, the aesthetic of destruction, a 'godless spirituality, bound to the material as its counterpart, such as can only be concretely experienced through evil' (Benjamin, 1985, p. 230).

If the allegory of the baroque ethic is one form of the aestheticisation of politics, Benjamin's study of the technology of mechanical representation is an even more celebrated second form. Like allegory, the movie camera is not just determinative of the content of experience; it represents an aestheticisation of politics, or is itself also a form of experience. The loss of intimacy between object and observer, called the loss of aura by Benjamin, is brought about by the mechanical reproducibility of those objects. Reproduction, as representation, is politically significant here as the representation of the same for the viewing of all. This has obvious links to Adorno's argument concerning the way representation can command mass experience. Where distance from the original object—for example, a holy relic—provides unique experience, the illusion of intimacy made possible by the mass reproduction of the object destroys aura. The closer the masses get to the reproduction of the object, the less intimate is their experience. Equally, the more the actor performs for the camera, the greater is his alienation from the audience. The dialectic of aura, significant politically, concerns the distance and the relation between object and viewer. In the movie, however, the distance is abolished and the reproduction of the actor is turned into 'common property' (Benjamin, 1992, p. 225). As Baroque allegory cradled the spirit of Fascism in the representation of the loss of dialectical relation to the universal, so, now, reproduction serves the spirit of Fascism in the destruction of dialectical relation.

The response to this 'shrivelling' (p. 224) of aura by the film industry is twofold, says Benjamin: it involves not only the commodification of the personality of the actor but also the fragmentation of reality by the camera, which then assembles the pieces 'under a new law' (p. 227). Appearing free of mechanical interference, this new law opens up for us the distraction of new and 'unexpected field[s] of action' (p. 229). The more 'closely' we are enabled to adventure into our cultural life by the movie, the more is aura destroyed. The more closely we are able to dissect, analyse and learn about our lives, our neighbourhoods, and our cultures from films, the more our relation through distance to each other, to tradition, to law and to the universal is destroyed. The illusion of relation is contained in the representation of a relation, a distance, between individual and mass. 'Individual relations,' says Benjamin, 'are pre-determined by the mass audience response they are about to produce . . . [T]he moment these responses become manifest they control each other' (pp. 227–228). In short, the more particularly our lives are represented, the more quantitatively and qualitatively the same we become. This is Fascist 'universality'. Allegory, which represented creatureliness aesthetically, is replaced by technology, which represents bourgeois social relations aesthetically. In both cases the distance, the relation, to the universal is destroyed and replaced by a pseudo-universality, viz., the represen-tation of this destruction as enjoyment. As Benjamin comments, mankind's 'self-alienation has reached such a degree that it can experience its own destruction as an aesthetic pleasure of the first order. This is the situation of politics that Fascism is rendering aesthetic' (p. 235). The Baroque ethic and mechanical reproduction, desertion and distraction, are the representation of the loss of the universal and the opportunity for its reproduction as aesthetic—in *Trauerspiel* as the absolute intrigue of politics, and in mechanical art as the absolute enjoyment of art as free from politics or the universal. Fascism and representation in Benjamin are both the effect and the determination of a dialectic denuded of its own law.

The significance of Benjamin's critique here is that culture becomes the reproduction of an experience that hides itself in the experience. Culture becomes a pre-determined way of relating to objects, to each other and to notions of the eternal and the universal, in such a way as to mask its pre-determination. Those within this culture are left to surmise that culture is their experience, realised by them and through them. They are not invited to comprehend how their experience is really the distortion of culture. Nor, therefore, are they able to learn of the political forms that underpin their experiences and their cultures. As such, the relation between culture and experience can only be experienced according to the culture that shapes the experience. The only experience that can contain this contradiction in and as its own form and content is speculative or philosophical.

THE END OF CULTURE

Before assessing the implications for theory and practice of the forms of representation and their relation to culture explored here, I want to offer a further analysis of culture in terms of its epistemology. Inside the now commonplace observation of Enlightenment rationality as characterised by teleological imperialism and totality, there lies another form of the relation between representation and culture that is relevant to the way we are constructing the philosophy of the teacher. In essence, and masked by the critique of the absolute as dogmatic, there is a domination of philosophical relation here that we can call the end of culture—where 'culture' is taken in the sense that we have been using it, as the philosophical recognition of thought's own re-formation in and for itself.

'End' here carries two related meanings. First, the end of culture means that the re-presentation of experience and its social, political and philosophical re-formation is exhausted. It is no longer capable of carrying any import as critical thinking. This is not just a different way of describing the theory of total reification. It is to realise the impotence that lies within such a realisation. As thought and critical thinking no longer have a relation to their being known, they are no longer of any educational or philosophical import. This end of culture must mean the end of philosophy, for experience is never allowed to become subject and substance. Another way of describing this end of culture is as the dialectic of nihilism.[6] Second, the end of culture refers to its own *telos*—that of re-presenting social and political relations as separate from experience. Put together, the end of culture represents its victory of abstraction over philosophical education as without philosophical significance. In this 'end' of culture, then, is the unification of the separation of abstraction from experience, with the (modern, political) experience of abstraction. The end of culture is culture's own end, as exhaustion and *telos*.

Within the field of education, the end of culture manifests itself where it is least observed, in the ubiquitous arguments for education as non-totalising, pluralistic and non-teleological. In a word, in the assertions that education must be 'open'. This openness refers not just to the learning of new things or to being open to new experiences, but also to the idea that education must not close itself down with any definition or systematic knowledge of itself. The claim for education as openness can be made on two grounds. First, it can be asserted epistemologically as the universality of possibility. Education here is deemed as not true to itself if it is seen to close down possibility. Second, and in ethical terms, education is deemed to be domination and imperialism if it is seen to rule out of court things that are different from itself. Possibility and tolerance are posited as the theory and practice of openness. However, this epistemology and ethics suppress the philosophical character of openness. As we saw above, both Carr and Burbules suppress the experience of the difficult relation of philosophy and education, or the broken middle, by positing, respectively, objectivity and aporia abstractly and without a notion of culture. Both practise the end of culture in the abstract opposition of education and philosophy. Noddings posits a relation of care against its formation and re-formation in experience, or against philosophy itself. She, therefore, practises the end of culture as the suppression of spirit. In all three cases, as in many others within the philosophy of education and educational theory, there is here a fetishism of education as openness. Experience is freed from its social and political determination in order to claim freedom for itself. Openness is here the re-presentation of bourgeois freedom freed from re-presentation. Its openness is precisely its fetishism. It is a fetishism that ensures stasis in the opposition between theory and practice.

What kind of representation of the true and of the relation of consciousness to the true, does this concept of openness reflect? How is it now *de rigueur* to argue for—to assert—the absolute impossibility of knowing the absolute? The answer lies, I think, in the way that representation has assumed for itself the new form and content that marks the high point of the culture of *Verstand* or abstract reason. This new form of representation is the form and content of the end of culture. Put differently, representation has as one of its dominant and current features a form of epistemology that can be termed 'pure culture'. This is, I think, to be distinguished even from Adorno's, Horkheimer's and Benjamin's critique of technological culture. Pure culture expresses a freedom from culture that even the movies cannot attain. Its distinguishing characteristic lies in its total refusal (*contra* notions of totality) of culture as the (self-) determination of philosophy: that is, as thought able to participate in its own act of thinking about itself; as able to present those acts as the science or doctrine of this work—its own culture; or as able to know that in this work it has come to know itself differently. In short, philosophy is stripped of its ability to learn about itself, from itself. It is denied the truth of itself as culture because the *concept* of culture (and, therefore, the *concept* itself) has become totally abstracted from such participation in its own work. Where culture is denied self-determination, not only is philosophy rendered nugatory as education, but culture itself becomes the final form of representation where any experience is equivalent to any other experience.

It is ironic, is it not, that in the destruction of the science of philosophical education, in the name, often, of difference, there is, in fact, no difference left at all. The philosophies of openness that characterise post-foundationalist and post-enlightenment thought, as well as those of pragmatism, ethics and even moral objectivity, are a relatively new and perfidious form of the abstraction of culture from experience that Adorno,

Horkheimer and Benjamin highlighted. This new abstract mastery has succeeded in re-forming the notion of culture by separating it absolutely from an idea of itself as re-formative. For culture, now, all content is seen as unessential, assuming therein the identity of pure possibility for itself. When re-formation, or culture, is re-formed without in turn being re-formed by the contradictions of this experience, the absolute significance of philosophy and education is comprehensively eschewed. The end of culture is thus the end of philosophical education, yet even this is a *telos* that the end of culture must suppress.

This can be expressed in another way. Reason has become culture as the form (but not the content) of its own universality. It re-presents itself not as art or religion or philosophy, which seek to re-present relation, but as culture *per se*, as the re-presentation of relation as the lack of relation. Thus reason here, as culture, is rational*ism*, turning diasporic reason into a reproduction of itself as self-satisfaction.[7] That this rationalism is often called 'post'-modern or 'post'-foundational reveals the emptiness of the form for itself. To be after reason is rationally to be of reason but without reason. Here representation posits that universalistic illusions—for example, grand narratives, imperialism, colonialism, discrimination, power-régimes—are known now as merely local contingencies dressed in imperial uniforms. But precisely therein they are *not* known. It is this lack of learning about the formative significance of illusion, or about how reason must educate itself about the way it distorts even its own critique of itself, that defines culture as the scepticism of an empty circle of rationalism. Rationalism is the grave of its own life and is despairing at its destruction of itself. In moments of bad faith it celebrates its despair, claiming the grave of its life as heralding new ethical relations and new possibilities.

Reason as pure culture or as rationalism is, therefore, the apotheosis of bourgeois property relations. It is the triumph of the relation to other as thing over the work that sees relation to other as self. Post-foundational culture expresses completely and comprehensively the illusion that defending contingency from unity means protecting reason from a self-determining relation. In fact, such culture is relation robbed of significance, or is no substantial relation at all, and is thus the very essence of bourgeois freedom.

Rose has met this challenge head on and has offered one of the most powerful and insightful critiques of pure culture in all its 'post' manifestations. An example of this is her critique of pure culture in philosophy as the overcoming of representation with respect to the Holocaust, or the Shoah. Against the piety of those who mystify the Shoah, who deem it ineffable and un-representable, Rose offers the chiasmus of the fascism of representation and the representation of fascism. Mirroring Benjamin's working of the aestheticisation of the political and the politicisation of the aesthetic, Rose is insisting upon the dialectic between power and its forms. The representation of fascism is fascist when its own power is effaced, or when its mediation between object and subject spares the audience its 'encounter with the indecency of their position' (Rose, 1996, p. 45)—that is, when relation and the experience of relation are suppressed. She distinguishes between the educational value of *Schindler's List* as informative—at this level it succeeds—and its refusal to implicate the audience in the crisis, a crisis that it makes 'external' (p. 47).

Such representation of fascism is fascist in two related ways. First, she argues, sentimentality—in the form of the Talmudic blessing that 'he who saves the life of one man saves the entire world' (Keneally, 1983, p. 52)—overcomes our complicity within the ambivalence of this 'pitiless immorality' (Rose, 1996, p. 45). Thus, and second, Schindler's dilemma becomes self-congratulatory of its morality, and therein the audience views the whole representation from the view of 'the ultimate predator' (p. 47) who can survey the cycle of life as voyeur. In this case, the fascism of the representation of fascism ensures not just a distance from the events portrayed but a lordly overview of them. Any emotion generated is for the myth of the heroes rather than for the sadness that is the condition of the whole. The fascism of the representation of fascism, as such, is our own fascism, that of the civil bourgeois whose relation to the universal is found in the commodity but not in the otherness of himself.

Rose does not make this critique in order to illustrate that the representation of fascism, in this case the Shoah, is impossible or in some sense beyond the scope of our experience or our thinking. On the contrary, those who traduce modern metaphysics into ontology, seeing in it the overcoming of 'the *imperium* of the modern philosophical subject and . . . the false promise of universal politics' (p. 55), converge 'with the inner tendency of Fascism itself' (p. 41). Rather, Rose argues, 'let us make a film in which the representation of Fascism would engage with the fascism of representation' (p. 50), or, where the dialectic of the aestheticisation of the political and the politicisation of the aesthetic is not suppressed. Reworked, Rose is arguing for a dialectic of representation in which our separation from the object is recognised as the condition of the possibility of its critique. The extent to which this is transformative (in terms of the teacher) will be returned to below.[8] Without the dialectic of representation, without the 'persistence of always fallible and contestable representation [which] opens the possibility for our acknowledgement of mutual implication in the fascism of our cultural rights and rituals' (p. 41), there will be no dialectic of enlightenment. Without its representation as philosophy and its implication in the universal, enlightenment will fail to 'examine itself' (Adorno and Horkheimer, 1979, p. xv). In Rose's terms, taking 'the risk of the universal interest [i.e., politics] . . . requires representation, the critique of representation, and the critique of the critique of representation' (1996, p. 62).

CONCLUSION

Such thoughts serve to remind us of why and how philosophy *and* representation must continue to challenge the forms of culture that denude such work of educational and absolute significance. For Adorno, in an age of mass production where thinking is determined always and everywhere as information only, experience conforms to the iron law that 'the information in question shall never touch the essential, shall never degenerate into thought' (1991, p. 73). The refusal to reproduce culture in this form leads, he says, to the suspicion of being 'an idiot or an intellectual' (p. 79). But he is absolutely clear that resistance to the totality of mechanical culture, and I would add now, to the totality of epistemology as the end of culture, is both necessary and possible.

Resignation belongs to the consciousness in which 'the feeling of a new security is purchased with the sacrifice of autonomous thinking' (p. 174). It is this act, says Adorno, that is resignation. This dialectic of myth and enlightenment dominates even the desire for resistance, not in any visibly brutal imposition where resistance can manifest itself, but in the enjoyment of free time wherein conformity parades as freedom. Our complicity here is not in question. On the contrary, 'the society that confronts human beings in such an impenetrable manner is these humans themselves' (p. 173). What is forced upon them is what they want, and 'what they want is forced upon them once again' (p. 165). As such, on representation and Fascism, Adorno concludes that 'it may well be the secret of fascist propaganda that it simply takes men for what they are ... [It] has only to reproduce the existent mentality for its own purposes; it need not induce a change' (p. 129); and change, as education within the end of culture, is exactly what is suppressed.

What, then, is the teacher, in all sectors of educational provision, to make of these problems, which seem endemic to modernity? If the critiques of representation outlined above—as mythical, mechanical, technological and epistemological—are in any way correct, then in some senses it is true to say that we have long since passed through the end of education as a re-forming of consciousness and of the world. Adorno rehearses this dilemma through the idea of resignation. In the *Dialectic of Enlightenment*, he and Horkheimer stage a brief dialogue between A and B in which B outlines his reasons for not becoming a doctor. He remarks that it is almost inevitable that the doctor will come to represent 'the establishment and its hierarchy' (Adorno and Horkheimer, 1979, p. 238), which will mean, in turn, that he must become the administrator, the controller, of 'life and death' (ibid.).[9] B is challenged by A that he is being somewhat hypocritical. After all, says A, B relies on the work of doctors and yet he criticises them and refuses, as it were, 'to get his hands dirty' (Adorno, 1991, p. 171). B agrees that it is better for doctors and hospitals to exist than for the sick to be left to die. Nevertheless, he says, he must face this seemingly hypocritical stance if he is to commit himself to trying to understand the dilemma of the doctor better, and indeed if he is to 'explain more clearly ... the terrible state in which everyone lives today' (Adorno and Horkheimer, 1979, p. 239). It is the person who capitulates to the demand that something be done who is 'spared the cognition of his impotence ... It is this act—not unconfused thinking—which is resignation' (Adorno, 1991, p. 174). By contrast, 'the uncompromisingly critical thinker, who neither subscribes his conscience nor permits himself to be terrorised into action, is in truth the one who does not give up' (ibid.). To engage in such critical thinking, he concludes, 'the contradiction is necessary' (Adorno and Horkheimer, 1979, p. 238). In our terms, the aporia of theory and practice is necessary. Of course, we have met this same contradiction between theory and practice in the difficulty of thinking the truth of education and learning, and we saw it above reproduced in the work of Carr, Burbules and Noddings. What we must now take from Adorno and Horkheimer is not a fatalism regarding the possibility of reconciling theory and practice in education, but rather their unfailing commitment to thinking critically about what teachers do and the conditions under which they do it. Even if these conditions make such thinking extremely difficult, and even if it appears that such thinking can change nothing, nevertheless, they say, our thinking '*must examine itself* (p. xv).

But *is* there any philosophical education possible after the usurpation by post-foundationalist thinking of the concept of relation as *all* possibility and without a necessity—an education—of its own? The answer is already in the question. This is the philosophy of education and the education of philosophy that I want to bring to bear in order to articulate a philosophy of the teacher. Part II, which follows now is, for the reasons described above in the Introduction to this book, written with a different voice and, at least potentially, to a different audience. It concerns the contradictions and oppositions that teachers face and the theoretical interventions that are available to them in trying to comprehend these experiences. It is an attempt to broach these difficult matters in an idiom that will address the concerns and experience of the practising teacher. As stated at the outset, Part II is written in anticipation of a reader who is not familiar with any of the material that will be drawn upon. The more usual academic style will return later in Part III.

NOTES

1. I know from experience that such statements arouse the criticism that this can be nothing more than a kind of quietism, a 'conservative hermeneutics' as one reviewer put it. We will see below in Chapter 6 that Hegel lamented the ways he had been interpreted but also predicted such 'fates' as inevitable within existing social relations.
2. There are three versions of this essay. The one translated in *Illuminations* is the third version, written between Spring 1936 and Spring 1939.
3. This article is also reprinted in Rose, 1998.
4. Rose writes about this in relation to the Judaic concept of *agunah* (desertion). She says that her intention is to deal comprehensively with Benjamin's work such that it will 'yield the difficulty of his relation to Judaism'. For Rose this means reading Judaism and modernity in and out of each other.
5. Rose translates this slightly differently: 'This is the kernel of the allegorical view, the baroque, earth-bound exposition of history as the story of the world's suffering; it is only significant in the stations of its decay' (Rose, 1978, p. 38).
6. This is the title of a book by Rose, 1984.
7. It can be added here that all *isms* are re-presentations of cultures but that they lack a notion of culture that can speak of their formation and re-formation within modern culture itself.
8. Perhaps we should remain mindful of the fact that Adorno stated that no matter how barbarian and lacking universality culture becomes, 'in the West, at least one is allowed to say so' (Adorno, 1973, p. 367). This represents the ambivalence of the commodification of critique.

9. Elsewhere Adorno examines the way that the ethos of administration also works to undermine the agency of doctors. He records the fallen alcoholic (Paul Verlaine) who, 'even when he was down and out, found friendly and understanding doctors in Paris hospitals who supported him in the midst of the most extreme of situations. Anything similar would be unthinkable today ... such doctors—with an eye towards their administration—would probably no longer have the right to give shelter to the vagabond genius, to honour him and to protect him from humiliation' (1991, pp. 103–104).

Part II

The Experience of the Teacher

Introduction

A teacher of mine, Gillian Rose,[1] died from cancer in 1995. Before she died, she published a brief account of her experiences with two consultants. This is what she said.

> A year ago, when I first developed effusions in the pleura (build-up of fluid in the lining of the lungs), which can be aspirated or tapped off, my local GP recommended that I see Dr Grove. He said, 'This is the person I would want to see if I had your condition.' In order to ensure that I did not lose the connection with Dr. Land, who is at the forefront of international research into chemotherapy for ovarian cancer, I telephoned her to explain that, for the nonce, I intended to consult Dr Grove, who is based at a hospital in Coventry, not far from the university where I work.
>
> Dr Land said slowly and measuredly, when I had explained the latest development in my condition: 'This means your cancer is active; this means you will become ill; this means you will need more treatment. How long do you intend to continue working?'
>
> Disconcerted by her predictions, delivered in such apparently judicious tones, I went to see Dr Grove. He invited me to arrive after his clinic so that he could begin to get to know me. With a deliberate gesture, Dr Grove pushed aside the proliferating reports on my condition which littered his desk. I found myself looking into the smiley, impish eyes of a youthful forty-five year-old with rounded shoulders, and, I would discover, a duck's waddle in his walk.
>
> 'Tell me,' he invited, 'who you are and how you are.'
>
> I spoke for ten minutes and told him the whole story of how one consultant had told me the disease was progressing, while his colleague, with the same access to it, insisted that it was static.
>
> Dr Grove examined me and then he said: 'You are well; you are not dominated by this disease; we will keep you in this equilibrium. Is there anything you want to do that you cannot do?'
>
> The difference in the set of statements uttered by Dr Land and by Dr Grove is the difference between a sentence of death and a sentence of life (Rose, 1999, pp. 43–44).

There is much here for the teacher to learn from. Rose goes on to say that in these encounters, philosophy provides the analogy for medicine. However, the different pedagogies or relationships that the two consultants engender also show how philosophy provides the analogy for education, and indeed for a philosophy of the teacher. Rose comments that Dr Grove is able to admit that he does not know what is causing this or that symptom and does not know what will happen next. He acknowledges, 'I don't know when you will die' (pp. 44–45). Here, Dr Grove is servant to medicine, just as Socrates, as we will see below, is servant to education and learning. Both recognise in their different spheres their vulnerability in not having all the answers. Dr Grove recognises that his independence as a doctor is wholly contingent upon the pre-condition of illnesses over which he is neither creator nor destroyer. In our studies of the philosophy of the teacher we will explore the work of teachers who, in exactly the same way, are servants of, and to, a process their lack of control and mastery of which makes them vulnerable and exposed to risks and mistakes.

In the same vein, Rose comments on the way the two doctors are able to cope with the ambiguities of their authority. Dr Land, misrecognising vulnerability as weakness, feels she has to compensate for her 'intrinsically limited knowledge' (ibid.), and its threat to her status, by speaking in such 'judicious' (p. 44) tones. She is mastered by illness and consequently sees others as mastered by illness. She has, therefore, missed the educational and philosophical complexities that accompany her vulnerability. Just as she suppresses her own domination within and by the limitations of medicine, so also is she free to become its representative as a master over others. Dr Grove, on the other hand, knows his authority to be mediated by his dependence upon conditions that he can neither choose nor control. He recognises his power to be limited by that which makes him powerful. This does not mean that he merely says 'I don't know', or conflates his powerlessness with irony. Nor does it mean that he refuses his authority and his responsibility as a doctor. On the contrary, Dr Grove accepts that he is both servant *and* master in regard to medicine, and he recognises his vulnerability in this dual role as the defining characteristic of his relation to his patients. It is by being master and servant that Dr Grove is able to offer Rose the ambivalence of freedom and self-determination even within the limits, or the contingency, of her terminal illness. Where Land, as master, expects you, the patient, to be servant, Grove, as master and servant, offers the gifts of uncertainty and doubt as positive, even authoritative agents for growth and self-development, especially, in the face of the absolute contingency of terminal illness. 'Dr Grove', says Rose, 'does not permit you to transfer your authority to him, and, so, paradoxically, you trust him more, because the trust is uncoerced and freely bestowed' (p. 45). The closer she came to death, the more she reported feeling well.

Rose's philosophy of the medical practitioner resonates with the philosophy of the teacher that will be explored below. Both teacher and doctor recognise 'that you have to find you own way between what can be controlled and what can't be controlled' (ibid.). They never confuse that limitation with a 'quest for control and fear of lack of control' (ibid.). Teacher and doctor do not pre-judge their relation or their authority in the light of any pre-conceived 'scientific map' (ibid.). Both, instead, have what Rose calls 'acceptance: acceptance that there is no solution, no cure for this chronic illness, but also no finality: and that there is no need to find a surrogate prediction for this intrinsically limited knowledge' (ibid.).

As Rose refuses to 'identify with cancer as a generality' (p. 46), so the philosophy of the teacher, as we will see, refuses to identify learning as a generality. Education is always a specific and actual relation; it is always the same, yet always different. If it were not, then it would not be *our* experience and indeed would not be an *experience* at all. We can retrieve a notion of wisdom and of vocation in teaching, but only when we recognise that teaching is a relation that has to be re-created by those who are themselves being re-created in it. This wisdom lies not only in recognising our vulnerability and our contingency, that is, our being servant, but also in our courage to risk this wisdom, again and again, as teachers, or as the master. We will come to see this duality as the philosophical experience of being a teacher.

NOTE

1. Gillian Rose was a lecturer at Sussex University in England (1974–1989) before moving to Warwick University to become Professor of Social and Political Thought. She published the following books: *The Melancholy Science: an introduction to the work of Theodor W. Adorno* (1978); *Hegel Contra Sociology* (1981); *Dialectic of Nihilism* (1984); *The Broken Middle* (1992); *Judaism and Modernity* (1993); *Loves Work* (1995); and posthumously, *Mourning Becomes the Law* (1996) and *Paradiso* (1999).

Chapter 3
The Master

INTRODUCTION

In the sixteenth century Martin Luther wrote the following about teachers:

> a diligent, devoted schoolteacher ... who faithfully trains and teaches boys, can never receive an adequate reward, and no money is sufficient to pay the debt you owe him ... Yet we treat them with contempt, as if they were of no account whatever ... nowhere on earth could you find a higher virtue than is displayed by the stranger, who takes your children and gives them a faithful training—a labour which parents very seldom perform, even for their own offspring (Monroe, 1905, p. 414).

Let us imagine, first that you are someone who is thinking about becoming a teacher? If so, perhaps you have already felt something of the nobility of the job of a teacher? Perhaps you have experienced for yourself the lasting impact that a truly devoted teacher can have on your life and you feel inspired to try and be that kind of influence for others? Perhaps also you have looked at the employment market and seen that the really high salaries are not to be found in teaching, yet you still feel called to a form of work that will engage you in the development of people, and especially perhaps young people? And maybe in teaching you see just such a profession, or at least the possibility of such? Let us hope so. Perhaps then you have been drawn to this book, and specifically to this section of the book, because you want to think about what it is to be a teacher, perhaps to find its inner significance and meaning, and to reflect upon its importance in the world—in the life of a student, and for you, the teacher, in your own life. If so, our project in this book is to follow a line of thinking about precisely what it means to be a teacher so that, in time, we might begin to understand, with Luther, the virtues of such work.

Or again, let us suppose a different reader. Perhaps you are already a teacher and, reading Luther's words, know that you have lost that optimism and faith in the job that you once had back when you started teaching? Now you are drawn more to his statement that teachers are held in contempt and undervalued. Or, perhaps you are a teacher who feels weighed down by the need for conformity and compliance to government requirements. Perhaps you despair of any longer being able to make a difference in students' lives? We know that retention of teachers is a huge problem. We have to ask: how is it that, in England at least, within four years of embarking on training for this career something between a third and a quarter of new teachers leave, or are seeking to leave, the profession? How is it that the *experience* of being a teacher so quickly and effectively undermines the *desire* to be a teacher?

There are of course many reasons, but there is one in particular that this book seeks to address. Whilst salary, status, conditions, health, paperwork and compliance all play their part in demoralising teachers, of much greater significance in the long run is that teaching has lost its sense of purpose, its *telos*, indeed, its own soul. It has lost any sense of virtue and nobility as an activity in the world. Bluntly, teaching has lost all meaning about its contribution to humanity.

I want to try and address this issue head on. What is the point of teaching? What is it for? What does it gain anyone to become a teacher? Is it still possible in this age of compliance and testing to find a meaning and significance to teaching that transcends the mundane and speaks to higher ideals? I think so, and that is what I now want to try and show. I intend for us to move swiftly through a number of different perspectives on the teacher[1] towards an intriguing and difficult conclusion—difficult not in the sense of how easily it can be understood, but in terms of how far it can be lived up to. If you feel drawn, now, to thinking hard about some of the contradictions that characterise being a teacher, and to learning some remarkable things from these contradictions, then we can begin together to investigate Luther's contention that there is no more virtuous occupation.

*

What I mean by the term *philosophy of the teacher* is argued in more detail in Parts I and III of the book. However, at this stage what can be said is that such a philosophy certainly does not promise a solution to all of the difficulties and challenges that face teachers. I recognise how frustrating this repeated refusal to offer solutions can be. Let me recount something I heard whilst I was a PGCE student.

Tutor: (summing up his lecture) And so, those are the perspectives that can be applied to understanding the classroom. Are there any questions?

Student: I have one. How does any of this help me with the struggles I am having on my teaching practice?

Tutor: That wasn't the point of the lecture.

Student: It never is.[2]

For now, it will suffice to say that the kind of philosophy that lies at the heart of Part II of this book is phenomenological. This means that it is grounded in real experiences that teachers have in their dealings with students every day, and at all levels of education from the primary age right up to PhD level. A phenomenology allows us to think about the structure and the content of our experiences in ways that teach us much about ourselves. The complication of such an approach is that a phenomenology asks us to experience one thing at the same time as experiencing its opposite or its negation. Thinking two things at once that do not, at first view, seem compatible, is one of the characteristics of the philosophy of the teacher—but then juggling with more than one thought at a time is something teachers are routinely expected to cope with. But whether or not you are a teacher, you do not have to learn how to do phenomenology. It is not so much a method that can be employed as it is a way of understanding the experiences we are already having.

One experience in particular that lends itself to this kind of analysis is that of freedom. Freedom in education is inescapably bound up with power. Indeed, probably the most frequently cited dialectic or relationship between something and its opposite in education is that found in the teacher–student relationship: namely, should the teacher use their power and authority to make students learn, or should the students be left free to discover things for themselves? In educational writing and training this dilemma is often referred to as the conflict between didactic teacher-centred pedagogy and experiential student-centred pedagogy. But seldom are these two pedagogies experienced in practice in anything like such a strict separation from each other.

Like it or not, in all aspects of their practice, teachers are embroiled in relationships of power. As such, teachers are inextricably involved in the business of freedom. Every decision one makes as a teacher is in some way related to freedom, authority and power. Indeed, as I hope to show in what follows, teaching is the very stuff of freedom's own difficulties and ambiguities. If you experience power in all its ambiguities, one might say *dialectically*, you are experiencing power as something that you cannot control, something that ebbs and flows with alarming alacrity. Some days with some students you have it; other days with the same students you seem to have lost it. In such experiences power is not a thing; it is a balance of relations. The effective teacher knows how to manage the balance in different situations. But all teachers at some time feel their vulnerability in relation to its vagaries and its capricious nature. Yet, and let us state this at the very beginning of our exploration, it is by taking the risks that freedom demands that teachers serve the emerging freedom of their students *by becoming students to themselves*, and doing so by *thinking philosophically*.

The structure of Part II of this book is very simple. For reasons that will quickly become apparent it is divided into three chapters. This shorter first chapter, Chapter 3, looks at examples of teachers who use power for *mastery* over their students. Chapter 4 explores examples of teachers who try to re-negotiate this power by endeavouring to *serve* the needs of their students' development and their freedom. The final chapter in Part II, Chapter 5, looks at three *spiritual* models of the teaching relationship and shows how, in some ways, these models begin to see the teacher as playing both of these roles, of master *and* servant. At the end of Part II I will return to themes raised at the beginning and ask what, if anything, we have learned along the way about the teacher in particular and education in general. Then, in Part III, I will return to philosophy to pursue the ambivalence within this contradictory relationship of the teacher as master and servant, not just in Hegel's own description of the relationship, but in its re-presentation, also, in Nietzsche and Kierkegaard. If you are a practising teacher, you may find resonances here, it is hoped, with some of the aspirations and dilemmas that underpin everyday decisions, practices and relationships. If you are intending to teach, you may perhaps find in what follows some reflection of the teacher you hope to be.

This first chapter of Part II explores a number of examples of ways in which teachers have used, some might say abused, their power as masters over their students. It takes a broad and rather fast historical sweep, but the message that comes across is clear. The Western tradition of education has held to a notion of education that sees teachers as justified in having domination over their students both in terms of what will be learned and how it will be taught. In large part the teachers considered here believed that their power over the students was ultimately for the students' own good. At the heart of this assumption lie various versions of a notion of education as *enlightenment*. It is here, with the classical model of education as enlightenment, that we will begin.

WHAT IS EDUCATION?

Plato famously wrote *The Republic* some 2,400 years ago in Ancient Athens. In that book he described the process of education as one of enlightenment. His allegory of the Cave is perhaps the most famous articulation of how education happens and what it is for. Plato describes the Cave in the following terms. Men and women sit chained in a Cave with their backs to the entrance and to the light outside in the upper world. They are unable to turn around. A fire burns behind them, the light from which projects shadows of objects onto a wall in front of them. Knowing only what appears before them, the prisoners believe the shadows to be reality, to be real objects. The shadows are the only things they know and thus they believe them to be the truth. Indeed, they measure each other's intellectual capacity by the degree to which they can memorise the sequence in which the shadows appear. In fact, the shadows are of objects carried by people between the fire and the prisoners, objects that are unknown to the prisoners.

Plato suggests that if one of the prisoners were released and 'forced suddenly to stand up and turn his head, and look towards the light' (Plato, 1992, p. 204) at the back of the Cave, he would undoubtedly feel pain and not a little confusion. Contrary to the wishes of the prisoner, and despite the pain, Plato suggests that this prisoner might then be dragged up 'the steep and rugged assent' (ibid.) towards the entrance and held on to until 'he had been dragged up to the light of the sun' (ibid.) outside the Cave in the upper world. The person doing the dragging—the 'teaching'—is, it is assumed, a 'philosopher king', one of a small élite who govern the state. The upper world represents the realm of philosophical thinking and knowledge.

The released prisoner, who has been used only to the darkness of the Cave, will at first be blinded by the light of the upper world. In time, however, his eyes will grow accustomed to this new world and he will gradually be able to see again. This prisoner is undergoing what, for Plato, constitutes enlightenment. At first this person sees only the shadows in the Cave. When he is turned round, however, his world is turned upside down as he is suddenly faced with things that he has never previously thought possible. He sees how the shadows are produced and realises, of course, that he has never before questioned their appearance. This reveals to him that the truth of the Cave is only an illusion. The illusion is maintained because no one has been able to see that what the prisoners take to be real are in fact only shadows of something else. At the same time, the prisoner sees another world, the upper world of which he has so far been in complete ignorance. As he emerges into this upper world, the light from the sun outside the Cave blinds him, and momentarily he sees again only shadows ... then reflections, then the objects themselves, and finally the sun that is providing the light that makes these perspectives possible. Now he is enlightened, for now he knows not only that the Cave world has been merely an illusion maintained through ignorance, but also that the truth of the world lies not in the Cave at all but outside in the upper world, in thinking philosophically.

We will return to the Cave, to explore a further aspect of the allegory, in the conclusion to Part II below. This same educational process can, however, be understood in more familiar terms. Consider the following example.[3] A mature undergraduate student begins a course of study at degree level studying the 1944 Education Act, the act that established the selection process for secondary schooling in the decades following the Second World War. As it happens, she is someone who attended a secondary modern school in the 1970s, having 'failed' the Eleven Plus examination. She found school boring and never relevant to her own imagination and thinking, and left with few qualifications. Neither her home circumstances nor her teachers encouraged to think about further education and certainly not about university. So after leaving school, she worked her way through a number of jobs. She eventually married and had children, and saw them grow up and become independent. Now she feels the need to do something more with her life, so she returns to education, gains an Access qualification and finally achieves a place at University. As she reads about the 1944 Education Act, and as its philosophical and ideological underpinnings are called into question, she begins to see her own educational history, and indeed her life as a whole, quite differently. The Eleven Plus, so it now seems, in effect determined that she and a large proportion of students like her would not get to the grammar school. It meant that she would never have expectations beyond her working-class station in life. Her teachers labelled her a 'failure' by the very fact that she attended their school. There was no need to stretch her or to raise her expectations, for it was decided in advance, as it were, that she would leave school at fifteen or sixteen and soon start a family.

Now, in thinking about this for the first time, this student begins to see that her world has been *designed* for her. Things that she accepted as *naturally* true, now appear as contingent—that is, things have been designed by someone else deliberately to engineer a specific outcome. The way she has understood herself and her life now changes. She had been made to feel stupid and an educational no-hoper, but it had been designed this way! She becomes angry, for now what she had taken to be the truth of her life becomes mere shadows cast by those in power, those who had made decisions about her and about those like her without telling her. Now, as the prisoner turns round, she sees another way of understanding the world open up before her. Now she sees shadows everywhere: she sees the ideology; she sees the 'spin'. Now she begins to think for herself rather than simply to accept the version of the world that is presented to her. She has moved from the world of appearances to the intelligible world, the world of thinking for herself. She is embarked upon a personal voyage of discovery, or enlightenment, out of the Cave.

But this questioning is unsettling, even dangerous to her and her life. As Plato said, she will be blinded by the new light and will not be able to see clearly. Her newly discovered independent thinking for herself will most likely change what she thinks about life and about herself. It will affect her relationships, and her work. It will change what she wants from life, what she wants to talk about and think about. It will threaten existing relationships as new ones are formed that are more in tune with the newly emerging person. In sum, such enlightenment is painful, difficult, and disruptive. So, one must wonder, is it worth it? Or, is ignorance bliss? Should she be left alone to live her life in the Cave, believing in the shadows? Or, on the other hand, is it simply immoral to hide things from someone and, in turn to obstruct their own self-determination and freedom?

There is a wonderful response to this dilemma in Aldous Huxley's book *Brave New World*. In it, he describes a world controlled at every turn by an élite who take it upon themselves to ensure social stability. They keep everything that is unpleasant from the population by means of genetics, drugs and consumerism so that people are 'happy' with their lives, and never seek to disrupt the social order. But this 'happiness' is problematic. It is not genuinely their happiness; it is a happiness engineered for them by the élite. When, towards the end of the book, the Savage,[4] a representative of a more natural and autonomous way of life, meets the Controller, the latter boasts,

> The world's stable now. People are happy; they get what they want, and they never want what they can't get. They're well off; they're safe; they're never ill; they're not afraid of death; they're blissfully ignorant of passion and old age (Huxley, 1977, pp. 218–219).

> You're so conditioned that you can't help doing what you ought to do. And what you ought to do is on the whole so pleasant . . . that there really aren't any temptations to resist (p. 235).

The Savage replies that this has all been achieved at the cost of liberty. Everything has been so easy that the experience of learning through suffering has been removed. He says to the Controller, 'I don't want comfort. I want God, I want poetry, I want real danger, I want freedom, I want goodness. I want sin ... I'm claiming the right to be unhappy' (p. 237). 'You're welcome' (ibid.) replies the Controller.

The nub of the discussion concerns the right of people to learn for themselves and not to have self-appointed guardians protect them from unpleasant or difficult things on their behalf. This makes life more unsettled, but it ensures that life is genuine and experienced by each of us freely, in our own ways.

The philosophy of the teacher lies at the very heart of this dilemma. If education is enlightening, unsettling and potentially destructive, is it right to teach for this? Is it right to teach for the shadows or to prepare the path out of the Cave? Freedom is compromised, however the story is considered. If you leave people in the Cave, you deny them their freedom. If you force them out of the Cave, you impose a model of truth upon them that they have not freely chosen and that they may even reject. Many have interpreted Plato's model of enlightenment in *The Republic* as the first Western example of the power of the teacher as master over the will, the mind and the bodies of the students. Karl Popper's critique is famously clear and unremitting, concluding that 'Plato's political programme, far from being morally superior to totalitarianism, is fundamentally identical with it' (Popper, 1962, p. 87).

Making a similar observation, Isaiah Berlin sums up very clearly the problem with the enlightenment model of education. Is there, he asks, a higher self within me 'which I can attain to only by a process of education or understanding, a process that can be managed only by those who are wiser than myself, who make me aware of my true, "real," deepest self?' (1999, pp. 62–63). If there is then one may experience these 'teachers' as oppressors. 'I may feel hemmed in—indeed, crushed—by these authorities, but that is an illusion: when I have grown up and have attained to a fully mature, "real" self, I shall understand that I would have done for myself what has been done for me if I had been as wise, when I was in an inferior condition, as they are now' (p. 63). In short he says, 'they are acting on my behalf, in the interests of my higher self' (ibid.). But—and it is a considerable 'but'—he adds, 'there is no despot in the world who cannot use this method of argument for the vilest oppression' (p. 64). The conclusion that we can draw from this, then, is that this kind of argument for enlightenment rests on the assumption that

> there is only one true answer to every question: if I know the true answer and you do not, and you disagree with me, it is because you are ignorant; if you knew the truth, you would necessarily believe what I believe; if you seek to disobey me, this can be so only because you are wrong, because the truth has not been revealed to you as it has been to me. This justifies some of the most frightful forms of oppression and enslavement in human history (pp. 65–66).

Here, then, is the *Catch 22* of the enlightenment model for the teacher. You can teach for the shadows, but that denies freedom, or you can teach against the shadows, but that imposes freedom. You are damned if you do and damned if you do not. In either case, you assume the position of the master over the student, knowing what is best for them, on their behalf.

THE EDUCATION OF MEMORY

In 1887, the philosopher Friedrich Nietzsche wrote a wonderfully provocative philosophical essay about the relationship between cruelty and morality entitled *On the Genealogy of Morals*. We do not need to rehearse the whole of his argument here. However, one aspect of it is pertinent to thinking about some of the examples of the teacher as master that follow below. Nietzsche suggests that what counts as right and wrong throughout history is decided by the strong. In other words, what is 'right' is what the lives of those who are powerful can and wish to enforce! In teacher- or parent-speak, it is the 'because I say so' school of morality. One form of morality that Nietzsche concentrates on is the Jewish/Christian conception. Here, he notes, it is seen as 'right' for people to develop a conscience so that they can take responsibility for their own actions, and overcome their instinct for exercising power over others. Power over the self thereby replaces the desire for power over others. The way to induce this conscience is through the development of memory. This is because without memory conscience cannot be held accountable. If we have no record of what we promised to be like, or what we promised to do, then it will be impossible to feel guilty about not living up to our promises.

By extending Nietzsche's argument to teaching, we can note that something very interesting happens here. We can observe the irony that when teachers have tried to instil a conscience into their students in order to overcome their desire for power over others—or as it is more usually described, to learn to treat others with respect—then the teachers themselves have done so by using *their power over others*, perhaps even by the employment of incredibly harsh and cruel strategies. This becomes apparent in those instances when, to punish a child for bullying, the teacher in effect bullies the child. '"If something is to stay in the memory,"' notes Nietzsche, '"it must be burned in: only that which never ceases to hurt stays in the memory"—this is the main clause of the oldest (unhappily the most enduring) psychology on earth' (Nietzsche, 1968, p. 497). Thus, for Nietzsche, cruelty and 'moral education' are inextricably linked. This goes some way to explaining why the history of Western education over the last 2000 years reads like a history of the changing relationship between memorisation and punishment. Indeed, the relationship of mastery over the physical bodies of the students is one of the most fundamental characteristics of the history of the Western teacher.

There are some remarkable examples of this over the last two thousand years. It is rare to find a current view of teaching that explicitly advocates this tyranny of the master, yet there are few of us who have not seen it and felt it first hand at some time in our educational histories. We all have memories of teachers who behaved like tyrants and dictators. Such teachers can often permanently scar one's experiences of school, indeed of education itself. The most lasting damage is done when such experiences destroy a person's confidence about their ability to succeed in education. These scars can be carried all through one's life, and certainly can put them off returning to education—for fear of being made to look stupid again by teachers who enjoy humiliating their students. Many mature students, who have left school years before with no qualifications, return bravely to higher education finally trying to overcome the fear that has been instilled into them regarding learning and its ever-present shadow— failure. It is not surprising that such students are often on the defensive, assuming that their teachers will be bullying and dismissive.

The seventeenth-century educationalist and teacher Jon Amos Comenius provides a very well-known example of the disciplining and training of the memory (mnemonics), one that displays many of the characteristics of a pedagogy of the teacher who is master over the students through memory. It portrays the teacher as the master having complete control over the production of the student and the student as a 'blank slate' on which knowledge must somehow be impressed and then recalled through memory.[5] Comenius writes this of his new method:

> The art of printing involves certain materials and processes. The materials consist of the paper, the type, the ink, and the press. The processes consist of the preparation of the paper, the setting up and inking of the type, the correction of the proof, and the impression and drying of the copies. All this must be carried out in accordance with certain definite rules, the observance of which will ensure a successful result.

> In didachography the same elements are present. Instead of paper, we have pupils whose minds have to be impressed with the symbols of knowledge. Instead of type, we have the class-books and the rest of the apparatus devised to facilitate the operation of teaching. The ink is replaced by the voice of the master, since this it is that conveys information from the books to the mind of the listener; while the press is school-discipline, which keeps the pupils up to their work and compels them to learn (Comenius, 1910, p. 289).

To our modern ears, this kind of dehumanising mechanisation, treating students merely as equivalent objects that are to be pressed into a uniform shape, is offensive.[6] It pays no heed to individual student need, to student-centred activity or to creativity and imagination, preferring instead a uniform procedure that demands conformity and compliance. Moreover, it clearly demonstrates a view of education as teacher-centred. The master is in control of the process. He knows on the student's behalf what she must learn and how it must be learned. In addition, he sees the student as a blank slate on which knowledge must be impressed, for only if knowledge sticks in the memory can it be said to be known, and only then can the student thereafter be held to be morally accountable. To this end the teacher can also discipline the student, should she in some way reject his authority. Comenius notes that students must be continuously supervised for they cannot be trusted to be diligent in their work. They must be blamed if they 'leave the beaten path' (p. 291).

Let me introduce now some other historical examples—some rather extreme!—from within the Western tradition of the teacher as master.

EDUCATION AND PUNISHMENT

From Ancient Greece, the Western curriculum has passed down a characteristic and indeed dominant form of learning that has ensured the continuing relationship between cruelty and memory. An educated, and indeed a moral person, knew Latin and Greek. Training in these languages therefore became training in memorisation of grammar and poetry. As long as there were (are) grammar schools, the relationship between education and mnemonics (has) continued. Quintilian (c.35AD–c.95AD), a remarkably progressive Roman educator who cared that learning should be pleasurable, nevertheless saw that the surest indication of the ability and character of a child 'is his power of memory' (Quintilian, 1921, p. 55; Book I. iii. 1.) Literary training is 'solely a question of memory, which not only exists even in small children, but is specially retentive at that age' (p. 29; Book I. i. 19). Indeed, says Quintilian, 'at the tender age of which we are now speaking ... memory is almost the only faculty that can be developed by the teacher' (p. 39; Book I. i. 36).[7] The job of the master therefore became that of training pupils in the art of rhetoric, which in turn required memorisation through imitation or repetition. The teacher's job became to ensure this memorisation and repetition. If harsh punishments were required to keep a student on task, then this was for the long-term benefit of the student. Thus the master had the responsibility to ensure conditions most conducive to the rigour demanded for memorisation and repetition—that is, long hours of exercise backed up by the threat of force for those who slackened.

From Socrates' dialogue with Protagoras we learn that parents and teachers in Ancient Athens decided what was just, honourable and holy for their students. Then, 'if he is obedient,' says Protagoras,

> well and good. If not, they straighten him with threats and beatings like a warped and twisted plank. Later on when they send the children to school, their instructions to the masters lay much more emphasis on good behaviour than on letters or music (Plato, 1956, para. 325d).

Keeping in mind the fact that the purpose of education was memorisation and repetition, and the relation of this to cruelty, it is appropriate to look briefly at a number of examples of ways in which this has been manifested in the work of teachers in the Western tradition over the past 2000 years. Although what follows is obviously selective, it is clear that Western education has in large measure sustained the idea of the teacher as master over the bodies of the students so that the minds of the students might be correctly formed and shaped. The repetition of prose and poetry that characterised so much Greek and Roman education was transferred to the Europe of the Middle Ages through Cathedral Schools. We find records, for example, in the twelfth century from Cathedral Schools of exercises in reading, in composition and in verse that had to be chanted without the aid of a book. One extant record of life in a Cathedral School in the twelfth century notes that

> since the memory is strengthened by exercise and the wits are sharpened by imitating what is heard, [the master] urged some by warnings, and some by floggings and punishments [to the constant practice of memorisation and imitation]. They were individually required on the following day to reproduce some part of what they had heard the day before (Binder, 1970, p. 98).

Grammar was practised in evening drill and students 'repeatedly wrote prose and poetry every day' (ibid.).

There were opponents of this connection between learning (repetition and imitation) and punishment. For example, Erasmus (c.1467–1536) announces: 'I have no patience with the stupidity of the average teacher of grammar who wastes precious years in hammering rules into children's heads' (Binder, 1970, p. 142). And Montaigne, (1533–1592) in 1580, complained of schools as

> gaols in which imprisoned youth loses all discipline by being punished before it has done anything wrong. Visit one of these colleges when the lessons are in progress; you hear nothing but the cries of children being beaten and of masters drunk with anger (Montaigne, 1958, p. 73).

Nevertheless, despite such protests, the relationship between learning and punishment continued unabated. At Eton in the sixteenth century 'Latin was almost the only subject of study ... the lower boys had to decline and conjugate words and their seniors had to repeat rules of grammar for the illustration of which short phrases called "Vulgaria" were composed and committed to memory' (Binder, 1970, p. 152). Some two hundred years later we learn from the same school of its most renowned 'flogger', one Dr. Keate, who was Headmaster from 1809–1834. It was said that 'in his sixtieth year [he] still found the energy to flog 80 boys in one day' (Evans, 1975, p. 47). This, however, pales into insignificance against one German schoolmaster in a latin Grammar School from the 1750s, of whom it is said,

> in the course of his fifty one years and seven months as a teacher ... had, by moderate computation, given 911,527 blows with a cane, 124,010 blows with a rod, 20,989 blows and raps with a ruler, 136,715 blows with the hand, 10,235 blows over the mouth, 7,905 *notabenes* with the Bible ... He had 777 times made boys kneel on peas, 613 times on a triangular piece of wood, had made 3001 wear the jackass, and 1707 hold the rod up,

not to mention various more unusual punishments he had continued on the spur of the moment (Cubberley, 1920, pp. 455–456).

Who knows how much of this is true? The point is that it adds to our picture of teachers as masters who saw learning as the external imposition of internal discipline. Students were beaten for their own good, and there was indeed virtue in it, for it helped, so it was supposed, to point their lives in the right direction and to make them moral.

The benefit of this punishment, as a means of ensuring moral lives, was not always restricted to the élite who attended the grammar schools. After the revolution in France in 1789, ruling classes across Europe feared that the masses might revolt and overthrow the existing order of things. To have to protect themselves through the militia might involve the unwelcome recognition that there was indeed a crisis. More effective would be to 'educate' the masses out of any rebellious aspirations. Schools could be established specifically for these lower classes in which they could be taught morality, devotion to God, hard work, and above all obedience and respect for the natural authority of their masters. Adam Smith commended the education of the trades people out of the public purse in no small part because the state, he says, 'derives no inconsiderable advantage from their instruction. The more they are instructed the less liable they are to the delusions of enthusiasm and superstition which, among ignorant nations, frequently occasion the most dreadful disorders' (Smith, 1958, p. 269).

But this concern for the teacher as the master's representative who must instil into the lower classes respect for the masters in general, is even more clearly spelled out through the elementary school system in nineteenth-century England. From Kennington Oval Elementary School we learn that

> the Object in forming Establishments of this nature ... is, to train the Infant Poor to good and orderly habits,—to instil into their minds an early knowledge of their civil and religious duties,—to guard them, as far as possible, from the seductions of vice,—and to afford them the means of becoming good Christians, as well as useful and industrious Members of Society (Silver and Silver, 1974, p. 1).

More infamously still, in 1867 the President of the Board of Education, Robert Lowe, told the Philosophical Institution of Edinburgh that 'the lower classes ought to be educated to discharge the duties cast upon them. They should also be educated that they may appreciate and defer to a higher cultivation when they meet it' (Sylvester, 1974, p. 35). If the grammar schools saw teachers or masters punishing in order to stimulate the discipline necessary to achieve enlightenment, the elementary schools used teachers as masters to enforce the discipline necessary to respect the enlightenment of others and to 'bow down and defer' (ibid.) to it when they met it. But although the methods of punishment increased in ingenuity, the relationship between punishing and learning continued uninterrupted. Now the body of the lower-class student had to be externally controlled so that it might learn conformity, a quality that was itself imbued with moral worth. It becomes clear that the punishing elementary school master was not using his authority to lead his students out of the Cave, but rather to control any dissatisfaction they might have with their lives within the Cave. This master was charged with disciplining the students to lead good 'Cave lives' and be compliant 'Cave citizens' who would not seek any changes in its structures and its hierarchies, and would not question its shadows.

Charles Dickens, in *Hard Times*, paints a vivid picture of the stultifying form of education that was practised in these Elementary Schools, whilst other sources record the kinds of punishments at the masters' disposal. In the early Monitorial Schools one of the founders, Robert Lancaster,

> worked out an elaborate code of rewards and punishments, among which was 'the log', a piece of wood weighing four to six pounds, which was fixed to the neck of the child guilty of his (or her) first talking offence . . . More serious offenders found their appropriate punishment in the Lancastrian code; handcuffs, the 'caravan', pillory and stocks, and 'the cage'. The latter was a sack or basket in which serious offenders were suspended from the ceiling (Craig, 1969, pp. 23–24).

As Dickens himself shows, the key to the mastery of the teacher, even some 2000 years after the Greek and Roman grammar schools, lay in the model of learning as imitation, repetition and memorisation. The famous example from *Hard Times* is worth repeating here. The teacher, Thomas Gradgrind, 'is a man of facts and calculations' (Dickens, 1969, p. 48). 'You can only form the minds of reasoning animals from facts' (p. 47), and students are to be brought into acquaintance with these facts by definitions. Girl number 20 in the classroom, Sissy Jupe, is unable to define a horse despite of, or because of, the fact that her father works with horses. Bitzer, on the other hand, is a student who knows and understands exactly what a horse is. It is a

> 'Quadruped. Gramnivourous. Forty teeth, namely twenty-four grinders, four eye-teeth, and twelve incisive. Sheds coat in the spring; in marshy countries, sheds hoofs, too.'
> 'Now girl number twenty', said Mr. Gradgrind, 'You know what a horse is' (p. 50).

Recent changes in European law have now made it illegal for teachers to hit their students. The master's freedom to rule by physical force has been removed. However, Michel Foucault (1926–1984) has demonstrated ways in which control over the body, and thereby the student, has continued without the need for the imposition of external physical coercion.

In his early work Foucault pointed out that at the end of the eighteenth century enlightenment came to mean 'a way of bringing to light' (Foucault, 1973, p. 64). In hospitals and schools, as elsewhere, pedagogical practices were introduced around this new discourse. In particular, that which was to be brought to light needed to be observed, and as such had to be made visible and available to the 'gaze' (p. xiii). However, Foucault argues that what is made visible is no longer under the power of a master. He differentiates between pre-enlightenment times, when power could be possessed by a sovereign individual and post-enlightenment, when power became a network of relations that no one individual could control according to his own will. This network of relations is what he means by the term *discourse*.[8] Hence, he argues that it is no longer human subjects who determine how power is to be used. Rather, it is the way that power is distributed in pedagogies that determine if and how human subjects are to appear. This is a very dramatic argument and one that is strange to many of our accustomed ways of thinking. We tend to think that the human being is an incontrovertible fact. Foucault is asking us to believe that the human being is really only a function of the arrangement of power in a particular discourse. Power is therefore no longer possessed; it is 'exercised' (Foucault, 1977, p. 26). This fundamentally changes the way we understand the relationship between the teacher and his power over the students. Foucault says that

> one doesn't have here a power which is wholly in the hands of one person who can exercise it alone and totally over the others. It's a machine in which everyone is caught, those who exercise power just as much as those over whom it is exercised ... Power is no longer substantially identified with an individual who possesses or exercises it by right of birth; it becomes a machinery that no one owns (1980, p. 156).[9]

In an influential book called *Discipline and Punish*, Foucault showed how this applied to the formation and organisation of schools. It is no longer the case that the teacher can exercise sovereign power over the students. There is, he says, a new kind of power that shapes the relationships between teachers and students—disciplinary power. Power is no longer possessed; now it is exercised through the bodies of the participants. Thus, teachers and students are only effects of power and 'the element of its articulation. The individual that power has constituted is at the same time its vehicle' (Foucault, 1980, p. 98).

In line with the discourse of enlightenment, discipline now requires the making of bodies visible, their being placed under the gaze. Thus classrooms were designed so that everyone could be seen; timetables were drawn up so that it could be known where every body was at any time throughout the school day; testing took the form of 'examinations' so that each body could be watched, judged, measured and allotted their deserved place in the hierarchy. The most interesting change, as far as punishment was concerned, was that now it was no longer possible or necessary for a teacher to wield sovereign power. Now discipline meant precisely that a student—or their body—would regulate itself. To be disciplined meant to have gained control over one's actions so that they conformed to the expectations that were carried by the discourse known as education. Bluntly, because students and teachers were constantly under surveillance as a result of being kept visible, disciplinary power became the sole controlling factor in schools. Pedagogy was now contained in the way the bodies were arranged rather than in any confrontation between them caused by inequalities in power. As such, for Foucault, punishment is no longer the personal prerogative of the teacher. It is rather the very structure and organisation—the pedagogy—of the school itself.

NATURE

It is not strictly accurate, however, to suggest that the history of Western education has been solely based in the idea of teacher as master and learning as memorisation through discipline and punishment. Eighteenth-century European thinking brought about attempts at a fundamental shift in the relationship between teacher and student and, in particular, away from the idea of the teacher as master. The idea that a child could, for example, be likened to a young tree that, in order to grow straight and true, required a gardener who would intervene at all points to ensure rigid and foreseeable progress, came in for much criticism. It began to be argued that in fact it was precisely the intervention in the development of the student that stultified his growth. There was, went the argument, innate in everyone a path of individual development that, if left alone, would allow each child and each student to develop naturally. Trying to better nature came to be seen as a crime against nature.

Jean Jacques Rousseau (1712–1778) is perhaps the best known example of a thinker who synthesised this law of natural development into a fully reasoned educational philosophy. For Rousseau, the most significant problem facing European society was its own sense of itself as civilised. It had become so dominated by social convention—the right way to do this, the wrong thing to say here, the correct form of dress, the importance of status, etc.—that mankind's true and genuine human nature had been completely lost. Thus, in civil(ised) society, says Rousseau, it became in the interests of men to appear to be something other than they truly were. The result was that people led lives that were fraudulent, none daring to show what or who they really were and preferring instead always to wear masks of social acceptability. Education, for its part, was a training in and for this deceit. Rousseau laments that 'sincere friendship, real esteem and perfect confidence are banished from among men. Jealousy, suspicion, fear, coldness, reserve, hate and fraud lie constantly concealed under that uniform and deceitful veil of politeness' (Roussseau, 1973, p. 6).

It was time then for a different kind of education to release the true person trapped within this social appearance, and better, for a new kind of education to prevent his being trapped in the first place. This could only be achieved through an education in which one's true nature could emerge and flourish without being suppressed by the hypocrisies and masks of civil society. In some ways, this resembles the point of view seen above in *Brave New World*. Rousseau is arguing for an education in which nature is the master, and in which the teacher would only serve this master, never dominating or interfering with it. As he famously begins his book *Emile* that describes such a natural education,

> God makes all things good; man meddles with them and they become evil
> ... he destroys and defaces all things; he loves all that is deformed and
> monstrous; he will have nothing as nature made it, not even man himself,
> who must learn his paces like a saddle-horse, and be shaped to his
> master's taste like the trees in his garden (Rousseau, 1993, p. 5).

As the Savage in *Brave New World* demands not to be unprotected from
life's evils and difficulties, so Rousseau commends just such a natural life
for all children, exemplified by his fictitious student, Emile. To be left
alone will be their education. His philosophy of the teacher is *do nothing*.
The most important thing a teacher can do is 'to prevent anything being
done' (p. 9) that will in any way hinder nature's own plans. Indeed, to
teachers he says: 'reverse the usual practice and you will almost always do
right' (p. 68). This conjures up the picture of a wild child growing up
unconstrained and out of control. Rousseau acknowledges that such a
pupil is more likely to injure himself because this teacher 'shall not take
pains to prevent Emile hurting himself; far from it' (p. 49):

> Instead of keeping him mewed up in a stuffy room, take him out in to a
> meadow every day; let him run about, let him struggle and fall again and
> again, the oftener the better; he will learn all the sooner to pick himself
> up. The delights of liberty will make up for many bruises (ibid.).

There is a teacher here, but it is not the tutor: it is the child's own natural
abilities. The whole secret to a natural education for Rousseau is not that
the child will grow up to be wild, uncontrolled and unconstrained. On the
contrary he will, through the hard natural lessons of pain and frustration,
learn to adapt his desires to his abilities. He will learn to curb his appetites
to that which he can, through his own efforts, meet for himself. The man is
truly free, says Rousseau, 'who desires what he is able to perform, and
does what he desires' (p. 56) and has put these two in mutual equilibrium
through his own natural education. Nature is the master here, and the tutor
only its by-standing servant.

Rousseau's philosophy of the teacher has been very influential,
particularly in Europe. It gave birth to a number of so-called child-
centred pedagogies that emphasised allowing the student to develop
naturally. Such philosophies provided a counter to the mnemonic
pedagogies seen above and indeed reversed such thinking. No force was
necessary now for there was no pre-determined plan to which a student
should be made to comply. There was no pre-ordained person they were
supposed to become, and thus the 'moral' authority of the master to inflict
punishment for the child's good was undermined. This progressive
education has taken many forms and, in different ways, can be seen in
educational work as varied as that of Pestalozzi (1966), Montessori (1964,
1965), A. S. Neill (1962) and Carl Rogers (1969). It is not overstating the
case to say that some of the thinking in *Emile* was replicated in the child-
centred Plowden Report of 1967, and that it lay behind a great deal of the
controversy regarding progressivism that characterised educational debate

in England in the 1960s and 1970s. Indeed, it could be argued that the backlash against such progressivism led directly to the National Curriculum and testing in the 1988 Education Reform Act.[10]

However, there is a problem with the idea that the teacher as master can be replaced by nature as master. It is a problem that Rousseau himself understood. He acknowledges a paradox, at best, and a deception at worst, admitting that in order for the teacher not to intervene and to let the student learn naturally, the art of teaching still 'consists in controlling events' (Rousseau, 1993, p. 251). The student must believe he is learning naturally, but the teacher needs to arrange these natural experiences very carefully. In short, Rousseau says, 'let him always think he is master while you are really master' (p. 100).[11] What Rousseau's insight makes clear is that even when child-centred pedagogies try to overturn the domination of the teacher's role as the master, they can, it appears, only do so *as masters themselves*. This contradiction haunts progressive philosophies of the teacher that seek to replace the shadows of the Cave with the autonomy of the students to learn for themselves. Inevitably, for or against the Cave and its illusions, the teacher must always assert a vision of what a student *ought* to be learning. As Berlin noted above, it seems that all visions of how others are to become enlightened are charged with a moral value in terms of what teachers think is good and right for their students. This presents a contradiction for the teacher who sees himself as servant to God or to nature. To be the servant, he must also be the master. This is a contradiction that as yet we are not in a position fully to comprehend, but it is one we will return to again.[12]

KANT AND THE RELEASE FROM TUTELAGE

Why do these stories of imposition, punishment, memorisation and so on produce in us feelings at the very least of unease and perhaps of outrage and disgust? It is easy to say that it is wrong for teachers to have the right to abuse students physically (and the law prevents this), but, as teachers, or potential teachers, can we clearly and articulately defend why we should not interpret the world on their behalf? Politically we might do so in terms of the individual human rights of students; educationally we perhaps feel that students' learning is something that comes from within, and cannot be imposed from without; philosophically it is also the case that this treatment of students offends our notions of equality, autonomy, self-determination and freedom.

A thinker who can help us better to understand our opposition to the idea of the teacher as master is Immanuel Kant (1724–1804). Kant is one of the philosophers who shaped our modern understanding of the concept of freedom. He argued that freedom could not be separated from the will of the person. An action can be called free if it is solely your decision. It must be un-coerced by anything external, including a teacher, and must be grounded in your own reasoning and your own thinking. Freedom thus requires us to make our own minds up. When the teacher makes up our minds for us, this, for Kant, cannot be freedom. In trying to link the ideas of enlightenment and freedom, Kant writes:

> Enlightenment is man's release from his self-incurred tutelage. Tutelage is man's inability to make use of this understanding without direction from another. Self-incurred is this tutelage when its cause lies not in lack of reason but in lack of resolution and courage to use it without direction from another. *Sapere aude!* 'Have courage to use your own reason'—that is the motto of the enlightenment (Kant, 1990, p. 83).

The teacher who is master clearly opposes this vision and concept of enlightenment for he ensures that students do not think for themselves. The master enjoys the power of tutelage. He prevents the students from thinking and acting autonomously. He demands that they learn what he wants them to learn. Indeed, very often the idea of the students' freedom or thinking independently for themselves is seen as a threat to the power and authority of the teacher. Such a master holds the student's will in subservience to his own. Thus, rather than acting autonomously, the student is forced to act heteronomously, that is, always according to the will of another, and never according to his own will. This student is not free, nor is he learning to be free. He is rather learning to become dependent, and this, for Kant, can never lead to universal equality and freedom but only to a perpetuation of an unequal relationship.

What we can take from this is that, on Kant's view, freedom is fundamentally an educational concern. The teacher who is master perhaps stands opposed to freedom, to enlightenment, to the use of one's own reason, to action grounded in one's own will and, ultimately, to the nurturing of the student into a person brave enough and rational enough to know that freedom requires him to take responsibility for his own decisions. On occasions the master will defend his tyranny by saying that the will of the student must be broken. This is necessary for the student because if he is to be an integrated member of society he must learn to co-operate with others and suppress his selfish desires. That may be so, but if the education about the relation between the self and others is forced, physically or mentally, by the will of another, then the very relation it is supposed to produce is already corrupted. Respect for the other has to be freely given, or it is not freedom.

For Kant, then, education must be for the enlightenment of each individual and must take seriously the idea, *the vocation*, of producing responsible people and enlightened citizens who think for themselves, freely and autonomously. Respect from fear is not self-respect, and a lack of self-respect devolves into abusive relationships. It is, as Kant argues, only our trust in the risk of freedom that can break the repetition of the cycle of abuse. This is why the kind of teacher as master that we have looked at above has perhaps had his day, Modern freedom, as defined by Kant, demands a different kind of teacher, one that respects the freedom of all individuals to grow and develop into autonomous persons, able to think for themselves.

In Chapter 4 we will explore some of the forms that this new kind of teacher can take. We will see that the teacher who believes in freedom seeks to be neither master over the students nor surrogate master on behalf of God or nature. Rather, the *critical* teacher aims to be *servant* to the emancipation of students from all forms of tutelage, self-incurred or externally imposed, and to their free and un-coerced development. From teachers in the Cave who shaped their students to pre-conceived models of development, we now move to teachers who not only are critical of the Cave's illusions but also seek to emancipate their students from the hold that the shadows have over them.

NOTES

1. This lends the need for a particular kind of approach in Part II. I am concerned to employ educational perspectives and theorists only to the extent that they contribute to our understanding of the philosophical significance of these experiences. This will, I am sure, offend some readers who find the treatment of perspectives and theorists a little too one-sided. I am not interested here in different interpretations of these perspectives or theorists—there are many books available that do just that, and far better than I could—but rather in the way their contributions can be seen within the bigger picture of philosophical experience that is being re-presented here in the book overall. Of course, some readers, new to some of this material, might seek out for themselves just such alternative conceptions and interpretations of these perspectives.

2. It is natural, of course, at times of greatest difficulty for teachers to think and to hope that there are techniques that will 'work' in the classroom—and there are things that can usefully be said to trainee teachers to help them in this respect. However, even these techniques rely on teachers establishing good working relationships with their students. The desire for answers to challenges and difficulties comes directly from teachers feeling vulnerable and exposed in front of students who will not 'behave' or co-operate. Sometimes these vulnerabilities lead to teachers in schools pushing the 'problem child' upwards through the hierarchy of the school, on the principle: 'You deal with them. You're paid more than me'. Another more general reaction to vulnerability is to blame school managers for not being strict enough: 'They're too soft, and the kids know it'. I am not suggesting that school managers are never to blame. However, what the philosophy of the teacher asks us to think about are different ways of understanding the vulnerability that teachers can feel in their relationships with students. It is possible to think about this vulnerability as something positive—indeed, as something educational for the teacher. It is possible to find a meaning in it that speaks quietly yet powerfully of the ways in which teachers can understand their continuing education about freedom and authority on the strength of the relationships they have with their students. I will say more about this later.

3. The example is taken from a course in education studies, but similar cases could easily be found across the range of higher education.

4. The term carries cultural baggage now that was unrecognised even in Huxley's time.

5. The term 'blank slate' in education is more usually associated with John Locke (1632–1704). In his *Essay Concerning Human Understanding* he states that we can suppose the mind 'to be, as we say, white paper, void of all characters, without any ideas' (1975, Book 2, Chapter 1, para. 2).

6. We should try to understand, however, the excitement that such mechanisation produced for its contemporaries and how they saw in the new processes a means of extending the opportunities for education quickly and efficiently.

7. Quintilian asks that the teacher must be of good character in order that he will 'govern the behaviour of his pupils by the strictness of his discipline' without austerity, temper, sarcasm or, 'above all abuse' (1921, p. 213, book II. ii. 4–7).

8. He says that a discourse is a 'group of statements that belong to a single system of formation' (1972, p. 107).

9. Foucault, 1980, p. 156. We will look at this idea of the non-subject again in Chapter 4.
10. For example, in tracing the ideological roots of the 1988 Education Reform Act, Denis Lawton has argued that 'child-centred teaching methods' were blamed for a fall in 'standards'. 'The remedy' for the Conservative Party, he says, was 'to give more power to parents . . . But just in case, a national curriculum was set up which would enforce standards' (Lawton, 1992, p. 47).
11. See also here Hansen, 2001, p. 65.
12. In some ways, of course, I have presented a rather one-sided picture of some of these thinkers. Many of the educational philosophies wherein teachers become masters defend the actions of the master in the classroom on religious grounds. As we have seen, for some it is a moral mission to enlighten the souls of the young so that, through imposed discipline, they might come to learn self-discipline. For others, mastery is necessary to save the souls of those who will be distracted from God by the temptations of the world. Comenius is one such example. It is very easy to quote the famous passage about the practice of teaching resembling the technology of the printing press and to make a dramatic point about the impoverished vision this conveys of the creativity and independence of the student. But behind this Comenius sees himself not just as a master but, more importantly, as a servant of God. Indeed, not only can Comenius be seen as a servant of God, but also, like Rousseau, as a servant of nature. Even though Comenius sees the mind of the child as a blank slate that needs to be written on, he does not believe in giving priority to memorisation over direct experience. Only if the child sees and experiences things for himself will he be said to have truly learned them. 'Man must proceed from sense experience (physical knowledge) to the knowledge disclosed through reason' (Murphy, 1995, p. 86), he says. He opposes the scholastic notion that a child can learn from being told, and champions the student's own discovery. 'The schools have not taught their pupils to develop their minds like young trees from their own roots, but rather to deck themselves with branches plucked from other trees, and, like Aesop's crow, to adorn themselves with feathers of other birds' (Comenius, 1910, p. 147). The somewhat one-sided picture is justified on the grounds that it helps to clarify and streamline the broader story that needs to unfold.

Chapter 4
The Servant

INTRODUCTION

We have seen how, in the model of enlightenment, the teacher is caught in a dilemma of domination. On the one hand, if he teaches his students that the shadows are the truth, he is keeping them in the dark, preserving their ignorance and their heteronomy. If, on the other hand, he forces them out of the Cave, with the resulting pain and confusion, he is imposing freedom and enlightenment upon them. Either way, his intervention contradicts the idea that the person must think and learn for himself.

However, there is another possibility. There is a way in which the teacher can be aware of this dilemma, yet still be a servant to the free development of the students. Such teachers locate themselves as in service to a sense of social, political and historical *contingency*. In short this means that instead of merely teaching within the Cave, teachers may now teach *about* the Cave. To understand this better, we need first to try to comprehend the meaning of this notion of contingency and its sociological and political significance for education and for the teacher.

At its most basic, the experience of contingency is the experience of the dependence of individuals upon the society in which they live. Sociologically it is the experience of being shaped and formed in and by the norms, values and customs of their society. Individuals are socialised into its language, its fashions and its ideas. When these factors are totally assimilated by individuals they appear merely as things that are taken for granted and as constituting common sense. In general terms, what we are and what we think, even our most critical thoughts, are all contingent upon the social conditions and definitions that make them possible. Nothing about us can be said to be uniquely our own for there is nothing that is not determined by our social environment. Philosophically, therefore, contingency raises questions about our sense of identity. Perhaps there is no individual essence, no independent 'I', that can be claimed as one's own or as one's unique individuality. Perhaps everything that we believe ourselves to be is only at best a social construction?

Contingency is also highly significant for education. In terms of the Cave we might say that it marks an educational development over the perspective of the master that we have explored above. The master never questioned whether the model of enlightenment that underpinned his practice was itself just another shadow masquerading as truth. Two serious and fundamental implications flow from this awareness of the totality of contingency. First, that *everything* is a shadow, even that knowledge that thinks that it can see through the illusions of the Cave (or society) and overcome them. What is a teacher to teach if even the critique of the shadows is only another shadow? Second, some people in the Cave benefit from people believing these illusions. If the mass of people are kept in the dark about the true nature of their situation it doubtless follows that this will be to the advantage of those who maintain this ignorance. Put these two together and you have a very dismal picture of a society ruled by illusions that serve the interests of a few over the many, but that cannot be overcome. Indeed, as we will see later, perhaps the more teachers believe they can overcome such illusions, the greater is their own illusion! Thus, not only is the model of enlightenment seen as unavoidably *political*; so, also, is the work of the teacher.

Not surprisingly this perspective on contingency presents a new and even more complex dilemma for the teacher who wants to teach about the Cave, or about the society in which she lives and works. On the one hand, the student who is to be made aware of the illusory nature of the shadows becomes aware also that his teacher is part of the structure that perpetuates those illusions. Teaching about unequal power relations could be seen here to reproduce those very same relations. The prisoner, in being enlightened about the Cave, thus remains a prisoner to his teacher. A new purpose for education therefore suggests itself to the radical teacher: that is, to emancipate the prisoner from this reproduction by enabling him to see its political function, and therein to empower him to change the power relations in the Cave. But for this teacher, if she is not to be part of this reproduction, she must find a different relationship with her students than that practised within the enlightenment model. She must find a way of teaching that educates but does not dominate. We will now explore some of the ways in which critical teachers have sought to be *servants* of the emancipation of their students without simply becoming their masters. This new teacher understands that her teaching is compromised by its own contingency, and she understands therefore that her own identity and the content of this teaching are problematic. They both depend upon the very thing that they are designed to teach against. Somehow this teacher has to teach the truth of political contingency at the same time as revealing the role that she plays in its reproduction.

We saw earlier, in Chapter 3, how the teacher as master fails to adopt this self-critical perspective. In recent years in social theory and philosophy, however, there have developed new, more self-critical perspectives on this experience of contingency. In turn, these critical experiences have produced more critical perspectives on education and on the teacher. As we will now see, it is no longer universally accepted that the job of the teacher is to teach facts about the world as if they were true, or as if they were not themselves politically, historically and socially contingent. It falls to the critical teacher precisely to reveal to the students how and why the view of the world that they have grown up to believe in may only be one particular version of what is true. There may be other ways to understand the world, which they have not yet been taught. There may even be reasons why they have been taught to believe certain things as true and immutable. Indeed, even the idea of truth itself may be seen as compromised by its contingency upon certain social and political preconditions. Perhaps the idea of transcendental moral and religious truths that could justify teachers as masters was itself only a Cave illusion, a social construction?

The new teacher, aware of this critique of the master, now becomes servant to the power and the implications of the experience of contingency as a social and political education in itself. To begin with he must expose his own mastery as a political fact and thereby as another shadow. This teacher becomes servant not only to raising the critical awareness of the student regarding their contingency upon the social world, but to his own sacrifice as master in doing so. This teacher, as servant to the students' experience of contingency, can never again justify his practice according to moral and religious visions that dominate the students and prevent them from thinking for themselves. As will become clear, elements of this new perspective on the teacher sit uneasily with and even reject the whole model of education as enlightenment and the role of mastery that it gives to the teacher.

There is a whole range of theoretical perspectives on the teacher in which education aims for the awareness not only of contingency *per se* but also of the contingency of the teacher in particular. We will explore two such broad-based perspectives. The first is from critical theorists in education who argue for the teacher as enabling the emancipation of the student from false ideas that are transmitted through the formal system of schooling. Here the teacher serves the critical and emancipatory thinking of the students, wherein they can come to understand and then change the world for themselves. The second group of perspectives is relatively new. They see the teacher in what can loosely be called 'post-enlightenment' or 'postmodern' terms. Here it is not the job of the teacher to serve any one idea of student development, but rather to listen to and encourage the many different views of the world that any classroom contains. These 'deconstructing' teachers will be servants of difference and pluralism, not masters of any one version of how education should be done or what must be learned and taught as if true. We will now look at each of these in turn.

CRITICAL PEDAGOGY
Karl Marx (1818–1883)

The thinking of Karl Marx may seem to be out of fashion today and certainly does not feature on many courses in higher education that train teachers. Nevertheless there are perspectives on the teacher that are to some extent grounded in the insights of Marx and of Marxist theory regarding contingency within and upon specific political relations.

At the time Marx was writing, in the middle of the nineteenth century, Europe was in the throes of the industrial revolution. The agricultural workers were migrating to the big towns and cities in search of jobs in the mills and the factories. For Marx this signified a new variation on the eternal relationship between rich and poor. In former times, labourers who worked on the land could at least sustain themselves, even if only to a meagre extent. Now, however, this new migrant labour force had no means of sustaining itself other than through paid employment. The workers had become wage slaves, which in turn gave enormous power to the owners of capital. The latter, the bourgeoisie, held all the cards. The former, the proletariat, simply had to play the hand that fate dealt them. In observing this new kind of slavery Marx made several insightful observations. He noted that the right by law for everyone to own property looked like a form of equality, for all were equal under the law of ownership. In practice, however, since the poor had nothing, their rights under the law meant nothing. Worse still, the legal protection of property instutionalised the privilege of the haves over the have-nots.

Marx also noted that the bourgeoisie ensured that not only civil society but also the state operated in such a way as to defend their own interests. The main weapon used by the state was 'ideology'. Bourgeois ideology ensured that the values and ideas that constituted common sense and taken-for-granted reality were those that reproduced the conditions that favoured the bourgeoisie. One of the most famous examples was religion. If the proletariat could learn to accept the idea that rewards should not be expected in this life, but rather in the next, then they would be more accepting of harsh working conditions and less likely to demand improvements. Similarly, the Protestant Work Ethic saw laziness as liaison with the devil, and workers were therefore encouraged to see hard work and long hours as a possible route to salvation.

For Marx, then, ideology was a key weapon in ensuring the dominance of the bourgeoisie over the proletariat. Whilst hunger and the need to survive won the battle with their material needs, ideology won the battle for their hearts and minds and the worker understood not only that he must sell himself for work to the factory owner but that it was morally right that he do so.

Since Marx's death, theorists have expanded upon these ideas, in particular regarding the role that teachers play in transmitting ideology to each succeeding generation of workers. This is a very important and controversial aspect of the job of the teacher, for anyone who already teaches or plans to become one. To what extent are teachers just lackeys of the state, educating students in ways that the state demands? Are teachers free to make their own decisions about the most appropriate education for their students, or are they merely passive conduits of the dictates of others? Many have argued that, whether consciously or unconsciously, teachers are always working on the side of the bourgeoisie against the proletariat. We will now look at one example that makes this case in a stark and dramatic way.

Louis Althusser (1918–1990)

The French Marxist, Louis Althusser, published an influential essay in 1970 called 'Ideology and Ideological State Apparatuses'. In it he outlined a theory of the way in which schools and teachers operated as instruments of the state. In contrast to the *repressive* state apparatuses, which used violence against those citizens who threatened the interests of the establishment, the *ideological* state apparatuses employed more subtle and hidden methods to achieve the same end. Althusser argued that, because of their role within the state, teachers had no practice except that determined 'by and in an ideology' (Althusser, 1984, p. 44). For one thing, this ideological function sees teachers employed to differentiate between those students whose future lies in production and those whose future lies in the management of production. All students are taught a number of useful techniques 'which are directly useful in the different jobs in production' (p. 6). But in addition it falls to teachers to reproduce in students the value system of capitalism and bourgeois morality. Thus, he says, students learn

> the 'rules' of good behaviour, i.e., the attitude that should be observed by every agent of the division of labour, according to the job he is 'destined' for: rules of morality, civic and professional conscience, which actually means rules of respect for the socio-technical division of labour and ultimately the rules of the order established by class domination (ibid.).

The real subtlety of this reproduction of ideology is that schools look on the surface to be politically neutral institutions. Althusser describes their ideological function as like a concert with a single score, 'although hardly anyone lends an ear to its music: it is so silent' (p. 29).

However, there is even worse news for teachers than that they reproduce bourgeois ideology. The cruellest irony of all is that the better the teacher is at motivating 'difficult' students to try harder with their school work, the more successfully he assimilates those students into the system that oppresses them. The more conscientious a teacher is, the more effective is his ideological function. In a passage that presents a bleak picture of the ideological role of the teacher, Althusser states,

> I ask the pardon of those teachers who, in dreadful conditions, attempt to turn the few weapons they can find in the history and learning they 'teach' against the ideology, the system and the practices in which they are trapped. They are a kind of hero. But they are rare and how many (the majority) do not even begin to suspect the 'work' the system (which is bigger than they are and crushes them) forces them to do, or worse, put all their heart and ingenuity into performing it with the most advanced awareness (the famous new methods!). So little do they suspect it that their own devotion contributes to the maintenance and nourishment of this ideological representation of the School, which makes the School today as 'natural,' indispensable-useful and even beneficial for our contemporaries as the Church was ... for our ancestors (p. 31).

The most dramatic thing that Althusser has to say, then, is that no matter how hard teachers try not to, they cannot help but represent the interests of the owners against the workers. Worse still, even the most inventive and caring teachers, who try to make schooling and learning more enjoyable for those to whom it might seem most remote, are still only reproducing the system that ultimately oppresses those students. This presents a very dismal picture of teaching, as unavoidably a political activity serving the needs of those in power. What more important job could there be for the bourgeoisie than that of the teacher who slowly indoctrinates students to accept the work ethic, to follow orders, to respect authority and to commit themselves to a life of wage labour? For Althusser, the teacher is always the agent of capitalism and works on its behalf.

Not surprisingly, many theorists and teachers, whilst sharing some of this kind of Althusserian analysis, do not accept the idea that the teacher is a helpless sap within the system of class relations. There are many perspectives upon the role of the teacher that try to show how the teacher can oppose this system of indoctrination and actually use education for emancipation rather than continued oppression. I shall now consider some examples of such thinking regarding the role of the teacher. Within what is generally called 'critical pedagogy', the job of the teacher is not only to help students overcome ideological distortions of their reality, but also to help them to create new realities.

Praxis

We saw above that critical teachers required a different relationship to their students than that merely of master. *Praxis* is the idea we must now explore if we are to understand this new type of relationship.[1] Recognising the importance of contingency, Marx argued that human thinking does not create its own social world; rather, the social world creates, shapes and gives content to human thinking. On the surface this looks as if it might support the view of teacher as master, for all that is required of education is that the teacher enable the world to fill the mind of the student—even perhaps as we saw earlier, by 'putting it in there' himself against the recalcitrant will of the student. However, this does not convey the subtlety of Marx's thinking. He also argues that our activity and the social world are separated or alienated from each other. In other words, there is a gap between us and the world we work on. There are two aspects to this. The first is that the worker is separated from what he produces. Unalienated work would have no such separation. The worker would express himself through his work, creating a unity between human activity and the material world. This type of work would be *praxis* and would see the world being transformed through the conscious activity of the human subject.

The second aspect is perhaps even more significant. It is not only physical work that alienates us from the external world; it is mental work as well. We can think about the world, but we cannot immediately turn our thinking into practice. A term that describes both aspects of alienation is *objectification*. With regard to work as production this means that our activity—which ought to be *praxis*, or a unity between our conscious and willed activity and reality—becomes divided. Work becomes split into my activity and an object out there that is not mine, even though it contains my work. My work has taken the form of an object; it has become objectified and I have lost a part of myself to it. (I shall return to this shortly.) With regard to the relationship between work and thinking, if we could unite our thinking with our actions, or with our work in the world, this would be *praxis*. For example, I might theorise about a world without private property, without rich and poor, without alienation and oppression, a world in which what I am, what I think and what I do are unified and indistinguishable from each other. But if I try to enact my noble universal and ethical thoughts in the real world as if there is this unity, then I will be likely to encounter problems. Thoughts about what I ought to be do not easily translate into my actions, because I cannot choose the conditions in which I act. What happens is that it looks as if I am saying one thing but doing another. I repeat the very separation between theory and practice that I wanted to overcome.

Nevertheless, if work/thinking and the world could somehow be united as theory *and* practice, this would be *praxis*. As such, *praxis* becomes the key idea whereby the radical teacher can struggle to change the world. If the radical teacher can somehow find ways of working and thinking that do not alienate and divide her from her students, and also if she can bring about the unification of her students' thoughts and actions, then the alienation of both will be overcome. Now we can understand what Marx means when he says that it is the social world that creates our consciousness. When the social world is characterised by alienation, then our work and our thinking are already separated into worker and object. But when the social world is characterised by *praxis*, our own work and our thinking are united with the world. It is still up to us to realise *praxis*, but for Marx, when we do, the world will be as our home. Moreover, being 'determined' by the world we live in will also be our own self-determination as human beings.

These are difficult ideas, not least because objectification is so powerful that it makes the reconciliation of theory and practice appear impossible. Nevertheless, before looking at how the idea of *praxis* has become an agenda for radical models of the teacher, there is a more simple way in which we can relate these ideas of alienation and objectification to the classroom. Teachers know that it is often difficult to motivate students to work. But 'work' in this example has the same characteristics and issues described above. When the teacher asks—tells—the student to do a piece of work, the student experiences alienation in carrying out the activity. Work in this example is learning. For those who struggle to realise *praxis*, learning ought to be an harmonious relationship between thinking and the world, and is or should be the most important way by which a student develops and grows, at one with the world. Students should learn about the world, work on it and in it, and they and their world should change as they do so. But when the work is forced upon them by another, it cannot be this self-determination, or *praxis*. Indeed, often students experience school work (learning) to be totally alienated from them. What they are asked to do, when and why, are all out of their control. What they make or write is not their own, indeed most often it is used to judge them. Thus, their work is produced in an objectified form and is returned to them in an objectified form as marks or sometimes even as punishment. Even if the work is praised, the students still understand that their work, their learning, is not *praxis*—valuable and worthwhile as an end in itself—but rather is a means to an end, perhaps for praise or to avoid the embarrassment of failure or punishment. As for the workers, so for the students, their work is not done for its own sake but merely as a means to other ends. In this way the students are alienated from their learning.

Critical pedagogues seek to address this alienation of the student directly. By doing so they propose a radical model of teacher practice that is servant to and not master of the students' emancipation. The radical teacher, in serving the idea of the student's *praxis*, is also politically committed to opposing and overcoming the causes of the alienation. You cannot work for *praxis* and expect to leave the student or the world as they are. If you work for *praxis*, you must also be working against those who profit directly from the objectification of physical and mental work.

Paulo Freire (1921–1997)

Perhaps the most significant contribution to a radical model of critical pedagogy is still that of the Brazilian educator, Paulo Freire. His most influential work was and remains *Pedagogy of the Oppressed* (1972), written in 1968. His radical perspective on the teacher emerges clearly in Chapter 2 of this book. It is worth spending just a little time looking at his argument. Freire sees the alienation of the student from her learning and her lack of *praxis* in the world as grounded in the way the teacher–student relationship reproduces a master–servant relationship. It is, he says, one where the teacher is active and the student passive, one where the teacher teaches about the world as if it is a fixed object, immutable and eternal, and the student simply has to collect this information. The teacher aims 'to "fill" the students' (Freire, 1972, p. 45) with contents that are 'detached from reality, disconnected from the totality that engendered them ... emptied of their concreteness and become a hollow, alienated and alienating verbosity' (ibid.). He refers to such a teacher–student relationship as the 'banking method' of education. Here, 'education thus becomes an act of depositing, in which the students are the depositories and the teacher is the depositor' (ibid.). It turns the students into 'receptacles to be filled by the teacher. The more completely he fills the receptacles, the better a teacher he is. The more meekly the receptacles permit themselves to be filled, the better students they are' (ibid.).

It is not hard to see how this description resembles very closely the idea of ideology mentioned above. The teacher becomes the agent who transmits to the students an ideological picture of 'how the world is', which the students then have to prove they have learned. Not only this: there is no *praxis* here, for learning is always separated from the reality of the students' own experiences and the curriculum never grants legitimacy to any knowledge that it has not sanctioned. This is not a creative enquiry or independent learning; rather it is merely the 'receiving, filing and storing' (p. 46) of deposits of knowledge that are placed in the containers called students.

Freire sees this as an issue concerning *praxis* and alienation, and seeks to change the way we understand the nature of work, and working relationships, in schools. The banking system of teaching suppresses any creativity or transformation that the student might wish to engage in. In this way it suppresses, Freire claims, their fundamental humanity, which can be fully expressed only as *praxis*, where work is unified with the world rather than objectified by it. This means, of course, that education directly serves the interests of those who profit from alienated work. Such people have no interest in seeing students become critically aware of their alienation, or of a notion of *praxis*, for that might see students rejecting the world as it currently is and working for radical social change.

This is precisely what Freire proposes. Instead of teachers fostering the credulity of their students, they should be working to arouse their incredulity, to raise their suspicions about what is happening to them. In other words, it is the teacher's job not to suppress but to encourage critical questioning. But here arises a fundamental question for this model of the teacher. How do you do this? Do you 'teach' critical questioning as if it were another deposit? Freire is very clear on this point: 'One does not liberate men by alienating them. Authentic liberation—the process of humanisation—is not another "deposit" to be made in men. Liberation is a *praxis*: the action and reflection of men upon their world in order to transform it' (p. 52). He coins the term 'problem-posing' for a form of educational practice or *praxis* that will facilitate forms of learning other than that of the banking method. Whereas the deposits of the latter act as answers to questions that the students themselves do not ask, problem-posing begins by seeing the world as still open to the negotiation of meanings. It begins with questions, not answers, and does not therefore prejudge the world on behalf of the student.

This has two related but very important implications for the radical and emancipatory model of the teacher. First, it challenges the mode of communication that is to be established between teacher and student, or, in essence, it challenges the whole structure of teaching. Problem-posing, says Freire, 'rejects communiqués and embodies communication' (ibid.). It establishes, therefore, a dialogical relationship rather than a relation of master to servant. Both are participants in a conversation about the world that can influence and affect that world according to their own perceptions and experiences; yet equally both are part of a dialogue over which neither exerts complete control.

This leads to the second implication. Problem-posing education fundamentally challenges and transforms the whole basis of the teacher–student relationship. In a difficult passage Freire tries to explain this. Dialogical education can overcome the established hierarchy of the teacher's domination over the student. If the teacher is as open to learning from this dialogue as the students, which she must be if she is to be working in the true spirit of problem-posing, then says Freire, 'through dialogue, the teacher-of-the-students and the students-of-the-teacher cease to exist and a new term emerges: teacher-student with students-teachers' (p. 53). The roles are no longer separated from each other or in opposition; now they are joined. Learning is no longer alienated from the learner and each becomes learner to himself, as well as teacher to others. In this different, dialogical practice, the actual teaching relationship itself has been changed. The world is questioned and criticised, and this critique produces a different world, one where the teacher and the student are no longer on opposite sides. Thus, in this radical model of education, problem-posing and dialogical education are seen to be *praxis* and potentially able to emancipate and liberate all who practise them.

Before looking at how critical pedagogy has developed since Freire, it is worth us addressing one question that might arise now in the mind of the teacher or the potential teacher. Is not Freire's suggestion actually undermining the authority of the teacher? In the real world how possible would it be to enter any classroom seeking dialogue, particularly if students for whatever reasons are already alienated and hostile? Would they not simply see this approach as soft and as a chance to take advantage of a teacher who has suspended her authority? Freire remarked on this in a talk he gave in London in 1993. He commented that his critical pedagogy is not

> saying that the teacher should lose her/his authority ... the authority of the teacher does not diminish the freedom of the student. One has to grow up through the contradiction of one with the other. In other words, there is no freedom without authority, there is no authority without freedom ... What I am saying is that both teacher and students must be subjects of the process of education (Freire, 1995, p. 21).

Critical pedagogy has developed considerably since the publication of *The Pedagogy of the Oppressed*. In particular the critique of the domination of the teacher in the banking model has been extended to cover any ideological domination of a minority group or suppressed voice in the cultural arena at large. The *praxis* of Freire, which destabilises the traditional identities of teacher and student is thereby extended into cultural fields other than education.

For example, Henry Giroux has employed the term 'cultural workers' (Giroux, 1992, p. 79) to encompass all those who work in the reproduction of ideological and social practices. This extension of critical pedagogy, says Giroux, 'ties education to the broader struggle for public life in which dialogue, vision, and compassion remain critically attentive to the liberating and dominating relations that organise various aspects of everyday life' (p. 137). As such, critical pedagogy moves from the classroom to social relations as a whole, and works now for social justice in all areas. Peter McLaren notes, 'it is Freire's particular strength that he has developed a critical vernacular that can help to translate both the other's experience and his own experience of the other in such a way that ideological representations may be challenged' (McLaren, 1997, p. 61). To paraphrase McLaren, critical pedagogy is relevant for all liberation struggles, the poor, women, people of colour, gays, lesbians and indigenous peoples (p. 64). For those who struggle for social justice, caught within but opposed to a master narrative, critical pedagogy 'speaks to the voiceless and the peripheralized, the marginalized and the excluded' (p. 13). It offers a 'space of hope' (ibid.) in which critical educators can now 'wage nothing less than war in the interest of the sacredness of human life, collective dignity for the wretched of the earth, and the right to live in peace and harmony' (ibid.). Here the model of the radical teacher becomes the practice of all whose work involves them with society's under-privileged and who, in destabilising the identity of the master, are prepared to become servants themselves to a notion of dialogical *praxis*, working towards 'a *praxis* of redemption' but in a space that 'can't be taken for granted' beforehand (ibid.).

Normalising education

Critical theorists have given special attention to the ways in which the workers' labour creates objects that have more value in the market place than the labour that made them. Objectification, explored above, refers to the way that the value of human labour is transferred into the value of commodities. The work of the human species becomes objectified, or exists in the world only in the form of objects. Marx calls this *commodity fetishism*, meaning that the value of human work appears to lie not in the activity of the workers, but in the objects that they make.

But critical theorists have taken this observation one step further. Now, they say, the worker himself is objectified. He has no value as a human being, only as an object in the market place, where his most powerful form of objectification is as a consumer. This human being is viewed as a potential source of profit, and is targeted by the media, by advertisers and by the pleasure industry—collectively, the culture industry—not to question that this objectified version of itself is indeed its true self and, rather, to spend our lives in the pursuit of personal pleasure through the entertainment industries.[2]

One critical pedagogue, Ilan Gur-Ze'ev, has argued recently that critical pedagogy must come to see itself as offering a 'counter-education' to this objectification of the 'I' within the culture industry. When education serves this objectification he calls it 'normalising education', meaning that it works to make us accept ourselves as the 'I' that the entertainment and marketing industries see us to be. This, says Gur-Ze'ev, is a 'de-humanisation' (Gur-Ze'ev, 2003a, p. 1), and one that is so powerful in determining our understanding of who and what we are that it prohibits us 'from detecting, questioning and challenging the violences of the apparatuses which construct them and determine [our] horizon' (ibid.).[3]

The task of the critical teacher, faced with the objectification of themselves and their students, is to try to counter this normalising education with a critical education that sees through these ideologies. Of paramount importance says Gur-Ze'ev is that teachers seek to educate for an 'I' that, through critical questioning, becomes an other to itself so that it might also then recognise the otherness of other people. What the teacher must try to combat is the normalising education that assimilates everyone into the market place of 'pleasure, cynicism [and] pragmatism' (p. 7). As such, this counter-education, through its teachers,

> inevitably collides with the ruling powers. ... It manifests a refusal to accept the present facts as the last and ultimate yardstick to evaluate reality, and it is committed to the effort of its own questioning and its own transcendence. It questions the self-evident and traces for the absent, for the forgotten, for the unrecoverable silenced voices and for the unfulfilled potentials (ibid.).

The real challenge here is that the educator must avoid pandering to the instant gratification of the objectified self and refuse any easy or certain solutions to the power of normalising education. For Gur-Ze'ev there can be no positive utopias, for, on the one hand, they turn the teacher into the master and, on the other hand, they come to serve, again, the process by which the 'I' is objectified, known and satisfied. This means that the teacher must teach in order to keep open the hope and possibility of what Gur-Ze'ev calls a 'negative utopia', one that is present in its absence. To do this the teacher will oppose an education that, Gur-Ze'ev writes, creates 'the subject as an object for manipulation' (Gur-Ze'ev, 2003b, p. 92) and work to produce 'the I as a centre for reflectivity' (ibid.). Ultimately his model of critical and emancipatory education asks two related things of the counter-educator. First, she will recognise that all human beings, her students included, are 'more than what the system has invested in [them]' (Gur-Ze'ev, 2003a, p. 9), and that as human subjects they have 'the potential of resisting the normalisation processes [and] becoming different than expected' (ibid.). Second, if the teacher is to know herself in the same way, then she must recognise her 'homelessness,' that is, that she also does not belong to the world that has sought to make itself normal for her. In keeping alive her own possibility, she can then teach from this homelessness for the homelessness of others. This, says Gur-Ze'ev, cannot

> overcome meaninglessness but it can offer a new readiness and vitalised responsibility for negating the given facts and pleasures. It is relevant in the counter-educator's refusal to abandon her own spiritual homelessness with and for the Other. This is the form of love that is still possible for counter-education. Yes, love, yes: offering the Other your hand in a Godless world is still an open possibility (Gur-Ze'ev, 2003b, p. 92).

Summary

Critical pedagogy, then, in many different guises, rests on the awareness that what counts as education in any given society is contingent upon and reproductive of the political relations that determine it. Teachers are inevitably caught up in this, and, at worst, act as agents for this reproduction. But awareness of this contingency, which we might call political awareness or political consciousness, is the beginning of the possibility of transforming these relations. Critical teachers teach for this awareness. They teach for students to understand how the system of formal education is designed only to release certain kinds of knowledge and to benefit only certain classes or cultures. They teach for students to recognise their own determination in a world that tries to make its education appear neutral and natural. They teach in order to raise awareness in the students that there are powers working behind the scenes that have a vested interest in maintaining the *status quo.*

Above all, critical teachers work to create the possibility that students might emancipate themselves from their condition as prisoners within the Cave. Such critical teachers recognise that their knowledge of social and political contingency does not make them masters of their students. On the contrary, it is this knowledge that calls such teachers to serve the emancipatory needs of the students.

POST-ENLIGHTENMENT PEDAGOGY

Introduction

There has recently emerged a different kind of criticism of the enlightenment model of education. Plato's Cave, described earlier, makes a number of presuppositions about education that impact considerably upon the role of the teacher. Above all it seems to lend itself to an hierarchical model of the wise and enlightened teacher who has the answers and his apprentice who will be taken along this same path to the same enlightenment. One recent French philosopher, Gilles Deleuze, has remarked that according to this 'infantile prejudice, the master sets a problem, our task is to solve it, and the result is accredited true or false by a powerful authority. It is also a social prejudice with the visible interest of maintaining us in an infantile state' (Deleuze, 1994, p. 158).[4] In Plato's model there is even an explicit reference to this hierarchy. He says that the prisoner may need to be dragged out of the Cave, against his will. Here the teacher is charged with forcing the student to become enlightened and is presupposed as having an authority over the student, an authority that the teacher can enforce for the good of the student. Most people can recall a teacher saying at some point 'I'm doing this for your own good ... You'll thank me later'. We saw above how this model of the teacher as master, and as the one whose greater wisdom and enlightenment is also their authority, could be manifested sometimes in a benevolent, and sometimes a not so benevolent, bullying and domination. Some have argued that even critical theorists assume the position of master because they still know how the student is to be enlightened and emancipated. Thus, not only the idea of the teacher as master but the whole notion of education as enlightenment and its related concept of emancipation have come under criticism. It is this I shall now explore as well as some of the different kinds of perspectives upon the role of the teacher that these criticisms have produced.

Teaching—the project

There is one main criticism of enlightenment education that has emerged from post-enlightenment philosophies that is relevant to and has far-reaching implications for the teacher. It concerns the way enlightenment models are used to justify what is to be taught, how it is to be taught, and by whom. Jean-François Lyotard is a theorist much associated with this critique. In his view, a model of enlightenment lies behind the way certain grand narratives legitimise some kinds of knowledge and actions in the world and repress or distort others. Grand narratives of this kind are 'total' explanations of the world that identify problem and solution at one and the same time. So, for example, Plato's model of enlightenment was part of the project designed to bring an end to the corruption of Athenian democracy. More recently in European history, the Enlightenment project (or the project of modernity), through its development of science, technology and the arts, sought to 'liberate the whole of humanity from ignorance, poverty, backwardness, [and] despotism' (Lyotard, 1992, p. 97). It was hoped that it would not only produce 'happy men, but, thanks to education in particular ... [would] produce enlightened citizens, masters of their own destiny' (ibid.). The legitimacy of this project lies not in the past but 'in a future to be brought about' (p. 61). This, says Lyotard, 'gives modernity its characteristic mode: the *project*, that is, the will directed towards a goal' (ibid.).

From Lyotard's perspective, then, education becomes the tool of the dreamer and the social reformer who has a vision of what ought to be and teaches in order to bring this about. The knowledge and actions that serve the dream are labelled legitimate; those that oppose it become illegitimate. The teacher who is legitimate therefore is the one who works for the project. We have seen this already represented above. Punishment by teachers was legitimate because it served the project of salvation; child-centredness was legitimate because it served the project of nature; critical pedagogy was legitimate because it served the project of emancipation. Whilst you would not call all of these 'modern', they nevertheless share a common structure: that the ends justify the means. Whereas much of European history has been a conflict about which ends and which means, post-enlightenment thinking is now questioning the very positing of ends. Perhaps we have reached the end of the idea of enlightenment and its form as a project. Perhaps we have come to the end of projects *per se*? If so, this has enormous implications for teachers, and we will look at these in a moment.

Lyotard's worries about the notion of 'the project' are threefold. First, he says that any project of enlightenment for a preconceived end relies upon a transcendental presupposition in order to justify itself. This means that all projects have to presuppose some kinds of truths that lie above and beyond the normal realm of knowledge and that cannot be known or tested in any of the usual ways. The real test of the transcendental pre-suppositions will be the realisation of the project, for this alone will prove the assumptions behind the project to have been correct. Examples of transcendental presuppositions might be projects that have to presume the existence of God, or the natural goodness of humanity, or even visions of human potential that lie beyond those that are currently possible. In the absence of proof, projects may have to rely on dogmatic assertions about why they are right and others are wrong.

Second, Lyotard says that the modern project for the betterment of mankind, which is based on the enlightenment model that freedom is rational and achieved by each person autonomously thinking for themselves, has dramatically and brutally failed. He says, 'for at least two centuries modernity taught us to desire the extension of political freedoms, science, the arts and technology. It taught us to legitimate this desire because, it said, this progress would emancipate humanity from despotism, ignorance, barbarism and poverty' (p. 110). But, he states, 'this promise has not been kept. It was broken not because it was forgotten but because development itself makes it impossible to keep' (p. 111). What does Lyotard mean by this? He means that the very thing that is supposed to solve the problems is in fact contributing to them.

> The new illiteracy, the impoverishment of people in the South and the Third World, unemployment, the tyranny of opinion and the prejudices then echoed in the media, the law that performance is the measure of the good—all this is not due to a lack of development but to development itself. This is why we would no longer dream of calling it progress (ibid.).

But there is an even more appalling example—Lyotard's third point—of the way in which the nature of enlightenment as a project has been (ab)used. This refers to the Holocaust of World War II, which is sometimes referred to in terms of *Auschwitz*. How, asks Lyotard, in the name of the 'fulfilment of all humanity' (p. 36) could one race be systematically exterminated? It is not just that those with power can define humanity in their own interests, it is also that the very idea of humanity as a project to be achieved enables them to do so. No wonder then that Lyotard defines the post-enlightenment (or postmodern) attitude against the enlightenment project as 'incredulity towards metanarratives' (Lyotard, 1984, p. xxiv).[5] Furthermore, Lyotard does offer some thoughts on how this incredulity can shape the work of the teacher (he is talking about philosophy teachers, but we can extrapolate from this). The problem as he sees it is this. Teachers who justify themselves according to the project, or within the enlightenment model of education, become part of the problem and not the solution. The real issue for such teachers is that they think they know in advance what they must teach, and what they are teaching for. In so doing, they perhaps risk closing down the possibility of education to that which is legitimated by the project. They suppress other projects and, worst of all, they assume that education *requires* projects. For post-enlightenment critics, this will, more often than not, result in a tyranny.

Against the prejudged certainties of the enlightened and the enlightening, Lyotard sees the post-enlightenment teacher refusing 'the consolation of correct forms' (Lyotard, 1992, p. 24) and learning to work 'without rules' (ibid.). We have, he says, paid a high price for the nostalgic dream of a universally transparent and communicable experience, and now is the time to wage 'war on totality' (p. 25) and to accept that not everything can be presented as rational knowledge. For the teacher, this requires a recognition that he is caught up in the dilemma of totality. The teacher as master represents closure and finality. His authority is the view that 'this is what must be learned because it is what has been learned before. It is what I know, and what you the student must come to know'. Lyotard's critique of the master is that 'you cannot open up a question without leaving yourself open to it' (p. 116). Accepting this means accepting that the teacher must renew 'ties with the season of childhood, the season of the mind's possibilities' (ibid.), rather than have his mind 'made up' (ibid.) before he arrives in the classroom. This is quite a challenge for a teacher— not to over-prepare but rather to keep open the space for unforeseen possibilities and not to prejudge what the learning must be. We will return to this in a moment.

Another similar critique of the idea of education structured by the enlightenment project comes from Zygmunt Bauman.[6] He argues that the modern project of emancipation and freedom through enlightenment only in fact 'emerged out of the discovery that human order is vulnerable, contingent and devoid of reliable foundations' (Bauman, 1992, p. xi). A total explanation of society was needed therefore in order to try to establish reliable foundations for such a society. Enlightenment thinking believed reason promised just such foundations, but the cost, as with any claim to totality, was that anything that did not fit the explanation, anything that was *different*, had to be controlled and suppressed. Thus, the educational project was twofold: to establish order and to recognise the moral righteousness of doing so. This became the justification for, and the authority of, the teacher as master. At its most horrendous, again, the project to control that which threatened the project became the Holocaust.

Bauman argues that rather than see the Holocaust as an aberration of the project for the goal of a unified humanity, we should understand that 'modernity contributed to the Holocaust' (Bauman, 1989, p. 88). It did so in two crucial ways. First, it provided the model for the project of Nazism, in that both modernity and Nazism believed that their ends justified the means. For both, 'the end itself is a grand vision of a better, and radically different, society' (p. 91, emphasis removed). Like the enlightenment project in general, then, 'modern genocide is an element of social engineering, meant to bring about a social order conforming to the design of the perfect society' (ibid.). Of course, we might want to say that the extermination of European Jewry (and others) and trying to educate for a better world have nothing in common. But Bauman is challenging us to consider that the same notion of education for progress underpins both. It then becomes not a difference in the vision of humanity that is at stake (although of course it is), as much as a shared model of means and ends by which each vision is to be achieved.

The second way in which Bauman sees modern reason as implicated in the Holocaust is that it provides a detached way of calculating the most efficient and effective ways of achieving the project. Throughout history there has been mass murder. But what gives the Holocaust its distinctively modern and rational character is the efficiency with which it was able to be carried out. Rational planning meant that the means could be divorced from the moral questioning of the ends, and how to kill and dispose of six million Jews becomes merely an exercise in problem-solving. 'Like everything else done in the modern—rational, planned, scientifically informed, expert, efficiently managed, co-ordinated—way, the Holocaust left behind and put to shame all its alleged pre-modern equivalents, exposing them as primitive, wasteful and ineffective by comparison' (p. 89). Chillingly, Bauman notes that the Jews, in a racially pure Aryan world picture, were the 'other' that could not successfully be integrated or assimilated or controlled. 'Like weeds, their nature could not be changed. They could not be improved or re-educated. They had to be eliminated' (p. 93). Again we might want to distance ourselves as teachers from the implications either that we divorce means from ends in our teaching, or that we have criteria by which some kinds of students are eliminated from the project. Yet we also know that both are to some extent true. Teachers often teach about how to solve problems in the absence of a discussion about the ends. And, of course, there are many criteria by which students can be excluded from education at all levels. Again Bauman is challenging us to see that in the nature of teaching within the enlightenment model, no matter how laudable our aims may be, we may be using methods to achieve them that become part of the problem rather than the solution.

To bring this discussion to a close, I am reminded of a text that I read when I was beginning my PGCE. At the beginning of a book on personal and social education, Richard Pring reproduces a letter that a Principal of an American high school sends to his teachers on the first day of school. It reads:

Dear Teacher

I am a survivor of a concentration camp. My eyes saw what no man should witness:
Gas chambers built by learned engineers.
Children poisoned by educated physicians.
Infants killed by trained nurses.
Women and babies shot and burned by high school and college graduates.
So, I am suspicious of education.
My request is: Help your students become human. Your efforts must never produce learned monsters, skilled psychopaths, educated Eichmanns.
Reading, writing, arithmetic are important only if they serve to make our children more human (Pring, 1984, introduction).

It is clear then that post-enlightenment thinking about the role and identity of the teacher has raised the stakes considerably. Now, the radical teacher, indeed any teacher with a vision for how education might contribute to creating a better world, could be said to be using the same model of education and teaching that allows for the tyranny of the enlightened over the apprentice. On this point Robin Usher and Richard Edwards state that,

> the end of education conceived as a 'project', of education as the vehicle for realising the modernist project, is one of the main characteristics of education in the postmodern. Coming to an end as a project implies that education can no longer be understood or understand itself as an enterprise standing above history and particular cultural contexts. It can no longer be dedicated—in its various forms—to the achievement of universally applicable goals—truth, emancipation, democracy, enlightenment, empowerment—pre-defined by the grand narratives (Usher and Edwards, 1994, p. 210).

So, are there post-enlightenment or postmodern perspectives on the teacher that can help us here? In fact there are many, and we will mention only a few. At heart, however, they share the view of Lyotard that we should be as the child, open to possibilities and to differences rather than closing them down.

Post-enlightenment teaching

Elizabeth Ellsworth provides a good description for us of the post-enlightenment teacher. We should, she says, entertain the idea 'that teaching is undecideable' (1997, p. 50). She means that even though a teacher may enter a classroom having decided what she will try to achieve, there is a gap between 'address and response' (p. 51). There are, she says, 'imperfect fits' (p. 50) between what this teacher attempts and what she actually achieves. In agreement with Freud, she argues that teaching is therefore one of the 'impossible professions' (p. 52) as no one can be sure, in advance, of the results they will achieve. As such teaching is by definition undecideable.

It could be observed that this undecideability might have been one of the reasons for the brutality of the master seen earlier. His harshness was a response to the increasing frustration, perhaps fear, that the teaching was not working, a failure that then became the justification for ever more severe methods being employed in order to achieve success. It could also be said that the critical pedagogue whose project was emancipation now has to recognise that education as a project will never be successful because education cannot be controlled. In addition of course, its undecideability challenges all models of education that are led by outcomes and measurable objectives.

Even though Ellsworth sees teaching as undecideable, she does not believe that we should not teach. It is often the case that where someone argues in favour of an orientation towards undecidability, on the grounds that some things cannot be rigidly planned for in advance, the response is either 'There will be chaos', or 'Since we can't do anything, we might as well not bother'. For Ellsworth, however, it is precisely here, in the space created by 'the undecideability of pedagogy and the indeterminacy of its address' (p. 55) that the real yet unanticipated possibilities of education exist. Faced with undecideability she says

I don't see any threat of paralysis or nihilism . . . there's no need to panic or despair. When I find myself despairing as a teacher it's not the paradoxes of my profession that have brought me down. Usually, what leaves me feeling hopeless is the way that the culture of teaching manages to ignore, deny or bull its way past its own ironies and impossibilities' (p. 139).

On the contrary, she says, in the undecideability lies the 'fecundity of teaching' (ibid.). Moreover, being asked to respond to these impossibilities 'empowers and condemns me' (p. 137) to keep teaching, but this time involved in disputes about 'which meanings will be valued and why' (ibid.). This post-enlightenment critique of the teacher understands that such a teacher is 'empowered to participate, but never as the One with the "right" Story' (ibid.), with consequences that she 'can never fully know, understand or control' (p. 138).

Such a post-enlightenment view of the teacher sounds exciting and full of risk and possibility. Of course, to those who, as Bauman has noted, crave order and predictability, 'the postmodern seems to condemn everything, propose nothing' (1992, p. ix). That is why the postmodern challenge seems to be 'a shaking of the foundations' (Usher and Edwards, 1994, p. 25) of everything that teaching seems to stand for. Usher and Edwards note that

education does not fit easily into the postmodern moment because educational theory and practice is founded in the modernist tradition. Education is very much the dutiful child of the Enlightenment and, as such, tends to uncritically accept a set of assumptions deriving from Enlightenment thought (p. 24).

Seeking a definitive post-enlightenment or postmodern philosophy of the teacher would obviously be self-contradictory. 'There is no uniform, unified postmodern discourse of education' (p. 25). That, precisely, is how and why it can remain open to unforeseen educational possibilities and is able to resist dogmas that prejudge totality or operate for closure.

Stuart Parker has offered a manifesto for education in postmodernity, arguing that the postmodern teacher will be an ironic teacher. His vision of a postmodern teacher sees a world that is framed and constructed but in ways that are not always transparent to common sense. The teacher's role is to deconstruct this world so that students may see through its appearance to the mechanisms that have put it together. This postmodern educationalist he calls 'the teacher-deconstructor' (Parker, 1997, p. 143). She will understand the world to be a text that has been written within the boundaries of certain genres and certain styles, boundaries that by definition legitimate some structures, some readings, and outlaw or marginalise others. Post-modern education thus becomes learning about the way 'in which a text achieves its effect ... highlighting the marginal, the concealed, the suppressed themes and assumptions' (ibid.). Again the challenging nature of the postmodern viewpoint becomes apparent. Teachers and students will deliberately misread the text 'with the intention of causing trouble' (ibid.). The lesson is likely to be that there is no one true reading of any situation, for each text is contingent, and each reading of the text is contingent. There is no foundation that one can discover and rely upon which will enlighten us as to the correct reading. All teaching, says Parker, all education, should reveal how everything in the world 'has no ultimate compelling justification' (p. 144).

How can a teacher truthfully teach that there is no one truth? Parker's ironic teacher must find a way of living a foundationless life, it seems, but doing so in a committed way. He writes:

> teachers and students will be encouraged to become ironic in reconciling the foundationless status of their beliefs and commitments—and the commitments of others—with the desire to create, develop and defend them. Possession of this ironic attitude—this unstable, dynamic oscillation of the rhetorical forces of deconstruction and position, or reactivity and creativity—is the signature of the postmodern voice and a central characteristic of emancipation in post modernity (p. 142).

A slightly different approach to a similar theme is taken by Ronald Barnett regarding the post-enlightenment teacher in higher education. He argues that modernity 'likes things to be orderly, measured (literally), fully calculable, uniform and rule-governed ... But postmodernity won't be put back into that bottle: the genie has now escaped. Multiple standards, multiple purposes, multiple knowledges and multiple consumers' (Barnett, 2000, pp. 20–21). This 'multiplication of frameworks' within which teachers in higher education now work Barnett calls 'supercomplexity' (p. 6).

What is it, he asks, 'to be educated under [these] conditions of radical uncertainty' (p. 153) that characterise the supercomplexity of this postmodern world? His response is that teachers do not serve their students if they do not expose them to the unsettling character of the supercomplex world. To learn to live in such a rapidly changing world students need to learn to let go of the myths of certainty and predictability. To become resilient to change they must, in their education, be exposed to change and then helped 'to live at ease with this unsettling' (p. 155). A new kind of pedagogy is required for this higher education, and a new kind of tutor. Barnett argues that the formal lecture is only a 'refuge for the faint hearted' (p. 159) and any unsettling it might evoke is 'barely skin deep' (ibid.). In the lecture 'the students remain as voyeurs' (ibid.) watching a performance but never required actually to engage with it. He notes:

precisely under the perplexing conditions of supercomplexity, lecturers will fall back on teaching approaches that appear to offer, in their pedagogical relationships, a degree of security and predictability. Indeed, the students themselves, faced with the corresponding challenge of a pedagogy for supercomplexity, are likely to resort to more orderly and predictable pedagogical situations. They will opt for dependency. In short, a conspiracy for safety develops between lecturers and students precisely when such curricular approaches should be jettisoned as the pedagogy of another age (p. 163).

In contrast, the pedagogy of the new age demands that the teacher 'step aside to some extent' (p. 160) or even that 'we have to give up the notion of teaching as such' (p. 159). If students are to be unsettled, the teacher cannot act as a dependable stabilising force. She cannot appear with first aid every time a student is injured by the 'radical uncertainty' (p. 164) of the times. This means that those forms of education and teacher–student relationships that have been engineered to promote the model of certainty and stability must be got rid of. The student can only experience supercomplexity for herself if the teacher does not ameliorate its effects. Only then will the student learn not just resilience but enjoyment in these bewildering times. The post-enlightenment teacher frees students from having to learn ways in which experiences, or indeed the history of the world, can be tied together within a common meaning. That idea of a grand narrative that can offer a coherence to all that appears disparate and heteronomous is over. Now, for Usher and Edwards, experience becomes an end in itself and is no longer servant to 'a hierarchy of foundational and transcendental reason and values' (1994, p. 11). Now, moving from one experience to another without the tyranny of having to understand them all together and 'properly', as high culture might demand, is a pleasure, even a desire.

Let me cite now two remarks to conclude on the postmodern attitude that underpins many different versions of post-enlightenment philosophies of the teacher. From Usher and Edwards the following:

> postmodernity, then, describes a world where people have to make their way without fixed referents and traditional anchoring points. It is a world of rapid change, of bewildering instability, where knowledge is constantly changing and meaning 'floats' without traditional teleological fixing in foundational knowledge and the belief in inevitable human progress. But the significant thing is that in postmodernity uncertainty, the lack of a centre and the floating of meaning are understood as phenomena to be celebrated rather than regretted (p. 10).

To which the following, from Bauman, can be added:

> we are bound to live *with* contingency . . . for the foreseeable future. If we want this future to be also a long one. . . . what is needed is . . . a practical recognition of the *relevance* and *validity* of the other's difference, expressed in a willing engagement in the dialogue (1992, p. xxi).

Summary

Clearly there are similarities and differences between recent emancipatory and post-enlightenment models of the teacher, but I do not propose to discuss these at this point. I want instead to end this chapter by asking a question of all of the models of the teacher explored here. The question is this. Regardless of whether teachers believe in serving nature, *praxis* or pluralism and difference, are they not all faced with the same problem— viz. that they know in advance what is to constitute an education for their students? In being servant to a particular idea of the teacher, and to a particular idea of the kind of educational developments they wish to work for, are they not also, again, becoming master over the student? Is it even possible for a teacher unambiguously to serve students when the teacher– student relationship is always mediated by an idea or a prejudged view about what education is for? Even the undecideability of post-enlightenment teaching has this very openness as its prejudged decision of the project that it seeks to achieve. Indeed, even irony can be a most powerful form of domination.

In Chapter 3 above we saw that Rousseau acknowledged this problem when he admitted that the art of teaching 'consists in controlling events' (Rousseau, 1993, p. 251) in such a way that the pupil does not realise he is being controlled: 'let him think he is master while you [the teacher] are really master' (p. 100). In a different way, McLaren also acknowledges the dangers that exist for a repetition of the domination of the master–servant relationship even in a *praxis*-based critical pedagogy. The latter, he says, can become 'dangerously domesticated' (McLaren, 1997, p. 55) because teachers can adopt it as a means to career advancement. Such teachers 'wish to enjoy the appearance of being radical without facing the hard decisions that could risk one's job security or possibility for tenure' (ibid.). Usher and Edwards also observe that the emancipatory teacher may easily turn into another master. Educators, they say, 'find it hard to accept that their emancipatory intentions, their desire to enlighten, may be implicated with the will to power and may, therefore, have oppressive consequences' (Usher and Edwards, 1994, p. 27). Postmodern teachers, they argue, 'need always to question *any* discursive practice, no matter how benevolent, for the configurations of emancipation/oppression within it' (ibid.). Their own response to the 'master's voice' of their own book is to assert at the end that in being forced to use language they accept that their mastery is already compromised and that their text therefore 'can be deconstructed' (p. 228). We also saw earlier, in Chapter 1, how Burbules summed up this dilemma, and it is worth repeating here. He notes:

> authority is inherent in any teaching-learning relation; it cannot be abrogated or denied even when one wishes to minimise its significance. But authority carries certain costs: It can foster dependency; it implies certain privileges of position that interfere with egalitarian social commitments; it becomes too easily taken for granted in the minds of both student and teacher. Encouraging students to question authority, even inviting challenges to one's own authority as a teacher, can foster

valuable learning—but only a person in authority can do that ...
Institutional customs arrogate dimensions of privilege to teachers that
conflict with our attempt to manage authority gracefully ... At a still
deeper level, we who have chosen teaching as a career must acknowledge
in ourselves the desires that motivate us. However modest we might
endeavour to be, the influence that comes with authority and the pride of
seeing our plans and intentions (sometimes) come to fruition are seductive
pulls back into the temptation to exercise our authority—though only for
the 'best' of purposes, of course (Burbules, 1997, p. 67).

Let us try and sum up what seems to be happening here. In this chapter we
have looked at two specific notions of the teacher, each serving an idea of
the potential of education, and describing a vision of pedagogy that would
effectively realise that service. But in each case, with *praxis* and
difference, the experience of the practising teacher may be much more
complicated and problematic even than is anticipated within some of these
perspectives. Teachers' good intentions may, in fact, produce the opposite
to what they intend. Education for emancipation cannot escape also being
education as tutelage; and education for difference cannot escape also
being education as the same. At the very beginning of this book we
recalled the concern of Max Weber that he was 'moved, above all, by the
fact that on its earthly course an idea always and everywhere operates in
opposition to its original meaning and thereby destroys itself' (Bottomore
and Nisbet, 1978, p. 362). Perhaps the unintended consequence, here,
of teaching that is designed to serve the cause of emancipation or
difference is that teaching unavoidably places the teacher in the master's
position. Every teacher teaches in the name of something, and in doing so
assumes the role of master, even if they do not intend this—even if they
refuse the title of 'teacher' and prefer, for example, something like
'facilitator'.

   This experience of the contradiction that lies at the heart of the teacher–
student relationship can be taken seriously and at face value. It is, of
course, very easy for the experience to be explained away as 'obvious'—
as it might be said, 'of course you have to take decisions on their behalf;
you have to teach them *something*'—and as having no real import beyond
this truism. However, educational theory and philosophy that pass over
this experience serve teachers poorly. This experience of the contradiction
of freedom and authority is absolutely fundamental to the teacher–student
relationship and to the dilemmas that the theory–practice divide
reproduces. Indeed, on a much grander scale, it is the problem of the
domination in modernity of instrumental reason, for it is the contradiction
that envelopes social critique. There is no way that alternative visions can
avoid becoming abstract and objectified as universal models, with the
consequence that they become separate from and thereby dominate the
very people whose truth they are supposed to represent. The philosophy of
the teacher, as it is being presented in this study, takes this contradiction—
the experience by both teacher and student of the abstraction of the teacher
from the student—to be the substance of its work. We will see now how

thinking about this contradiction and opposition as philosophical substance and subjectivity offers teachers the chance to reassess their understanding of what they do and how they do it, and retrieves meaning within the difficult relation of their successes and their failures. In short, it reveals otherwise hidden philosophical depths within the ambivalence of the relation of teacher and student.

Before leaving this topic, however, it is appropriate to look briefly at a teacher who, over two thousand years ago, took the idea of being servant to others' education even more seriously—Socrates. He is relevant for us at the end of this chapter for many reasons, but one stands out in particular: Socrates not only experienced the dilemma of being master over those he wished to think for themselves; he also, uniquely, turned this experience of the dilemma into an educational method, and became therein a 'negative' teacher.

SOCRATES (C. 469–399BC)

Socrates realised that when he questioned people about what they said they knew, it was not long before inconsistencies appeared in their defence of that knowledge. If they were honest, they would eventually have to admit that the certainty of their knowledge was pretty flimsy and that doubt had, in fact, replaced their certainty. What they learned from Socrates was that they did not know what they thought they knew. This is the same kind of education that Plato envisaged for the prisoners in the Cave—namely, that they would come to question and to doubt the illusory truths that the Cave reproduced. Where Socrates differs from Plato is that whilst Plato was prepared to argue for enlightenment and for enlightened teachers, Socrates refused to countenance such certainties. Crucially, what Socrates knew—the only thing he knew—was that as a teacher he did not know anything either. This was therefore the only thing he could honestly teach people. Famously, his response to this self-professed ignorance was that instead of trying to teach students some particular content, he chose instead to teach only for the negation, the doubting and the questioning of their existing knowledge. Since, as we have seen, the problem of the teacher as master over the student has always involved some prejudgement about what is to constitute their education, the solution that Socrates offers to this dilemma is to teach them nothing at all.

Here, then, is a very intriguing approach to the difficulties the teacher faces in trying to be servant to the education of his students. Socrates served the Delphic Oracle, which told him that there was no one wiser than him. Since the God could not lie, but equally since Socrates could not understand how this could be true, he devoted his life to trying to learn the truth of the Oracle. The only experience he knew to be true was that he never really knew anything for certain, and the more he interrogated those around him, the more he realised this was also true for them. Thus, as a teacher, he could never assume the identity of the master of knowledge, but only that of a servant of its continual questioning, or its negation. This he spent his life doing. At his trial he says that if he is spared the death penalty on condition that he gives up this truth of his life, he will not accept this. Here he states very clearly what he believes being a servant of truth means for the teacher. He declares that, for as long as he lives, he will continue to serve the truth of the Oracle that he is wise solely in knowing of his ignorance. At stake, here, for Socrates is the integrity of the teacher. If he teaches something he does not know, then he is being untrue to himself and that will cost him his soul. Raising this issue before the jury, he asks them, 'are you not ashamed that you give your attention to acquiring as much money as possible, and similarly with reputation and honour, and give no attention or thought to truth and understanding and the perfection of your soul?' (Plato, 1969, p. 61).

How, then, does Socrates actually practise this 'negative' philosophy of the teacher? How does he serve the truth of knowing nothing without becoming, as ever, the master or the teacher who knows what to teach on behalf of his students? Socrates responds to this in several ways. First, he distances himself from the idea of being a teacher at all. At his trial he notes there are respected teachers who charge for their services, but since he has never taken money under these circumstances, he is not a teacher of this kind—'I have never set up as any man's teacher' (p. 65). Indeed, when Socrates does try to define a philosophy of the teacher that applies to him, it is as a very particular kind of teacher—a midwife. His skills, he says, are the same as those of a midwife, except that he supervises the labour of minds, not bodies. Also, just as midwives often have no children of their own, so Socrates says he himself is barren of wisdom, and that it is this lack of wisdom that makes him question the knowledge of others in order, then, to test their ideas to see whether they turn out 'to be viable or still born' (Plato, 1987, p. 41).

Over two thousand years later Socrates' midwifery is still the subject of debate. From one point of view, it might be said that here is a teacher who sets himself to be the servant and not the master of his students. At no time does he have anything positive to teach anyone. All he does is to serve the Oracle, by which he has been given the task of understanding the truth of his lack of wisdom, and in serving this truth he is indirectly able to 'teach' others that his truth may also be their truth. He cannot tell them this, for that would be to know something. He can only work with them until they begin to see this truth through their own doubts and questions. If his negative education is successful, they will not have been taught anything except through and by themselves. But from another point of view, it might be said that he is a hypocrite. After all, he knows that he does not know anything, and this is still to know something. Or, he might even be seen as a destroyer, undermining beliefs but having none of his own.

Either Socrates is a near-saint who, at great personal cost, remained true to himself and to the service of education, refusing to make his life easier by compromising his integrity and pretending to know things that he did not know. *Or* he is a rogue, whose verbal acuity is sharp enough to reveal inconsistencies in everyone else's knowledge but who never risks any of his own. Indeed, perhaps his claim to know nothing is hardly credible, and is at best ironic, intended not to be completely believed. This would make him a practitioner of deceit. Such judgements about Socrates depend largely upon the extent to which one feels that he genuinely avoided abstraction (and therefore domination over the student), or rather masked it behind the dissemblance of not being a teacher.

Socrates ends this chapter by placing before us an intriguing challenge. If you set out to serve an educational ideal that has at its core the avoidance of inculcation and works instead for the free development of the student's own questioning and doubting mind, does this necessarily still place you in the position of master? Is the path out of the Cave inescapably one that has always already been travelled before by the teacher? Or, alternatively, and perhaps with Socrates: if a teacher recognises that her role is essentially negative, knowing nothing in herself and drawing from her students their negation of their own knowledge can she succeed in being a servant *to*, rather than a master *of*, her students' education? Is it negative teaching, rather than emancipatory or post-enlightenment teaching, which is really the foil of being the master? Does negative education finally achieve the overcoming of mastery and abstraction that has eluded our theorists thus far? If so, this offers us the perplexing idea that the teacher who successfully works for the free and critical thinking of the student has an inescapably contradictory identity. She must teach nothing in order to teach for the freedom of her students to think for themselves, and she must assume no other authority than that of the questioner. Carl Rogers has, so it seems, implicitly recognised the logic of just such a view: 'When I try to teach ... I am appalled by the results ... because sometimes the teaching appears to succeed. When this happens I find that the results are damaging. It seems to cause the individual to distrust his own experience and to stifle significant learning' (Rogers, 1969, p. 153).

Even if one accepts that Socrates achieved a negative pedagogy and was not teacher as master but teacher as servant, however, it is not easy to see how such a negative pedagogy could be employed by modern teachers. On the whole, they are not free to teach nothing, nor *only* to ask questions; more often, they have content that they must teach. Whilst Socrates can be seen to take seriously the question of authority that lies within the teacher–student relationship, it may be that we must also take the dilemma seriously but understand it in other ways. Bluntly, the modern teacher is set the challenge of finding ways to deal with their abstraction, their mastery, that enable them to serve the development of critical and thinking students whilst still being able to teach them *something*. Here, the contradiction of the teacher–student relationship takes its philosophical form. How can the teacher be both master and servant? The answer, within the philosophy of the teacher, lies in philosophical thinking about the significance and import of the experience of contradiction and dilemma: that is, by taking seriously the idea that there is something more, something deeper, to be learned from the difficulties of theory and practice.

It is towards this thinking that we now move in Chapter 5 but will be taken up in more detail in Part III below. In the following chapter we will look at three examples of perspectives on the teacher that find a *spiritual* significance in these dilemmas and oppositions, and in the unintended consequences that are repeated between teacher and student. This will open up the way to deeper analyses of the teacher–student relation, deeper in the sense that thinking around the spiritual significance of teaching is implicated with notions of vocation, service and even self-sacrifice. These may or may not be religious in character. We will see in the next chapter how this spiritual pedagogy fares both with and without a sense of the transcendent.

NOTES

1. This is one version of *praxis*, viz. revolutionary praxis. Another type of *praxis* would be the one that Aristotle writes about in Book 6 of the *Nicomachean Ethics*.

2. For example, this objectification sees the 'I' turned into an object that consumes pleasure, amusement and entertainment. Theodor Adorno and Max Horkheimer wrote a celebrated essay on what they called 'the culture industry'. They argued that the amusement on offer from the culture industry was only 'the prolongation of [mechanized] work' (Adorno and Horkheimer, 1979, p. 137). The manufacture of amusement was sought after by the workers as an escape from the tedium of work, but in fact it only served to commend 'the depressing everyday world' (p. 139) to which they must return. Adorno and Horkheimer argue that even laughter itself has become an ideological weapon in the objectification of the individual. They state that within the culture industry fun and laughter have become 'the echo of power as something inescapable' (p. 140). Fun, they say, 'is a medicinal bath. The pleasure industry never fails to prescribe it. It makes laughter the instrument of the fraud practised on happiness' (ibid.). It perpetuates laughter as 'a disease which has attacked happiness and is drawing it into its worthless totality' (p. 141). They conclude that 'a laughing audience is a parody of humanity (ibid.). See also Chapter 2 above.

3. This is in line with Adorno and Horkheimer who argue that no 'independent thinking must be expected from the [cinema] audience' (1979, p. 137).

4. I shall return to look in more detail at Deleuze in Part III below.

5. It is not just 'post-enlightenment' thinkers who draw attention to the relationship between education and the Holocaust. Theodor Adorno, one of the main figures in critical theory, opened a radio broadcast in 1966 by noting that 'the premier demand upon all education is that Auschwitz not happen again ... Every debate about the ideals of education is trivial and inconsequential compared to this single ideal: never again Auschwitz. It was the barbarism all education strives against' (Adorno, 2003, p. 19).

6. As with other theorists and perspectives in Part II I am presenting the ideas of Bauman uncritically. The overall aim of Part II is critically to comprehend the whole that is presented when these different interpretations of education appear in relation to each other within our experience.

Chapter 5
The Spiritual Teacher

INTRODUCTION

Our journey to this point, through Chapters 3 and 4, has been a difficult one. Our guides along the way have, in a number of different respects, all tried to help us deal with the fundamental issue of authority and freedom in education. So far, we have worked with the idea that the teacher can try either to be master of the students or servant to the students. We have not yet explored the idea that the teacher can experience herself in some way not just as *either* master *or* servant, but in the context of a different kind of relationship altogether, one where the relation of master and servant has spiritual significance. The teacher who is committed to her students' freedom, as was shown in the preceding chapters, experiences for herself the *aporia* of theory and practice. An *aporia* is a dilemma that seems to offer no path to its resolution. Here, then, the *aporia* of theory and practice is that teachers seem unable to put the theory of freedom successfully into practice and the result is that what the teacher *says* or *intends* is not what she actually *does*. The teacher who teaches for the freedom of the students' own learning finds herself having to use her authority over the students to do so. She has to be master of them in order to serve their educational needs. She has to know in advance how and what it is that the students must find out for themselves. Thus her goal of students' autonomy, whether it be through critical or post-enlightenment pedagogies, is compromised by a contradiction that she seems unable to shake off.

In consequence, the two approaches examined in Chapter 4 can provoke the thinking teacher towards a philosophy of the teacher but they can only take her so far along that road. They contribute to the philosophical education of the teacher because they acknowledge dependence and contingency as the fate of the teacher. But in teaching *about* contingency—indeed, in teaching *for* contingency—neither critical pedagogy nor post-enlightenment pedagogy has learned how to teach *as* contingency. Neither has succeeded in recognising how the contradictions that are inescapably part of the experience of contingency are themselves another and different kind of educational experience.

This is not to say that critical pedagogy or post-enlightenment pedagogies are not important. Their contribution to debunking some of the illusions of modern thinking and modern educational theory and practice in particular are vital. It is within these two broad perspectives that many of the teacher's contradictory (and negative) experiences are generated. The problem is that for the thinking teacher who needs to deepen her understanding of these difficult (negative) experiences neither perspective offers any help, because both fail to give due recognition and substance to the experience of contradiction in the teacher's work. They fail to give substance to the truth in education that the master in education always comes first. ('Fear of the lord is the beginning of wisdom', Hegel, 1977, pp. 117–118, and Proverbs, 1. 7.) Indeed, the post-enlightenment teacher who, through irony, asserts his lack of identity or of authority fails to be aware of the truth of irony. Irony requires that the teacher be both exactly what he appears to be and not what he appears to be. The teacher who misses the former gives up all rights to being a teacher. Worse, he becomes a dissembler, feigning not to be a teacher whilst using the fact that he is one in order to do so.

There could be a number of responses here to these difficulties. The teacher could, for example, give up teaching altogether in the certain but despairing knowledge that, despite her best efforts, the system, the institution, the instrumental method with its testing and tables of results, always wins through. Equally, she could become resigned to the conditions that oppose her at every turn and take the view that 'if you can't beat them, you might as well join them'. In fact, both of these responses are forms of resignation. The former resigns from teaching, the latter resigns to teaching. But there is within philosophy a different way of understanding this dilemma for the teacher. It is not an alternative to these difficulties; it is rather a different way of learning from them. It is a perspective that recognises the difficulties as offering something to learn from—about practice, about theory, and about the teacher. In this chapter we are going to examine three theorists who have, again in different ways, found the nature of these difficulties within theory and practice to have spiritual significance, particularly for the teacher who suffers them. In a sense, these three thinkers can be seen to take seriously the commendation from Adorno and Horkheimer that even when conditions make such thinking extremely difficult, and even when it appears that such thinking can change nothing, nevertheless, they say, our thinking *must examine itself* (Adorno and Horkheimer, 1979, p. xv). This is what we shall undertake now by exploring the ways in which Martin Buber, Simone Weil and Martin Heidegger have each discerned spiritual import in the asymmetry of the teacher–student relationship. For Buber, Weil and Heidegger, in different ways, the aporetic experience of theory and practice is an experience of the relation between teacher and student where individuality or identity is in some sense lost to and re-formed in their encounter. This re-formation can be called *spiritual* for it seems to transcend each individual person and to have a significance beyond each of them, a 'beyond' that can be said, at least to begin with, to be an experience of unity over separation. For Buber and Weil spirit is essentially religious; for Heidegger, as we shall see, it is more nationalistic and political.

MARTIN BUBER (1878–1965)

The first spiritual philosophy of the teacher that we shall explore comes from a recent Jewish thinker, Martin Buber. He has written a great deal about how religious insights can inform the understanding of everyday human relationships, but also within his work there are many references to education. In addition, the philosophy for which he is most famous, the *I-Thou* relation, can, as Buber himself shows, be applied in particular ways within education and in particular to the teacher–student relationship. It will be seen that with Buber, as with our other selected philosophers, what is offered here is not just an understanding of the teacher as pursuing *either* a project of enlightenment *or* its critique, not just a philosophy of the teacher as *either* master *or* servant, but a spiritual philosophy where both meet in a genuine encounter. Buber's philosophy of the teacher helps us to understand something of the spiritual significance of the identity and work of the teacher.

In one sense, Buber sees education as a struggle against forms of estrangement in a world where humanity, as we have already seen, becomes alienated from itself. For Buber, true human relations are to be found in 'dialogue' or in what he calls the *I-Thou* relation. In opposition to the *I-Thou* relation, however, he finds in the world another relation, the *I-It* relation. In the modern world this latter relation becomes dominant over the *I-Thou* relation. The *I-It* relation has a resemblance in some ways to the notion of objectification that was considered in Chapter 3: for Marx, objectification succeeded in treating people as things and converted the objects of their labour into commodities. In consequence, the value of the work—in effect, the essence of the human species—becomes invested in commodities. What is lost in and to objectification is genuine human relations between people, and between people and the natural world.

This is similar to Buber's critique of the *I-It* relation (although he does not have an economic theory of objectification). Buber says of the *I-It* relation that it enables an 'accumulation of information' (Buber, 1987, p. 5) between people whose relations to each other are thus characterised as between objects. Such people are, therefore, merely 'surrounded by a multitude of "contents"' (p. 12). In the *I-It* relation a man 'rests satisfied with the things that he experiences and uses ... [H]e has nothing but objects' (pp. 12–13). Buber argues that this reduction of the living process to things or to facts is the overriding characteristic of modern life: 'This is the exalted melancholy of our fate, that every *Thou* in the world must become an *It* ... As soon as the relation has been worked out, the *Thou* becomes an object among objects ... fixed in its size ... Life ... can again be described, taken to pieces, and classified ...' (pp. 16–17). Any communication between *I-It* (i.e. between the I and the object, or the information, or the person treated as the object) 'is prompted solely by the need of objective understanding' (Buber, 1947, p. 37), which, he says, is 'the inalienable sterling quality of "modern existence"' (ibid.). Against the *I-It* relation Buber sees the genuine human relation of *I-Thou*, where you and I experience ourselves in and as our relation to each other such that it is impossible for either of us to become fixed, classified or objectified. The relation of *I-Thou* is 'mutual' (1987, p. 15). 'My *Thou* affects me, as *I* affect it' (ibid.). Thus, he claims, 'all real living is a meeting' (p. 11).

In addition, the *I-Thou* relation is spiritual because 'spirit is not in the *I*, but between *I* and *Thou* . . . Man lives in the spirit if he is able to respond to his *Thou*. He is able to if he enters into relation with his whole being' (p. 30). In the *I-Thou* there is no object, only relation, and in this relation is to be found our spiritual life.

In view of this, Buber argues, the *I-Thou* relation exists as a dialogue in which there is 'a genuine change from communication to communion' (Buber, 1947, p. 21).[1] This dialogue does not consist in what is said for the 'what' is only its objective form. The *I-Thou* occurs 'when in a receptive hour of my personal life a man meets me about whom there is something, which I cannot grasp in any detail at all, that "says something" to me' (ibid.). That is, he 'speaks something that enters my own life' (ibid.). Thus, in the *I-Thou* relation someone addresses us through 'inner' (p. 27) speech.

An example might help here. Buber describes a meeting in 1914 of men from different European countries who had come together over the outbreak of the war. Even from the start, and because of the seriousness of the situation, 'the conversations were marked by that unreserve, whose substance and fruitfulness I have scarcely ever experienced so strongly' (p. 21). As the discussion moved to the subject of who should represent the countries, Buber recalls that 'a man of passionate concentration and judicial power of love, raised the consideration that too many Jews had been nominated, so that several countries would be represented in unseemly proportion by their Jews' (p. 22). Buber, inwardly sympathetic to the speaker's viewpoint, outwardly protested the injustice of the former clergyman's argument saying that the Jews had access to the Jewish being of Jesus in a way denied to the Gentile. 'He stood up, I too stood, we looked into the heart of one another's eyes. "It is gone," he said, and before everyone we gave one another the kiss of brotherhood' (ibid.). Buber interprets this by noting that 'the discussion of the situation between Jews and Christians had been transformed into a bond between the Christian and the Jew. In this transformation dialogue was fulfilled. Opinions were gone, in a bodily way the factual took place' (ibid.).

Buber gives two other examples:

> in the deadly crush of an air-raid shelter the glances of two strangers suddenly meet for a second in astonishing and unrelated mutuality; when the All Clear sounds it is forgotten; and yet it did happen, in a realm which existed only for that moment. In the darkened opera-house there can be established between two of the audience, who do not know one another, and who are listening in the same purity and with the same intensity to the music of Mozart, a relation which is scarcely perceptible and yet is one of elemental dialogue, and which has long vanished when the lights blaze up again (pp. 245–246).

Indeed, the participants in such a genuine dialogue do not need to say anything at all to each other for in the truly *I-Thou* relation, 'no matter whether spoken or silent . . . each of the participants really has in mind the other or others in their present and particular being and turns to them with the intention of establishing a living mutual relation between himself and them' (p. 37). Buber also distinguishes two other kinds of dialogue: technical dialogue, 'which is prompted solely by the need of objective understanding' (ibid.), and monologue, in which 'disguised as dialogue . . . two or more men . . . speak each with himself in strangely tortuous and circuitous ways' (ibid.).

This is of course only a very brief summary of Buber's notions of *I-Thou* and *I-It*. Nevertheless, what we now need to do is to try to draw out the implications of the *I-Thou* relation for education in general and for the spiritual significance of the teacher–student relation.

There are two points we can pursue here. First, that the *I-Thou* relation is an educational relation, and second that the *I-Thou* relation, seen as pedagogy, has a special form in the classroom between the teacher and the student. In both cases the *I-Thou* relation works against the objectification of its participants and for their genuine human relation to each other.

First, then, how is *I-Thou* innately an educational relation? It is so because in the *I-Thou* relation I have to relearn who I am, who you are, and to recognise or 'become aware' (p. 27) that each of us, now, is not merely a solitary individual but is, instead, a mutual relation. The learning here, we might say, is that in becoming aware of myself as a person only in relation to another person, I am also becoming aware of the fiction of the world of facts and of objectification. In addition this is an education for the teacher about his identity, for if he is a teacher only in relation to the students then his certainty, his autonomy and his mastery are therein negated. The *I-Thou* relation, therefore, is implicitly a critique of, or a re-education in regard to, our taken for granted assumptions about ourselves and others. Buber implies that there is such an educative import to the *I-Thou* relation when he says that, when we are truly in relation, we 'enter a realm where the law of the point of view no longer holds' (p. 23) and we must learn about ourselves and others all over again.

But at the same time Buber warns that our lives are becoming increasingly unreceptive to these educational moments where the factual content of the world of *I-It* is lost to the mutual dialogue of *I-Thou*. 'Each of us,' he says, 'is encased in an armour which we soon, out of familiarity, no longer notice. There are only moments which penetrate and stir the soul . . . [F]or most of the time we have turned off our receivers' (p. 28). Thinking of the work of some of the critical theorists explored above, we might say here that for most of the time we prefer the security of answers, facts, certainties, objects, property and even of entertainment to the unsettling but educative relation of *I-Thou*.

Second, then, what are the implications of this for teachers? What does the mutuality of *I-Thou* mean in developing a spiritual pedagogy? Buber finds *I-Thou* in the classroom, but not in its pure 'mutual' form. Equally, he does not find the spiritual made educational in either of the two pedagogical traditions that we looked at earlier in the book: the enlightened pedagogy of the master or the more critical pedagogy of the servant. Nor does Buber find the mutual *I-Thou* relation in a synthesis of these. In another essay, 'On National Education', he offers a summary of the two perspectives that have dominated educational theory and that we have already characterised above as those of the master and the servant. There are, he says,

> two basic approaches to education and the task of the educator. According to the first, 'to educate' means to draw out of the child that which is in him; not to bring the child anything from the outside, but merely to overcome the disturbing influences, to set aside the obstacles which hinder his free development—to allow the child to 'become himself'.

> According to the second approach, education means shaping the child into a form which the educator must first visualize, so that it may serve as a directive for his work. He does not rely on the child's natural endowment but sets up an opposing pattern which determines how such endowment is to be handled (1997, p. 149).

The latter, rather more old-fashioned approach, which we have met as the approach of the master and which is based on the unquestioned authority of the teacher, he compares to that of the sculptor. 'Like Michelangelo,' says Buber, 'he [the master] sometimes sees the shape hidden in the crude marble ... which he wishes to realise in the material [the student] at his disposal' (ibid.).

The new, more progressive approach, characterised by the teacher who seeks ways of serving the free and sometimes natural development of the student, he likens to gardening and to that of the gardener. This teacher 'fertilises and waters the soil, prunes and props the young plant, and removes the rank weeds from around it ... [Then] he trusts to the natural growth of that which is inherent in the seed' (ibid.). He concludes that the gardener's education 'indicates the care given to a soul in the making, in order that the natural process of growth may reach its culmination' (ibid.), whilst the sculptor's education 'means influencing a soul to develop in accordance with what the educator who exerts the influence considers to be right' (ibid.).

Buber is unhappy with both of these, for neither represents the relation of *I-Thou*. The gardener's approach is more humble: he believes in the fundamental goodness of man, but it is also 'more passive' (p. 150). The sculptor's approach 'shows greater initiative, but carries with it graver responsibilities' (ibid.). Buber concludes that the sculptor has too much confidence in his relation with the student. He, the master, knows too much. The gardener, on the other hand, has too little confidence in his relation with the student. He does too little.

Daniel Murphy, in his book *Martin Buber's Philosophy of Education*, comments that, being dissatisfied with both the traditional and the progressive approaches to education and learning, Buber 'did not attempt therefore to resolve the conflicting viewpoints of classical and progressive educators' (Murphy, 1988, p. 96). On the contrary, 'he writes of truths that are disclosed through the knowing, loving, believing and other relationships of everyday life, i.e. truths that are disclosed through relational rather than objectivist criteria' (p. 95).

In terms of pedagogy within the classroom and specifically in regard to the teacher–student relationship, Murphy argues that for Buber neither can be grounded in any kind of truth that is based on 'objective validity' (ibid.). On the contrary, Murphy claims, Buber sees genuine education to be 'grounded in the integrity and truth of the relation in which the teacher is reciprocally engaged with his pupils and by the various forms of relational truth towards which he can guide them by his word and example' (ibid.). As will shortly be apparent, the nature of this relation in the classroom is not as clearly or symmetrically reciprocal for Buber as Murphy might be suggesting.

Buber further explained his thoughts on education in a paper given in 1925.[2] This essay begins with a dualism or an opposition reminiscent of the gardener and the sculptor. This time the dualism is between the historical reality that the new born must conform to and the uniqueness of each child. A one-sided approach to this dualism is taken by the gardener who merely 'releases' the unique force of each child, and by the sculptor who nurtures by copying history into the child. Freedom, says Buber, is as misunderstood in modern educational theory as authority was in old educational theory. In the spirit of *I-Thou*, Buber has a different understanding of the teacher–student relation. The teacher can bring dialogue, or *I-Thou,* into the classroom if he practises 'inclusion', which means that he can live and work 'from the standpoint of the other' (Buber, 1947, p. 125). This is not empathy, for empathy still treats the other as an object to be understood. Inclusion means being aware that 'experiencing the other side' (p. 123) is also experiencing one's own being. Buber says of a teacher who practises inclusion that

> he enters the school-room for the first time, he sees them crouching at the desks, indiscriminately flung together, the misshapen and the well-proportioned, animal faces, empty faces, and noble faces in indiscriminate confusion, like the presence of the created universe; the glance of the educator accepts and receives them all (pp. 121–122).

This *I-Thou* relation of inclusion and pure dialogue becomes an *I-It* relation if the teacher seeks to dominate his pupils or to *interfere* in their lives. Interference misunderstands *I-Thou.* Interference treats the life of the pupil as an object, and results in the pupil treating the teacher also as an object, as something to be obeyed or to rebel against. Using the drawing class as his example, Buber distinguishes the 'compulsory' school of thought from the 'free' school of thought. The former begins with the rules; the latter eschews those rules. Buber, however, finds the third term of their relationship to each other in the 'hidden influence' (p. 117) that the teacher expertly practises. We saw above in Part I that 'the third term' can be taken as referring to the thinking or the experience of a dualism, a dualism, in this case, between the rules of drawing and the absence of such rules. Buber himself talks of the idea of 'the between' where *I* and *Thou* meet, and calls it 'a narrow ridge' on which 'a genuine third alternative is indicated' between individualism and collectivism (p. 246).

The difference here between interference and influence is the difference between the teacher as master or servant and the spiritual teacher. In the drawing class if the students are told the rules to which they must conform, then the drawing will have little risk of personal engagement for the student. Alternatively, if the student is left 'free' to draw the object, undoubtedly each drawing will be different, but each effort will also be untutored by any 'scale of values' (p. 115) or by any judgements or standards by which the work can be taken forward. It is here, says Buber, when the risk of freedom has been taken by the teacher and the student that 'the delicate, almost imperceptible and yet important influence begins—that of criticism and instruction' (ibid.). In the influence that the teacher practises, he is master in the sense that he must select those aspects of the world that are to be brought to the child as a condition of the possibility of drawing. But equally the influence that he brings to bear on the work is contingent upon each element of 'the created universe' that constitutes his classroom. In selecting the world the teacher does not usurp the world. He is only its 'hidden influence' (p. 117). In the compulsory school of drawing, then, 'the preliminary declaration of what alone was right made for resignation or rebellion' (p. 115). But when the teacher is able, through her own example, to bring the 'scale of values' to the student by which his own work may be put into relation with criticism and instruction, then, 'after he has ventured far out on the way to his achievement, his heart is drawn to reverence for the form, and educated' (ibid.).

The only way this relation can be practised is in the spiritual understanding of the teacher between authority and freedom. Such an experience, Buber writes, finds the teacher with an 'almost imperceptible, most delicate approach' (ibid.) to educating, one that can be as little as 'the raising of a finger, perhaps, or a questioning glance' (ibid.). Here Buber understands the contradictory experience of the teacher who must teach in order not to dominate. This is the experience of the teacher as master and servant, and it is the spiritual identity of the relation between the teacher and the student practised as influence. Buber states:

> if the educator of our day has to act consciously he must nevertheless do it 'as though he did not'. That raising of the finger, that questioning glance, are his genuine doing. Through him the selection of the effective world reaches the pupil. He fails the recipient when he presents this selection to him with a gesture of interference ... Interference divides the soul in his care into an obedient part and a rebellious part. But a hidden influence proceeding from his integrity has an integrating force (p. 117).

Such a teacher, therefore, appears to the student as only another of the influences of the world. As such, Buber is able to define education through the relationship of teacher, student and world: 'what we term education, conscious and willed, means *a selection by man of the effective world*; it means to give decisive effective power to a selection of the world which is concentrated and manifested in the educator' (p. 116, emphasis in original). The teacher does select the parts of the world to present to the student, but this selection is embodied in the teacher as his own life, his own example. The result is that he influences the child as the world does, but also, like the world, does not interfere. Buber concludes, 'the forces of the world which the child needs for the building up of his substance must be chosen by the educator and drawn into himself ... The educator educates himself to be their vehicle' (p. 129). It is here, in the spiritual relationship of the teacher who is, in a sense, both master and servant to the education of the student, that Buber believes he can find the spiritual renewal that he seeks.[3] And *contra* one of the modern tendencies that have caused the need for such a renewal, he sets himself firmly against those who hold that only egoistic or charismatic personalities can make successful teachers. On the contrary, Buber has high praise for the quiet work that is the hidden influence of the teacher. He says,

> in an age which is losing form the highly praised 'personalities', who know how to serve its fictitious forms and in their name dominate the age, count in the truth of what is happening no more than those who lament the genuine forms of the past and are diligent to restore them. The ones who count are those persons who—though they may be of little renown—respond to and are responsible for the continuation of the living spirit, each in the active stillness of his sphere of work (p. 130).

But whilst teachers might seek Buber's spiritual philosophy of the teacher in the reproduction of the *I-Thou* relation in the classroom, Buber himself notes that influence in the person of the teacher is necessarily characterised by a one-sided relationship between teacher and student. In reflecting upon the dualism of freedom and compulsion he notes that freedom is not the opposite of compulsion. In the spirit of the mutuality of the *I-Thou* relation, the opposite of compulsion is 'communion' (p. 117). Freedom in fact is the possibility of communion, and communion itself is the free desire 'to commune and to covenant' (p. 118) with others, the *I-Thou* relation. Thus,

> freedom in education is the possibility of communion; it cannot be dispensed with and it cannot be made use of in itself; without it nothing succeeds, but neither does anything succeed by means of it: it is the run before the jump, the tuning of the violin, the confirmation of that primal and mighty potentiality which it cannot even begin to actualize (ibid.).

In the primal potential for communion lies what Buber calls responsibility. Not just the responsibility of the teacher to influence without dominating, but the responsibility of all human beings to respond to the address of the other. The *I-Thou* relation in education manifests this responsibility as inclusion, and is practised as dialogue. But Buber acknowledges that a special responsibility falls to the teacher, one that both confirms yet also in one way exceeds Socrates' thoughts about the necessary negativity of the teacher's role. Because the teacher must select elements of the world on behalf of the student the relation of *I-Thou* can *never be mutual* between them. It would be very easy to say that the spiritual philosophy of the teacher requires that the teacher and the student be master and servant to each other. But this is not the philosophy of the teacher that Buber expounds. On the contrary, Buber holds the failure and the impossibility of the mutuality of *I-Thou* in education, and its implications for the teacher as both master and servant, to be the key experience and education of the teacher.[4]

Buber notes that inclusion between persons is when one 'lives through the common event from the standpoint of the other' (p. 125). In this way we are able to 'acknowledge' (p. 127) the living truth between us. However he very clearly notes that this mutuality, this pure inclusion, cannot be practised in education. Even though the 'true relation of the educator to the pupil is based on inclusion' (p. 126) and, as we saw above, the teacher must include all of the class that faces him, nevertheless 'the relation of education is based on a concrete but one-sided experience of inclusion' (p. 127).[5] Specifically,

> however intense the mutuality of giving and taking with which he [the teacher] is bound to his pupil, inclusion cannot be mutual in this case. He experiences the pupil's being educated, but the pupil cannot experience the educating of the educator. The educator stands at both ends of the common situation, the pupil only at one end. In the moment when the pupil is able to throw himself across and experience from over there, the educative relationship would be burst asunder, or change into friendship (p. 128).

We saw above that for Buber spirit existed in between the relation of *I* and *Thou*. Where, then, in this one-sided version of inclusion in education is spirit to be found? It is to be found in the experience of the teacher as both *I* and *Thou*. Since the student cannot be *Thou* as the teacher, it falls to the teacher alone to have the experience of mutuality. Obviously this experience is contradictory. The teacher cannot experience mutuality on his own. Yet it is precisely this relationship that constitutes the vulnerability, the risk, the negation and the truth of his identity now as master and servant. This does not mean that it becomes an experience unrelated to the other. On the contrary it is the relation to the other experienced as the teacher's own education about himself from the point of view of the student. The teacher's experience repeats the *I-Thou* relation, but here he experiences himself as both of the participants—that is, as educator of the other and as educated about (the lack of) mutuality as it appears from the point of view of the other.

> The man whose calling it is to influence the being of persons that can be determined, must experience this action of his (however much it may

have assumed the form of non-action) ever anew from the other side. Without the action of his spirit being in any way weakened he must at the same time be over there, on the surface of that other spirit which is being acted upon . . . Only when he catches himself 'from over there,' and feels how it affects one, how it affects this other human being, does he recognise the real limit, baptise his self-will in Reality and make it true will, and renew his paradoxical legitimacy (ibid.).

In short, the responsibility for selecting the world to present to the student, and the inclusion of the teacher himself as the paradoxical vehicle of its presentation, Buber calls 'self-education' (p. 129).

We can see now that this self-education includes the two elements that have guided our study of the teacher to this point. The teacher is master in that he selects those elements of the world that are to be taught. He is also servant to the students' own learning by risking his authority in the selection of the world that he makes and in seeing himself do so through the eyes of the students. The teacher is never more vulnerable to negation and to doubt than when he accepts the one-sided but dual-natured responsibility of educating as influence. To stand opposed to this vulnerability would be to adopt the stance of interference. This teacher would select the world but would not also be able to see himself from the other side. As such he would be unable to learn from himself about the necessity and the inevitability of his one-sided relationship to the students. In turn, this would render his integrity, his hidden influence and his being the third term between compulsion and communion, nugatory or worthless. Worse still, such a teacher would create the relation to the students of 'resignation or rebellion' (p. 115) for, in failing to be student to himself, he would confuse his authority with 'a quest for control and a fear of lack of control', a phrase found above in the Introduction to Part II (see Rose, 1999, p. 45).

Against this, the teacher who risks himself as selection and also negates himself from the other side, is the relation of self-education because he stands on both sides. Because he risks teaching an other, he is also student to himself. As such, and recalling Rose again, this teacher 'does not permit you to transfer your authority to him, and, so, paradoxically, [the students] trust him more, because the trust is uncoerced and freely bestowed' (ibid.). Mutuality in the teacher–student relationship, as we saw above, Buber calls friendship. The lack of mutuality, however, is what provides for the negation of the teacher. Only in this negation is the teacher working in and as the spirit of the educational relationship between the *I* and *Thou* who are teacher and student.

Buber is clear that the responsibility and inclusion that constitute this self-education are threatened if and when the educator fails to make his selection from 'the pupil's own reality' (Buber, 1947, p. 127). He is able to conclude that 'the influence of the teacher upon the pupil, of the right teacher upon the right pupil, is not merely compared to, but even set on a par with, divine works which are linked with the human, maternal act of giving birth' (Buber, 1997, p. 138).[6]

Buber adds a new and substantial dimension to our thinking about the role of the teacher. It is a philosophy that is grounded in the real and difficult experiences of the teacher–student relation, but equally in the recognition of the unequal and asymmetrical power of their relationship. Being able to work with this negative difficulty as an educational and spiritual experience marks Buber's philosophy of the teacher out from the critical and post-enlightenment theorists who, in one way or another in Chapter 4, refused it, or sought to overcome it.[7] The implication of the unequal and difficult *I-Thou* relation in the classroom is that the teacher is not unmoved or indeed unchanged by his relation to the student. On the contrary it is his education about being the teacher from his own risking of its authority.

SIMONE WEIL (1909–1943)

Our second example of a spiritual teacher is the French thinker and writer Simone Weil. Here, as with Buber, it is possible to uncover thoughts on teaching that find meaning and significance in the ambiguities and ambivalences experienced in being a teacher, and in the teacher–student relationship. In particular, as with Buber, the ambiguity of being the teacher who expresses herself as being both master and servant has a spiritual significance present in the difficult relation between them. In Weil's philosophy of the teacher a third term—attention—is present, as will be seen, in the contradictory relationship between authority and freedom. This middle term, as with Buber and influence, is the notion of doubt understood not as paralysing or merely ironic but as a formative experience for the teacher about how, in her practice, she has to be both master and servant.

We have seen above that one of the fundamental ways in which teaching is experienced as a contradiction is in the gap between theory and practice, or between thought and being. Weil's life provides a remarkable example of someone who attempted, at all times, to unite thought and being, and to lead a life that was true to her thoughts and doubts. Her largely ascetic existence infuriates some and inspires others. In relation to our explorations of the philosophy of the teacher, she provides a challenging and difficult example of someone who lived her life in the anxiety and with the doubts of being both master and servant. Indeed, this example was not restricted to her time in the classroom but extended to her work as a political activist against dehumanising factory conditions in France, and later against the Nazi occupation of that country and in the context of the war effort in general. In order, then, to understand a little about the spiritual nature of Weil's philosophy of the teacher, it is helpful to have some details about the way she lived her own life, both as a teacher and outside formal education.

Simone Weil was born in Paris on 3 February 1909 and died on 24 August 1943, aged 34. As a teenager she became interested in the working conditions of low-paid workers and attended meetings of the unemployed. She was educated at the Ecole Normale Supérieure, where in 1928 she met

Simone de Beauvoir, and in 1929 she had her first publication, which attempted to define 'work'. She was ill for most of her life, and suffered from severe and virtually incapacitating headaches. In 1931 she achieved her degree and was described in her final report as 'a brilliant student' (Anderson, 1971, p. 26). Thereafter she became a teacher in various schools. Notably during this period she used her supplementary pay towards the purchase of books for workers' study groups that she attended and taught. She lived on five francs a day, which was the same as unemployment benefit. She is said to have been careless in dress, often with cigarette burns in her clothes, and she spoke in a rather monotonous voice.

At the end of 1932 she determined to ask for time off from teaching. Publicly the reason she gave was that she wanted to write a philosophical treatise on the relationship between modern technology, industry and culture. In fact it was her intention to gain experience as an industrial worker, and this she did for nine months between 1934 and 1935, including a period working in the Renault factory. We shall see why in a moment. In 1936 she fought in the Spanish Civil War. Around this time she had three significant religious experiences and began, in her life and her writing, to use the word 'God'. When the Germans entered Paris in 1940, she left, hoping to go to London to continue struggling against the Nazi occupation of France. She joined the resistance in Marseilles, but eventually went to New York in 1942. Finally, she reached London and worked for the French provisional government, but she was refused permission to return to France on grounds of ill-health. In April 1943 she was found unconscious, having tuberculosis, and she died on 24 August 1943. It turned out that she had restricted her diet to what was available to her compatriots in Occupied France.

It is significant that here again it is possible to make a link between, on the one hand, the spiritual and, on the other, the ambiguities of power and authority found in teaching. At times, in Weil's books, it is not easy to see where teaching stops and preaching begins. She has an overwhelming concern for the poor. She believes in a God, but she is not prepared to become a member of the Church, and she sacrifices her own happiness and desires so that she can share the suffering of others. She states,

> the suffering all over the world obsesses and overwhelms me to the point of annihilating my faculties and the only way I can revive them and release myself from the obsession is by getting for myself a large share of danger and hardship ... It is not, I am certain, a question of character only, but of vocation (in Miles, 1986, p. 44).

She was a teacher for much of the last twelve years of her short life and we have records from some of those she taught describing what it was like to be her student. Weil is spoken of as 'a uniquely gifted and sympathetic teacher' (p. 6). Despite the fact that she appears to have taught her students in a tone that was 'low and monotonous' (Anderson, 1971, p. 26), nevertheless her dedication to education seems to have carried itself over to them. David Anderson notes that she treated her pupils as equals, seeking to awaken in them a response to great ideas rather than to cram them for examinations. Her methods were open to criticism by her superiors, who looked for solid academic results rather than diffuse Socratic inquiries, but Simone Weil seems to have been ahead of her time in her way of encouraging free and creative thinking (p. 27).

Not surprisingly, therefore, the exam results of her students were notoriously awful. Clearly, as a teacher, she taught her students what she thought was important, which most often did not coincide with the examination syllabuses. One of her students has said:

> our class was a small one and had a family atmosphere about it . . . when the weather was good we had our lessons under the shade of a fine cedar tree, and sometimes they became a search for the solution to a problem in geometry, or a friendly conversation . . . The headmistress [used to come] to look for marks and positions which she [Weil] usually refused to give (Miles, 1986, p. 12).

Her career as a teacher was accompanied wherever she went by her controversial teaching and by angry complaints from school inspectors and parents about the examination failures of her students. Her teaching did not fulfil their expectations of an education designed for success in bourgeois French society.

We can gain an insight into some of Weil's most important philosophical ideas from things she wrote about teaching and education. She wrote a piece, probably in 1942, called 'Reflections on the Right Use of School Studies with a view to the Love of God'. Central to Weil in education was the importance of what she termed 'attention'. She argued that studies in schools are not interesting for their particular content— what they are about—but only to the extent to which 'they really call upon the power of attention' (Weil, 1977, p. 53).

What does she mean by 'attention' and why is it so central to education for her? In one very important way her description of attention is close to Donald Schön's idea of *the suspension of disbelief*, a phrase borrowed from T. S. Eliot (see Schön, 1987, p. 94). Following Socrates, Schön points out that students cannot know at the beginning of their course of study whether or not they are doing the right things. Students cannot know at the beginning what they will know at the end, and do not know enough at the beginning for the teacher to be able to explain to them everything they need to know. It falls, therefore, to students to 'suspend their disbelief' in what they are being told by the teacher until such time as they can understand it for themselves. Obviously this requires students to proceed without certainty and requires trust and faith on their part. Weil's idea of attention is similar to this. It sees the process of learning to be a suspension of actively seeking or, in particular, grasping at the truth. Instead the learner, whether she is the teacher or the student, must suspend her desire for an answer in favour of waiting patiently for the truth of the object to reveal itself. This waiting, like the suspension of disbelief, requires faith in education *per se* in order to sustain the waiting, or attending, that is required.

As such, there is a spiritual import to teaching and learning to be found in her idea of attention and one that has important implications for the teacher. She argues that

> attention consists of suspending our thought, leaving it detached, empty and ready to be penetrated by the object ... [A]bove all our thought should be empty, waiting, not seeking anything ... [A]ll clumsiness of style and all faulty connection of ideas in compositions and essays, all such things are due to the fact that thought has seized upon some idea too hastily and being thus prematurely blocked, is not open to the truth (p. 58).

She concludes: 'we do not obtain the most precious gifts by going in search of them but by waiting for them' (ibid.).

There are several important and educative aspects that should be noted here regarding this notion of attention. First, speaking in religious terms, Weil says in *Gravity and Grace* that 'attention, taken to its highest degree, is the same thing as prayer. It presupposes faith and love' (Weil, 1987, p. 105).

Second, she remarks that faith and love also require what she calls the 'decreation' of the self, suggesting that we must try to negate or overcome the 'I' in order to understand better the other, or, indeed, the universal that is all humanity. In attention the 'I' is suspended. In *Gravity and Grace* she says that 'in such work all that I call 'I' has to be passive. Attention alone—the attention which is so full that the 'I' disappears—is required of me. I have to deprive all that I call 'I' of the light of my attention and turn it on to that which cannot be conceived' (p. 107). In her biographical details it becomes clear that Weil spends her life trying to pay attention to all that is not the 'I', and this, perhaps, is exactly why for Weil suffering and truth are so intimately connected. This suspension or sacrifice of the 'I' in prayer and in teaching is a faith in and a love for the spiritual education that it produces. As with Buber, where spirit was between self and other, so, now, for Weil, spirit is in the space left between the decreated 'I' and those she is concerned to work with, be they her students or her factory workmates. Weil believes that we learn best, and we learn most deeply, when we work for and wait for something other than the self. Learning or attention for Weil is then 'a negative effort' (1977, p. 57). Clearly this has resonances with Socrates, and its significance for the philosophy of the teacher will be explored shortly.

Third, in her piece on school studies, she hints that learning is by nature contradictory. Weil says that a contradiction must be accepted as a fact in itself and not necessarily overcome. If, when one has worked hard to resolve a contradiction, it proves impossible, then, she says, both of the incompatible thoughts must be accepted. 'Contradiction itself, far from always being a criterion of error, is sometimes a sign of truth. Plato knew this' (Weil, 1988, p. 173). Weil says that opposites characterise our entire being. 'No human thinking can escape from contradiction' (ibid.), and in the face of this, 'faith is the indispensable condition' (Weil, 1977, p. 54) for a kind of deep learning about the human condition, of which the capacity to attend others is, for Weil, the highest quality.

Fourth, putting attention, faith, the decreation of the 'I' and contradiction together, Weil can see the important contribution that teachers can make in the spiritual development of their pupils. 'Teaching should have no aim but to prepare, by training the attention, for the possibility of such an act [of faith]' (Weil, 1987, p. 108). Of equal significance for the teacher is the fact that they may never see the result of this teaching. Their pupils will leave them and move on, as they must. But 'every time that a human being succeeds in making an effort of attention with the sole idea of increasing his grasp of truth, he acquires a greater aptitude for grasping it, even if his effort produce no visible fruit' (Weil, 1977, p. 55). In a thought that will ring true for many teachers who recognise that the fruits of their work may take a long while to blossom, Weil concludes that, 'even if our efforts of attention seem for years to be producing no result, one day a light which is in exact proportion to them will flood the soul' (ibid.). Therefore, and this explains her controversial teaching methods and poor student performance in examinations, 'students must . . . work without any wish to gain good marks, to pass examinations, to win school successes . . . [all their work should] aim solely at increasing the power of attention' (ibid.). Thus, she says, 'our first duty towards school children and students is to make known this method to them, not only in a general way but in the particular form which bears on each exercise' (p. 59). Her last sentence in her notebook before she died reads: 'the most important part of education—to teach the meaning of "to know" (in the scientific sense)' (Miles, 1986, p. 51).[8]

Fifth, and lastly, she believes that the education of attention is for truth and good and against evil: 'the true road exists. Plato and many others have followed it. But it is open only to those who, recognising themselves to be incapable of finding it, give up looking for it, and yet do not cease to desire it to the exclusion of everything else' (Weil, 1988, p. 157). Desire is crucial to the work of attention for desire leads the intelligence. She writes: 'for there to be desire, there must be pleasure and joy in the work. The intelligence only grows and bears fruit in joy. The joy of learning is as indispensable in study as breathing is in running. Where it is lacking there are no real students . . .' (Frost and Bell-Metereau, 1998, p. 54). When desire aims at truth it sets aside all questions of what 'I' want in favour of giving attention to truth. To do so, for Weil, is to give oneself to working and learning in the world for the good. She believes that since illusion blocks truth, illusion is, therefore, evil. Here, education as attention can be enlisted against evil, setting itself the task of freeing itself from the illusions that are rooted in human ignorance and misunderstanding. Although we might call this process of education 'enlightenment', clearly it is not the one-sided model of enlightenment seen in Chapter 3 above. It differs from it not least because whilst the master of Chapter 3 teaches truth, attention for Weil teaches openness to truth.

We can try now to relate this educational philosophy more closely to the relation of the master and the servant that is structuring our approach to the philosophy of the teacher. It can be observed, first, that Weil herself explores the teaching relationship in the language of the master and the servant. The teacher who teaches for attention in the student is embarked upon a vocation that works for the soul of the student. In this work, the teacher is helping the student to attend to the true process of learning so that, when the time is appropriate, he, the student, may be fully open to the truth of the object that penetrates him. In a manner similar to that of Gur-Ze'ev, as we saw in Chapter 4, the teacher is helping the student to detach himself from the short-term entertainments that distract him from the work needed to sustain attention. In this way, the student also finds that attention is best sustained when the selfish desires of the 'I' are suspended. The goal, therefore, of Weil's spiritual teaching is in the effort to negate the 'I' by waiting in faith and love for the 'most precious gifts' (Weil, 1977, p. 58). In the language of master and servant, Weil writes:

> [Thus,] may each loving adolescent, as he works at his Latin prose, hope through this prose to come a little nearer to the instant when he will really be the slave—faithfully waiting while the master is absent, watching and listening—ready to open the door to him as soon as he knocks. The master will then make his slave sit down and himself serve him with meat (p. 59).

We have already seen above how teachers can experience their work within the contradictions of the need to be both master and servant. This is a contradiction that Weil too finds at the heart of the educational relationship. Only the waiting and the attention of the student, brought about by the teacher who risks her authority for the education of attention, 'can move the master to treat his slave with such amazing tenderness' (ibid.). The service of the teacher is in the decreation of the 'I' of the teacher who attends her students. Weil recognises that such service 'is a condition of love' (ibid.), but on its own, she says, it is not enough. In addition to love for her students, the teacher must attend the student in each 'particular form' (ibid.). Weil understands that the teacher can only attend her students by enabling them to attend to truth for themselves. The truth of the teacher's work is not as master over student but as master dependent upon the truth of the work of the student. Her call to the teacher to be both master and servant is summed up in her description of the kind of teaching and learning that attention commands:

> In every school exercise there is a special way of waiting upon truth, setting our hearts upon it, yet not allowing ourselves to go out in search of it. There is a way of giving our attention to the data of a problem in geometry without trying to find the solution, or to the words of a Latin or Greek text without trying to arrive at the meaning, a way of waiting, when we are writing, for the right word to come of itself at the end of our pen, while we merely reject all inadequate words (ibid.).

She concludes, 'every school exercise, thought of in this way, is like a sacrament' (ibid.).

This concept of teaching and learning as attention and decreation of the 'I' may, in the climate of testing and league tables, seem slightly luxurious. Who has time to attend to the National Curriculum (in England and Wales for example) in such a way that their students can wait for the deeper truths of each exercise to penetrate them? Who can afford the patience required to achieve an empty and waiting mind 'ready to receive in its naked truth the object which is to penetrate it?' (p. 58). It is more the case that the mind of the student be filled so that this content can be reproduced in the testing régime. Nevertheless, for the teacher who despairs of such a regimen, and the teacher who, despite the contradictions that it produces, still works for the freedom of her students to think for themselves, Weil's thinking speaks directly to the pain and struggle of those efforts. Indeed, it speaks of the significance of those efforts and struggles even though they may always seem to fail.

To work for attention and decreation is, Weil claims, to teach for love; not only love of God, but also 'love of our neighbour, which we know to be the same love' (p. 60). The meaning of the struggle by the teacher to exceed the formal curriculum goes beyond 'warmth of heart' or 'pity' (ibid.). It has at its core the struggle to put others before ourselves. Weil is clear in pointing out an elective affinity between academic work and the spiritual struggle involved in our relations to others, particularly those less fortunate. Those who suffer in the world, she says, need above all else 'people capable of giving them their attention' (ibid.). This quality is not achieved overnight, and indeed will be accompanied by many failures. 'The capacity to give one's attention to a sufferer is a very rare and difficult thing' (ibid.). But the truth of attention is in the struggle of the 'I' against its desire to know in advance or to settle the issue. Attention enables a relation to the academic project and to the sufferer that never seeks to evade or to overcome its difficulty. Only from within the struggle can the truth of the relation *as struggle* be recognised.

We saw, earlier, in the Introduction to Part II that Gillian Rose spoke of her consultant, Dr. Grove, as understanding the truth of his limitations within the difficult relation to his patients. But equally, he attended the truth of Rose's illness; he did not mask his limitations by seeming to know the illness too well. Dr Grove's pedagogy here is, in Weil's terms, an implicitly spiritual and educational philosophy of the teacher, for it too is an attending to difficulty and dilemma as they are actually experienced in work. To learn to be open to the difficulty of any particular form of academic work is to learn the same openness required to attend to the suffering to others. Weil writes:

> so it comes about that, paradoxical as it may seem, a Latin prose or a geometry problem, even though they are done wrong, may be of great service one day, provided we devote the right kind of effort to them.

Should the occasion arise, they can one day make us better able to give someone in affliction exactly the help required to save him, at the supreme moment of his need (p. 61).

Perhaps it is this asceticism, this struggle against selfishness that makes Weil's spiritual philosophy of the teacher too difficult for teachers? But it is not the end-point of the struggle that is most important here. There are very few saints. What Weil is offering is a philosophy of the teacher that speaks to the failings, the limitations, and the vulnerabilities of the teacher who risks attending the other. As master she must take responsibility for teaching and for the content she provides. As servant she must find ways of teaching that content that open up the space for attention to truths that are unanticipated by the content. The teacher who serves the freedom of her students is in this case the teacher who herself practises attention and decreation. It is 'only watching, waiting [and] attention' (p. 60) that enable the teacher who is master also to be the teacher who is servant.

Weil's philosophy of the teacher as master and servant can be summed up by noting that teaching and learning require the same suspension of certainty and knowledge in both teacher and student. The teacher must await the truth of the student as the student must await the truth of the lesson. The challenge for teachers, with or without a national curriculum, is, therefore, that in geometry and Latin (as in all subjects) they struggle to teach for the truths that lie not in the content itself but in the relationship that the student has to the content. And they do this through having the same relationship to their students. For those teachers who find themselves able to attend their students, by letting their students attend the truth of their objects, there is a spiritual import to their work. The giving of one's attention to learning is of the same quality as the giving of one's attention to suffering. Weil writes: 'the love of our neighbour in all its fullness simply means being able to say to him: "What are you going through?"' (ibid.). This embodies the recognition that the sufferer is a human being like us, who requires to be looked at in the manner of attention. 'The soul empties itself of all its own contents in order to receive into itself the being it is looking at, just as he is, in all his truth. Only he who is capable of attention can do this' (p. 61). She concludes: 'academic work is one of those fields which contain a pearl so precious that it is worth while to sell all our possessions, keeping nothing for ourselves, in order to be able to acquire it' (ibid.).

From our brief exploration of the concept of 'attention' as a form of teaching and learning, we are perhaps in a better position now to understand why Weil led the kind of life she did. To suffer with others was a way of expressing her attention, her negation of the 'I' and her openness to truth. She lived a life that tried to express the not-I (perhaps we can say the *I-Thou*) of herself, or the human *relation* that she shared with others.[9] In a sense, Weil is offering 'attention' as a way of coming to understand or to learn about the way humanity is suppressed and distorted in the world. Christopher Frost and Rebecca Bell-Metereau argue that, whether in the schools or in the factories, Weil was practising her educational philosophy. She was following her doctrine of the 'popularization of knowledge, and she strived to achieve this goal both by educating herself about the lives of the people she wished to serve and by serving the people with whom she worked' (Frost and Bell-Metereau, 1998, p. 14).

But what are we to make of such sacrifices on the part of Weil? Is this a life reflecting merely a somewhat pious ideal of service, or does it reveal something more spiritual within the demands and the struggles of the contradictory relation of servant and master? Is the truth in fact that Weil was from a reasonably wealthy family and chose to go into factories in the secure knowledge that her own life circumstances meant that she did not *have* to do this. Was this not somewhat patronising? Critics have recently wondered whether, 'considered within the context of certain endeavours that she attempted, she can even be seen as downright ludicrous or pathetic, most particularly in her attempts to be a factory worker, an occupation for which she could not have been more ill suited' (p. 22). T. S. Eliot, no less, in his introduction to Weil's *The Need for Roots*, says that 'one is struck, here and there, by a contrast between an almost superhuman humility and what appears to be an almost outrageous arrogance' (Weil, 1995, p. vi). Weil's response to Eliot's insight about her being both master and servant at the same time might be found in the following:

> nothing gives me more pain than the idea of separating myself from the immense and unfortunate multitude ... I have the essential need, and I think I can say the vocation, to move among men of every class and complexion, mixing with them and sharing their life and outlook, so far that is to say as conscience allows, merging into the crowd and disappearing among them, so that they show themselves as they are, putting off all disguises with me. It is because I long to know them so as to love them just as they are. For if I do not love them as they are, it will not be they whom I love, and my love will be unreal. I do not speak of helping them, because as far as that goes I am unfortunately quite incapable of doing anything as yet (Weil, 1977, pp. 6–7).[10]

Perhaps we can say that, like Buber, she chose the philosophical and spiritual struggles of relation over the evils of separation and self-interest. In the language of master and servant, we might also say that she rejected being master of those she attended precisely by risking the pre-emptive understandings of their suffering that led her, as master, to the factory in the first place. In this way, she accepted that her own difficult experiences were necessarily those of master and servant: master because she could observe suffering, and servant because that mastery was then risked by attending the truth of that suffering. In seeing the dialectic of humility and arrogance in Weil, Eliot touches the truth of Weil's educational philosophy. Only the arrogance of the master can lead her to want to understand those who suffer; and only the humility of the servant knows that precisely it is this arrogance that must be risked. If we see Weil only as master then she is the middle-class reformer come to enlighten and liberate the workers. This is the master of the enlightenment model. If we see Weil only as servant, then she appears as a pious ascetic who believes that she should become as those who suffer. But if we see Weil as understanding the necessity of being master and servant, then we recognise the spiritual significance of her acceptance of the contradictory struggle that not only attends attention but is the very substance of attention embodied in this philosophical teacher. We should not forget that Weil did not merely observe the sufferings of others in some objective or clinical fashion. She worked in the contradiction of teacher and student, and of freedom and domination, both in the factories and in the classroom.

For a conclusion we can look again to the recent book by Frost and Bell-Metereau. The authors note that in the question of how much in life to give and to sacrifice, Weil insisted that the truth required painful experiences. They note that Weil 'put herself at both physical and emotional risk, recognising this stance as essential to any quest for genuine truth' (Frost and Bell-Metereau, 1998, p. 107). Of this risk, Weil says: 'there is nothing that I might not lose ... [But this] state of extreme and total humiliation ... is also the condition for passing over into truth' (ibid.). Such is the spiritual philosophy of the teacher that is Simone Weil. The authors end their book by asking:

> why do so few people seek the high standards of perceptual acuity and intellectual rigour that Weil herself sought? Perhaps her life offers the best reply. The answer, it seems, is one of cost. Readers of Weil may focus primarily on the outcome of her life because doing so reminds them of the potential cost of such a life course. However, if one remembers Simone Weil's own criterion—that one must choose a life of attention without regard for results—then her life is a model not of failure but of near perfection (p. 110).

MARTIN HEIDEGGER (1889–1976)

Our third spiritual philosophy of the teacher, which is drawn from Martin Heidegger, is significantly more controversial. Although Heidegger's writings that are relevant to the philosophy of the teacher are brief, they contain some potentially educative insights about the philosophical nature of the teacher–student relationship and the work that the teacher performs in serving that relationship. There is, however, a dark side to Heidegger's work that we cannot ignore, and it serves as an important warning to us.

The teacher as explored in this chapter recognises the spiritual nature of his work. Both Buber and Weil have argued that in the relation between teacher and student there is a third partner, the *work* and the *experience* of relating. This work for Weil was attention and for Buber influence, and both recognised in this work the spiritual nature of the difficulties of power and authority that necessarily accompanied teaching. Equally both, in different ways, mediated their authority through their openness to vulnerability.

The spiritual teacher who understands himself to be the contradictory relation of master and servant knows that he must treat the contradictory *telos* of authority and freedom with great care. Its negative authority is delicate yet unforgiving. But what happens when that spiritual import of teaching becomes deformed? What happens when the teacher avoids the necessity of being both the authority of negation and the negation of (his) authority? In such avoidance the teacher becomes master even of spirit itself. There is great danger here, for our difficult experiences still call for resolutions. When spirit is deemed to be that resolution, it becomes a political weapon wielded towards an end other than itself by a teacher who assumes for himself mastery of spirit. Here difficulty becomes the opposite of itself. It becomes spirit as certainty. This changes fundamentally the relation between teacher and student and is at least one interpretation of the fate of Heidegger's philosophy of the teacher, as we shall now see.

To understand something of Heidegger's relevance for the teacher it is first necessary to try to give a flavour of his more general philosophy. For Heidegger learning is always connected to thinking. Both set in motion a process that in a sense calls us to an awareness of our own selves or of our own Being. (What is intended by this capitalisation will become clearer below.) Thinking and learning are at the same time the being of Being—or, we might say, where we are being our own Being. Similarly, to ask a question tells us more in some ways than answering the question. To ask a question is to be already part of the possibility of asking the question in the first place. The questioner is implicated in the question; or, the question is his being called to the awareness that he *already is*. Heidegger says, 'we ourselves are, in the strict sense of the word, put in question by the question' (in Krell, 1993, p. 385), and to be put in question is to know or recognise that we are Being.

But there is a complication. Thinking, learning and questioning provoke an awareness of our Being, but when we try to get closer to this awareness, to Being in itself, it withdraws from us. This is because if we ask of the origin of every question that provokes awareness, it can be known only as something lost in the asking. To ask the question 'what is Being?' is to ask the question that Being has made possible. The question is always the effect of Being. As such, we can say that Being withdraws from direct contact with us and is known by us only through these effects. It is in the question but cannot be known as the answer to the question. The name Heidegger gives to this possibility that is already Being is *Dasein*. In *Being and Time* he puts it like this:

> Looking at something, understanding and conceiving it, choosing, access to it—all these ways of behaving are constitutive for our inquiry, and therefore are modes of Being for those particular entities which we, the inquirers, are ourselves. Thus to work out the question of Being adequately, must make an entity—the inquirer—transparent in his own Being. The very asking of this question is an entity's mode of *Being*; and as such it gets its essential character for what is inquired about—namely Being. This entity which each of us is himself and which includes inquiry as one of the possibilities of its Being, we shall denote by the term '*Dasein*' (Heidegger, 1992, pp. 26–27).

This is difficult stuff. Let me try to put it like this. What is at stake for Heidegger is that whatever I do, whatever I think, whatever I might ask, I have to accept that they are only possible because I am in some sense already alive. My Being, or my being alive, is the necessary pre-condition of any activity, any thinking at all. If I miss this, I might take myself to be the master who is independent of such preconditions and that would be an illusion. His point, then, is that in asking questions I am drawn to the fact of my own Being, but in such a way that, while I can only repeat my implication or contingency within it, I can never know it objectively from a detached or privileged viewpoint.

> It is we ourselves to whom the question 'What is called thinking—what calls for thinking?' is addressed directly. We ourselves are in the text and texture of the question. The question 'What calls on us to think?' has already drawn us into the issue in question. We ourselves are, in the strict sense of the word, put in question by the question. The question 'What calls on us to think?' strikes us directly, as a lightning bolt. Asked in this way, the question 'What calls for thinking?' does more than merely struggle with an object, in the manner of a scientific problem (in Krell, 1993, p. 385).

This perhaps becomes a little clearer when we assess its implications for Heidegger's philosophy of the teacher. Clearly Heidegger's argument about Being has some connection with one of the most important themes in our discussion of the philosophy of the teacher, namely the practice of asking questions. If the teacher is to be the questioner he needs to understand himself as *Dasein*, that is, as an effect of the possibility of Being. Furthermore, if the *Dasein* of the teacher is charged to call others to their *Dasein*, this teacher is setting himself up as the Being that must withdraw in the face of the students' questions. I shall quote at length here a much-cited passage from Heidegger that tries to describe this philosophy of the teacher:

> Teaching is even more difficult than learning. We know that; but we rarely think about it. And why is teaching more difficult than learning? Not because the teacher must have a larger store of information, and have it always ready. Teaching is more difficult than learning because what teaching calls for is this: to let learn. Indeed, the proper teacher lets nothing else be learned than—learning. His conduct, therefore, often produces the impression that we really learn nothing from him, if by 'learning' we now automatically understand merely the procurement of useful information. The teacher is ahead of his apprentices in this alone, that he still has far more to learn than they—he has to learn to let them learn. The teacher must be capable of being more teachable than the apprentices. The teacher is far less sure of his material than those who learn are of theirs. If the relation between the teacher and the learners is genuine, therefore, there is never a place in it for the authority of the know-it-all or the authoritative sway of the official. It still is an exalted

matter then, to become a teacher—which is something else entirely than becoming a famous professor (pp. 379–380).

What a beautiful passage. On the surface it defines teaching as learning, teacher as learner, and suggests their conjunction to be difficult, and the difficulty, precisely, to be the learning. It shows how the purpose of education and, therefore, of the teacher is not to fill students with knowledge, but to let them learn and, most importantly, to let them learn learning itself. It highlights the necessary humility of the teacher, for the success of his teaching will not seem to reflect on him at all. In this, the teacher must above all be teachable and this teachability alone must be his only authority (see Tubbs, 2003a, pp. 75–90). Moreover, Heidegger seems here to have described a philosophy of the teacher where the teacher is master because he must anticipate the *Dasein* of his students and call to it, but also servant to *Dasein* because the success of this calling requires his own withdrawal so that the students come to think their own *Dasein* for themselves. A sense of humility and vulnerability could be said to be integral to being teacher in Heidegger's philosophy of the teacher. Thus, the teacher's identity falls to the movement that is learning.

Integral to the notions of calling and withdrawal as authentic education and learning is the idea of the current or draught that is produced by the withdrawal of Being from the question, and the withdrawal of the teacher from the student. This current is the calling of that which withdraws. Thus, the calling by a teacher to his pupils—'learn from me'—is not in this sense intended to be any kind of mastery or command over against the pupil. It is rather 'an anticipatory reaching out for something that is reached by our call, through our calling' (in Krell, 1993, p. 386). The call of the teacher is not just to his own *Dasein*, it is to the anticipation of the *Dasein* of others. What prevents his dominating them is that what the teacher calls, or points towards, is at the same time his withdrawal from it:

> What withdraws may even concern and claim man more essentially than anything present that strikes and touches him. Being struck by actuality is what we like to regard as constitutive of the actuality of the actual. However, in being struck by what is actual, man may be debarred precisely from what concerns and touches him—touches him in the surely mysterious way of escaping him by its withdrawal. The event of withdrawal could be what is most present throughout the present, and so infinitely exceed the actuality of everything actual (p. 374).

One of the reasons that Heidegger's philosophy has proved so appealing is that it seems to ensure that the results of thinking about Being are not known in advance. As we saw in Chapter 4, post-enlightenment thinkers find the notion of the project that knows in advance the ends or truths it must achieve to be tyrannical, totalitarian and a suppression of difference. Heidegger would seem to offer a model of just such 'undecideability'. He argues that when we point towards what falls away or withdraws, although we are called into the resulting current, this is a sigh 'without interpretation' (p. 375). This open-endedness of questioning and learning makes Heidegger's philosophy of the teacher attractive to those who wish to combat the seemingly closed and totalising narrative of the enlightenment model that we explored above. It is this notion of learning and teaching as 'without interpretation' that seemingly ensures the respect for and the tolerance of difference in the students' education. Education cannot be deemed to have reached its end because 'arrival' is only a prejudice of the intellect. As the cabinetmaker learns from the wood what slumbers within it, so the teacher must learn of the student without interpretation and, therefore, without any closure of possibility (pp. 379–381).

Beyond formal education itself, Heidegger extols the importance of the whole of one's life as the questioning and learning *Dasein*. Questioning, he says, is not

> to serve those who have grown tired and their complacent yearning for comfortable answers. We know: the courage to question, to experience the abysses of existence and to endure the abysses of existence, is in itself already a *higher* answer than any of the all-too-cheap answers offered by artificial systems of thought (in Wolin, 1993, p. 51).

In the same year, 1933, he added that this kind of philosophical questioning that goes to the heart of our own Being 'will then no longer be simply the preliminary stage to the answer as knowledge ... but questioning will itself become the highest form of knowledge. Questioning will then unfold its ownmost power for disclosing the essence of all things' (p. 33), including, as we have seen, the essence of the teacher as the possibility of teaching for the students' own *Dasein*. Thus, in his philosophy of the teacher, both teacher and student will be expected to practise 'the most constant and most uncompromising and harshest *self-examination*' (p. 29). To risk the danger and the excitement of questioning, both in ourselves as teachers and in the withdrawal of our students is, says Heidegger, actually to 'will ourselves' (p. 38).

In a way very similar to that of Plato, Heidegger sees how this philosophy of the teacher, and this kind of philosophical thinking, has the spiritual significance of serving the society or community in which one lives. Just as Plato argues for a republic divided into the wise, the courageous and the skilful, so Heidegger argues for a community or a people wherein, through questioning and self-examination, students will learn and practise three kinds of service, each in their way embodying the spirit of the whole society. They will learn to share the physical work of the community—labour service; they will learn to share in the protection of the community—military service; and they will learn to embrace the difficulties of understanding the history and destiny of the community—knowledge service. This latter, he says, is not to be 'the dull, quick training for an "elegant" profession' (p. 35). Rather it is to embrace the Being of the community by placing oneself within its 'overpowering' Being (p. 36). He intends that this threefold model of education as service will reform university study in particular so that it will no longer serve the professions but rather the reverse. The professions were to serve the spiritual mission of the questioning student. Of this spiritual mission, he claims: 'all capacities of will and thought, all strengths of the heart, and all capabilities of the body must be developed *through* struggle, must be intensified *in* struggle, and must remain preserved *as* struggle' (p. 37, emphasis in original).

There are themes here that we can pick out as relevant to our own exploration of the spiritual nature of being the teacher. Clearly of paramount importance for Heidegger, as for Buber and Weil, is the idea that the teacher must be a questioner. He must question himself at the same time as he provokes questioning in others. Heidegger grounds education and the Being of the teacher not in an objectified vision *per se* but in the vision of struggle as spiritually educative and formative in itself. There are few philosophers we can draw on who have so clearly identified the difficulty of being a teacher to students as the very essence of the job itself.

There are other features that spring from this that in some ways complement what we have already seen in Buber and Weil. For example, by putting thinking at the heart of our Being, Heidegger offers no rest from the withdrawal of the teacher from the *Dasein* of the student, or from the decreation of the taken-for-granted self, or from the call to the living relation that is the work of the teacher. Questioning calls us to the vocation of Being because it makes us realise our dependence upon other more overpowering elements. As the *I-Thou* relation and 'attention' both lead the I into the kind of spiritual work where its certainty decreases as its work for the other increases, so, now, in the education for and of *Dasein*, what we are becomes less and less certain as the recognition of the precondition of Being grows ever more irresistible. In each case the spiritual is the meaning of the negative experiences about ourselves and our practice that we have as teachers. In each of the cases mentioned, the spiritual is present in the ways that our negotiation of the authority of the master teaches us to become students of its difficulties, dilemmas and contradictions. It is present in our commitment to work for others, but more so in the failures that accompany our attempts. Heidegger's particular emphasis and special contribution to the philosophy of the teacher is, I think, that he shows how we can become servant of the struggle by risking our own authority, our own mastery, so that others may hear the call of the question that comes from themselves. As the master succeeds, so also the master fails to secure himself. As the students' questioning grows, as they answer their own call, so the lessons get harder for the teacher, not easier. *Dasein* is not an answer; it is—on its most sympathetic reading—a question. As the *Dasein* of the student emerges, so the power and the calling of the question increases. In this philosophy of the teacher, the latter is master and servant, living and working in the question rather than resolving it.

But, if all of this is true, then how is it that this same Heidegger is 'a member in good standing of the Nazi Party from 1933 to 1945'? (see Wolin, 1993, p. vii). How is it that there are, from around 1933, speeches in which he extols the virtues of Hitler as 'the present and future German reality and its law?' (p. 47). How is it that this teacher, who seems to recognise the necessity of the spirit of the teacher to contain his own withdrawal, also writes that 'knowledge means: to be *master* of the situation into which we are placed?' (p. 58).

One answer to these questions is that Heidegger not only extolled spirit as the Being of the question and the question of Being: he also believed that the spirit of the struggle was the truth of the German people (*Volk*) and the German state. In short, Heidegger grounds spirit, or struggle, in German National Socialism or Nazism. Where Buber and Weil find the import of the third partner between authority and freedom in the negation of will, Heidegger locates it in the mastery of the properly educated will of the German people and the state.

What is the tenor of Heidegger's rhetoric around the time of 1933? When this will of the German people, this third partner between authority and freedom is enacted, therein is realised 'the new reality' (Farias, 1989, p. 143) of the German people. The education of this new reality, he says, is 'that act of questioning that is born from the movement of the future that erupts into the present' (ibid.). And again, 'asking questions is always marching ahead, sounding the future' (p. 147). As such, the movement requires 'the new Teacher' (p. 139) whose will embodies the truth of the German people. Heidegger saw this new teacher emerging from the politicised youth in Germany who constituted 'the new student' (p. 142). Such students were members 'of the SA or of the SS' (ibid.). From their energy and will would emerge 'the new order' (p. 146). They were the ones with the necessary courage to act for the realisation of the new reality. They were to be the leaders, the Führers, whose own will would lead to the binding unification of all wills into 'the one great will of the state' (Wolin, 1993, p. 59). It is the true comradeship found in the moment of vision, the *Augenblick*, that 'educates the Führers' (Farias, 1989, p. 145). Heidegger summarises his educational philosophy as 'learn to know ever more deeply: from now on every single thing demands decision, and every action responsibility' (Wolin, 1993, p. 47). He advocates this education as a 'spiritual will to serve' (Farias, 1989, p. 149), sacrificing the self for a genuine understanding of Being as this destiny, here and now, in the *Volk* and in the National Socialist revolution that will engender 'the total transformation of our German existence (*Dasein*)' (Wolin, 1993, p. 46).

In sum, the will of the leaders was legitimate because they worked for the destiny of the German people, a destiny known and recognised in advance and served by those whose spirit matched that future reality.

It is significant that the university was to play a key role for Heidegger in serving this spiritual vision of the national community of the future. When he was made Rector of the University of Freiburg, he made a now infamous address from his new position, 'The Self-Assertion of the German University'. In it, he called on the teachers and students of the university to commit their will spiritually and intellectually to the true 'essence of the German university' (p. 29). He states: 'this essence will attain clarity, rank, and power . . . when the leaders are, first and foremost and at all times, themselves led by the inexorability of that spiritual mission which impresses onto the fate of the German Volk (people) the stamp of their history' (ibid.). This will require, as we just saw, 'the most constant and most uncompromising and harshest *self-examination*' (ibid.). The self-examination will require strength, and the assertion of will. What the will must aim to realise is the '*spiritual* world' (p. 33) of the German people, a power that, says Heidegger, 'comes from preserving at the most profound level the forces that are rooted in the soil and blood of a Volk' (pp. 33–34).[11] He concludes, 'a spiritual world alone will guarantee our *Volk* greatness' (p. 34).

We could continue listing quotations that illustrate the links that Heidegger makes between the mission of the National Socialists in Germany before World War II and his vision of philosophy and education. But we need now to draw out two criticisms of Heidegger's ideas as they relate to the philosophy of the teacher. The first is his carelessness with the spirit of the teacher–student relation, and the second is his carelessness with spirit *per se*.[12]

A philosophy of the teacher that is contained in the contradictory relation of the teacher and the student requires the negation of the teacher for the truth of its theory and practice. The teacher who teaches for doubt, for questioning, and for the realisation of contingency is not only concerned with the negation of certainty in theory, or in principle. In his practice he knows that he must bring it about and that he, as teacher, cannot remain immune from this practice. The teacher can 'attend' the student or can 'influence' the student, but in neither case does the teacher remain only the teacher. On the contrary, the spiritual struggles that attention and influence contain mean that the teacher cannot remain the same after the work as before it. The work is his education, a work that requires the learning of both teacher and students.

In Heidegger's description of the teacher–student relationship seen above, however, it is the teacher who calls the student to self-examination and questioning, or to his own *Dasein*, his own Being. We saw that Heidegger describes how Being withdraws from the question leaving only its trace as 'possibility'. The same is now true of the teacher. The teacher withdraws in order for the truth of his teaching to be present as the trace of its possibility. *But*, the negation of the teacher here is no more than mere rhetoric. The teacher withdraws in the face of that which is already known or presupposed in advance. His withdrawal from the student replaces his negation by the student. This both denies the student her own work, and protects the mastery of the teacher from the negative implications of that work. When Heidegger says that the difficulty of teaching is 'to let learn' (Krell, 1993, p. 380) and that the truth of the teacher is the 'spiritual will to serve' (Farias, 1989, p. 149), this is rather the dissemblance of the teacher who is and remains master. It is in the risk of the relation to the other, not in the withdrawal from that relation, that the truly philosophical teacher represents the truth of this dilemma and opposition that constitute his work.

This leads to the second, perhaps even more significant criticism of Heidegger's notion of a spiritual education. It becomes clear that whereas in the spiritual education of the teacher the outcome of learning is ambivalent, Heidegger's spiritual education is known to be grounded in the destiny of its own future. Like Buber's sculptor, this teacher knows too much in advance about the end of education—in the sense of its certain outcome as the will of the German people—to risk the difficulty and struggle of education in his own work, difficulties and struggles that will not stand being owned by any individual or any 'race'.

In Heidegger, then, at the nadir of his thought, the philosophy of withdrawal becomes the philosophy of mastery; the philosophy of letting learn becomes the dogma of the German will; the openness of education 'without interpretation' becomes the totalitarian certainty of nationalistic teaching; and the current or draught that calls to education becomes the power of 'the storm' (Wolin, 1993, p. 39) of Nazi ideology. Heidegger perceived what he called a general decline in the 'moribund pseudocivilization' of the West, whose spiritual strength was failing and starting 'to come apart at the seams' (p. 38; see also his 'Letter on Humanism,' in Krell, 1993, pp. 217–265). We should not be surprised then that a concrete ontology, a definite way of Being, was employed against the arbitrary[13] freedoms of this pseudo-civilisation, or even that education itself degenerated into mastery as nationalistic fervour. But we need to be ever mindful that, in the face of the difficulties of spiritual education and the philosophical teacher, it is likely that seemingly plausible and attractive resolutions will be offered. Against this, the philosophical teacher continues to choose the harder path of being master and servant at the same time, and resisting pseudo-ends, such as nationalism, that can so easily and disastrously colonise it.

We have to understand Heidegger's contribution to the philosophy of the teacher, therefore, as a warning about the uses and abuses that spiritual education can fall into.[14] How easily the third partner that accompanies teacher and student in their difficult relation becomes a spiritual certainty, and one that retains its spiritual appeal whilst in fact setting itself against all who are 'others', or are outside of the chosen people. We have to see through the spiritual rhetoric of Heidegger's educational philosophy and realise that it is nothing more than the mastery and domination of doubt, of questioning and of thinking posing as their essence or their truth. Against this 'jargon of authenticity'[15] the negative education that is the work of doubting, questioning and learning has its own truth, a truth that is not mine or yours, neither the teacher's nor the student's simply to own or to possess.

NOTES

1. This is the spirit of Freire's comment in *Pedagogy of the Oppressed* that in banking type education, 'instead of communicating, the teacher issues communiqués' (1972, p. 45).
2. This paper is translated as 'Education' in Buber's *Between Man and Man* (1947). It was an address to the Third International Educational Conference, Heidelberg, August 1925.
3. Buber was concerned that within Judaism the teachings of the Law (theory) and the actual lived life of Jews (practice) had become separated. He sought a spiritual renewal through

education that could reunite these elements with each other. See, for example, Buber 1967 and 1997.

4. Of course, we have to be cautious here for Buber is referring specifically to Jewish education and in particular the relationship between the Law and everyday modern Jewish existence. This is not the place to discuss the relationship between Judaism and modernity. (I have done so to a certain extent in Tubbs, 2004, Chapter 6.) Suffice to say that those who find in Buber a new ethical relationship, a new unity that can easily be transferred from Judaism to modernity—and this includes educators who argue for the purely mutual form of the *I-Thou* relation between teacher and students in the classroom—may not themselves be practising inclusion.

5. Buber makes the same point about the relationship of therapist to client in his conversation with Carl Rogers in 1957. Buber says of the therapist, 'you have necessarily another attitude to the situation than he [the client] has. You are able to do something that he is not able. You are not equals and cannot be' (Buber, 1998, p. 162).

6. This is taken from the essay 'Teaching and Deed', and is also reprinted in Buber, 2002, pp. 234–239.

7. I am aware that Buber would most likely not welcome calling responsibility and inclusion a 'philosophy' of the teacher. Philosophy was one of the elements he blamed for the separation of thinking and being, or theory and practice. The intellectualisation of Western philosophy, he says, has turned God into a (Kantian) idea and only a renewal of Jewish teaching will be able to overcome the 'depressing loneliness' (Buber, 1967, p. 158) of the intellectual climate of Europe. However, Buber also notes that the separation of thought and being 'transforms the Jewish question into a human question' (1967, p. 25). We might, therefore, risk calling his theory and practice of inclusion, in its one-sidedness in education, a philosophy of the teacher precisely because it does highlight the teacher's experience of paradox and contradiction in relation to freedom and authority, and, crucially, he finds this experience to be educational and formative. Equally, we might call this experience of influence and negation a spiritual education for the teacher because it learns of itself from within the separation of thought and being. This opens up for us the spiritual significance of the teacher's difficult identity. Lastly, we might call the spirit of the teacher in Buber—that raising of the finger or the questioning glance, the 'hidden influence'—a third partner in the necessarily one-sided relation of teacher and student. It is the same one-sidedness or experience of opposition and contradiction that has given momentum in Chapters 3 and 4 to our search for a philosophy of the teacher that is grounded in these difficult experiences.

8. 'Scientific' in this context, broadly speaking, means philosophical.

9. The others in whom she found the crisis of humanity most acute were the poor and, in industrial twentieth-century France, the factory worker. In her writing about her experiences of factory life she notes the way that that such work suppressed man's true humanity because it suppressed his ability and his will to pay attention, *to learn*, making him, in order just to survive, not want to be human. To suppress attention is to suppress man's need to learn, to crush his power of attention and thus also his ability to care for himself and for others. Here are some of Weil's observations about working in factories.

> It is inhuman; work broken down into small processes, and paid by the piece; relations between different units of the firm and different work processes organised in a purely bureaucratic way. One's attention has nothing worthy to engage it, but on the contrary is constrained to fix itself, second by second, upon the same trivial problem, with only such variants as speeding up your output from 6 minutes to 5 for 50 pieces, or something of that sort ... (Miles, 1986, p. 20).

> The situation itself automatically banishes rebellious feelings ... (p. 21).

> One dare not be insolent to the foremen and, moreover, they [the conditions] very often don't even make one want to be. So one is left with no possible feeling about one's own fate except sadness. And thus one is tempted to cease, purely and simply, from being conscious of anything except the sordid daily round of life. And physically too it is a great temptation to lapse into semi-somnolence outside working hours. I have the greatest respect for workmen who manage to educate themselves. It is true they are usually tough; but all the same it must require a lot of stamina (ibid).

In front of his machine, the worker has to annihilate his soul, his thought, his feelings, and everything, for eight hours a day . . . One submits in silence . . . One *cannot* be 'conscious' (p. 27).

And in the midst of it all a smile, a word of kindness, a moment of human contact, have more value than the most devoted friendships among the privileged, both great and small. It is only there that one knows what human brotherhood is. But there is little of it, very little. Most often, relations between comrades reflect the harshness which dominates everything there (ibid.).

10. Note that Rose is struck by Weil's inability to disappear or to pass unnoticed (Rose, 1993, p. 222).
11. Perhaps it is worth noting that there is a better defence here against Heidegger's being a racist than against his being a spiritual master. It is in the nature of the *Dasein* that he describes that it can never be assumed purely biologically or separated in some way from the conditions that constitute it. The extent to which this is contradicted by the idea that authentic *Dasein* is to be found in the soil and the blood of the *Volk* is obviously highly debateable. An incisive exploration of this theme can be found in Cohen, 2003, Chapter 1.
12. I use the term 'careless' deliberately here as Heidegger believed that 'care' was an essential property of *Dasein*. See Tubbs, 2004, Chapter 3.
13. In fact, Heidegger calls 'academic freedom' in particular 'arbitrary.' See Wolin, 1993, p. 34.
14. The contributors to the recently published *Heidegger, Education and Modernity* (Peters, 2002)—in which the first item, allegedly a transcript of the deposition of Heidegger before the Committee on De-Nazification, proves to be a hoax—generally give priority in their studies to the ways in which Heideggerian philosophy can be employed in education against instrumentalism in, for example, science (Copper); normalising education (Gur-Ze'ev); performativity (Smeyers); the technological dissolution of the historical essence of the University (Thomson); resistance to technology's totalising effect (Standish); calculative thinking (Fitzsimons); and the machinery of standardisation (Bonnett). The result is that in the same volume, Paul Standish apart—who argues that the lack of (mis)recognition of the other in Heidegger 'undermines his ontological project [which] founders toward a kind of nihilism' (Peters, 2002, p. 166)—the dangers of spiritual totality unmediated in and by real social relations, real subjectivity, are not explicitly recognised by the other contributors to *Heidegger, Education and Modernity*. In sum, the suppression of property relations in *Being and Time* is not recognised. I have argued elsewhere (Tubbs, 2004, Chapter 3) that Heidegger's notion of care in Part I of *Being and Time*, lacking actuality, has identity imposed upon it as time (and destiny) in Part II. The silence on the relation of *Being and Time* to Heidegger's Rectorship is a silence which also suggests that philosophy can be abstracted from practice. In addition, it is a silence that represents the political as if it was not a representation. It is the culture, the re-formation of education and philosophy, and modern subjectivity, which is silenced here. It is, finally, a silence that elides the retreat into the dualisms that Heidegger is being employed precisely to destroy—say, the dualisms of creative/standardising, *techne*/poetry, closure/openness. It is in this repetition of such dualisms that private property relations and philosophy mark their eternal return. It provides, at least, another contingent beginning for the philosophy of education to reassess the necessity of the philosophical resources that it has mistakenly and dangerously discarded.
15. This is the title of a book by Adorno that carries criticisms of Heidegger. It is helpful to note, here, that Adorno says of 'Heidegger's absorption into Hitler's *Führerstaat* [that it] was not an opportunist manoeuvre: it followed from a philosophic attitude of mind in which the *Führer* and the dominant power of being were virtually identified' (Adorno, 1992, p. 24).

Conclusion

At the beginning of our excursion into the philosophy of the teacher in Part II we separated the identity of the teacher into master and servant. Now, at the end of our study, we are coming to see the relation of master and servant itself as the whole of the teacher's difficult experience of the relation of authority and freedom in her work. In many ways, the separation of these elements is itself an abstraction from their coexistence in experience as contradiction, and as difficulty. But it is in their abstraction from each other that we experience most powerfully their return to each other, and it is this that has brought us now to begin to understand the complexities of their relationship within teachers' experiences. Equally, we started with a model of education as enlightenment taken from Plato's analogy of the Cave in *The Republic*. If, now, the teacher can be seen as necessarily both master and servant, and if the living out of this contradiction is the reality of her work, what does this mean for that model of enlightenment? Is it still a relevant model for the teacher?

It is, but only as a model re-formed in and by the real experiences and difficulties with freedom and authority that teachers face. We shall illustrate this in two ways: by returning to the Cave and by returning to the teacher who prefaced our study in Part II, Gillian Rose.

In Chapter 3 we observed teachers as masters who taught in the Cave but not, in general, about the Cave. In Chapter 4 we described two groups of theorists who promoted the idea of teachers criticising the Cave from within it, and trying to overcome or deal with the contradictions that this posed for them. For critical pedagogues, mastery was overcome in and by *praxis*, and for post-enlightenment pedagogues mastery was avoided by, for want of a better term, the difference that is respected in pluralism. However, we saw how, in both cases, the totality of the Cave returned to upset these plans, forcing both attempts into contradictions and aporias of abstraction and domination that teachers could experience repeatedly but seemingly never overcome. It was to these experiences of the self-defeating nature of teaching for freedom in the Cave that our spiritual educators in Chapter 5 looked in order to understand the deeper truths within the difficulties of theory and practice. The result is that, whilst our spiritual teachers have not freed themselves from the Cave, they have changed their relationship to it considerably. Their enlightenment about the shadows, about the reality that was uncritically taken for granted, and about the oppositions that reproduced themselves in attempts to reform the Cave, has made them aware that more is at stake here for the teacher than was realised in critical pedagogy or post-enlightenment theorising. These spiritual teachers know that relations inside the Cave imply or commend something also apart from the Cave, something that is not immediately 'present'. What is commended is a universal perspective, something that offers meaning and significance to their particular situations. But, equally, they know that such a total perspective is only present negatively, for universality can never be known by the individual except in some kind of spiritual way, as between, perhaps beyond, individuals. This is how the teacher-prisoner has appeared to us in the contradiction of both master and servant. She must serve an idea of truth and freedom that negates her ever being master of it, yet she must also be sufficiently master of it in order, therein, to serve it through the education of others.

From all our educators we recognise that life in the Cave is hard. We know that it does not immediately encourage its residents to think too much about the big questions or the truths that might offer universality over and above the illusions of the Cave. Our dreams and our hopes for justice, for peace, and for a fairer and more equitable world are often based on intuitions or feelings or concepts of this universality, but they are fleeting and retreat as quickly as they come. They are as likely to be overcome by the demands of everyday survival as they are by the distractions, abstractions and escapes from these demands that the entertainment industries of the Cave provide. And yet, at certain times in our lives, we may feel that we are in contact with these bigger feelings and ideas. It may be around death or at times of great fear, it may be in quiet moments when we suddenly feel the enormity of nature and its landscape, it may be when we look up at the stars and feel smaller and more insignificant than a grain of sand in the whole universe. Or it may be when, failing at school, we sit before the ocean and write poetry

There is no reason to think, however, that we cannot also learn something very important about enlightenment from these difficult experiences. There is no reason to reject out of hand the idea that these difficult experiences might actually be enlightenment. As such, we could say that enlightenment is not a result, a positive and definite something that, like a newly minted coin, we can simply pick up and put in our pocket. Education is not a 'thing'. Education is both experience and our relation to the experience that recognises it as learning. It is not enough to say that we learn from experience. We also have to learn *about* learning *from* experience. And what we learn about learning, from experience, is that it is difficult, elusive, essentially negative and unceasingly contradictory. Even this definition of learning, directly communicated, is not itself learning until, in your experience, it too is negated. Hence, we do not need to reject the big thoughts, the big ideas, because they are difficult and hard to understand. On the contrary, difficulty and its brethren might be the very stuff of such big ideas.

So, what kind of enlightenment is this? Perhaps it can be called a philosophical enlightenment—an enlightenment that is its own self-turning wheel, having its substance in the difficult experiences that negate our certainties repeatedly and without compromise. To learn of enlightenment in this way is to change our pre-conceptions, our prejudices, about what enlightenment and indeed what truth are. The Cave teaches us to expect truth to be something concrete when, as we have just seen, there is evidence for the teacher that it may have more spiritual import.

In fact, there is a reading of Plato's Cave that finds strikingly similar notions of difficulty in truth and education. Plato argued that despite the beauty and truth of the upper world outside the Cave, the philosophical world or philosophical knowledge (*sophia*), part of the education that is gained in the upper world is, nevertheless, that the teacher must *return* to the Cave. Teachers have a duty to offer this opportunity for *sophia* to others. It would be wrong, he says, to leave people in a worse condition when you could help them to realise a better one. It would be wrong to leave them in ignorance. Thus, enlightenment in and out of Plato's Cave offers no ivory towers for the enlightened to sit in, from which to watch, from above, the rest of the world. Life does not serve cognition, but rather cognition serves life.[1]

Plato makes this very clear in his description of the Cave where he highlights the necessity of return.[2] He is clear that the enlightened former prisoner would not wish to return to live as the other prisoners still do. For one thing, if he were to return, his new understanding would not be recognised or welcomed in his old world. Indeed, his new way of seeing would be interpreted as a dangerous illusion. Plato admits that all who become enlightened would, not surprisingly, be unwilling 'to trouble themselves with mortal affairs and that their souls [would be] eager to dwell above' (Plato, 1992, p. 203). Plato warns that the enlightened will be refused the liberty of remaining outside the Cave, in the upper world, however, and will be made to 'descend again to the prisoners and to share with them in toils and honours . . . ' (p. 205). In response to questions about the justice of this compulsion, two points are made. First, the reluctance of the philosopher king to want to rule is one of the main reasons why he can be trusted to rule. Second, the duty to return and to work for the truth of return is precisely what he has become enlightened about. Plato goes further, however, and argues that the return of the teacher is related to justice. He argues that the soul of an individual contains the same characteristics as the 'soul' of the city or the society. The soul and the city both consist in a relationship between desire, spirit and reason. When the soul and the city balance these constituents in the same way, this is justice for all. This balance is what is worked for in the struggles for enlightenment. Desire and reason, he argues, are in opposition in both the soul and the city. Desire seeks personal satisfaction, but reason demands truth and freedom. They are held in their difficult relation by spirit, which, siding with one or the other, is the work of that relation. In the analogy of the Cave this work is the return of the philosopher to the upper world from the Cave and from the upper world to the Cave. This return is the relation of spirit and reason over personal desire. To engage in this struggle to educate the soul and the city, for Plato, is in essence to work for justice.

This philosophy of the teacher, the one based in enlightenment that began our study in Part II, and quickly fell into disrepute, retrieves now the vocation of the teacher. It sees work as the substance of reason itself. The return to and from the Cave is really Plato's way of saying to teachers that they must never stop thinking about what they are doing, and that the embrace of this as a personal struggle is also tantamount to working for just relations as a teacher in the world. Here, then, enlightenment is not only the eternal return of thinking, doubt, action, further thinking, and further doubt, endlessly; it is also formative of who we are and how we live.[3]

So, what is the teacher to make of this model of enlightenment and education as struggle? She may strive to embrace it but she is undermined by having to impose equivalence through measurement and examination. She may dislike the current forms of education, yet she is pivotal in their continuation. Her heart may wish things were different, but her job sees her caught between the dilemma of freedom and authority. What is the teacher to understand of her entwinement within this self-defeating opposition of hope and despair? Is this contradiction of working *against* students when trying to work *for* them not the very stuff of disenchantment, despair and resignation in the profession?

It is appropriate to add here that some strands of recent postmodern writing engage in a dissemblance at this most difficult and troublesome point. For example, Gert Biesta says to this teacher that her experience of this contradiction and aporia is not *hers*. Any claim she makes *for* this experience is 'based upon a specific, individualistic definition of man' (Vanderstraeten and Biesta, 2001, p. 10) that grounds a view of education as an interaction between *subjects*. Her mistake leads her to view her experience 'either through the perspective of the educator, or through that of the child or student' (p. 11). Instead she ought to understand that education is constituted by the interactional space between teacher and student and that it is this 'new reality' (p. 17) or difference 'which educates' (ibid.). This new reality is not a contradiction—even though 'the possibility of [this] education is sustained by its impossibility' (p. 16)—for it would only be a contradiction *for subjects*, and they are only a 'fallacy of misplaced concreteness' (p. 11).[4]

How seductive this must seem for teachers when theorists posit a 'new reality' over against their actual experiences! How calming to replace the immersion in difficulty for the subject who teaches, and fails to teach, with 'an in-between space' (p. 17) But how dispiriting to displace the struggle of the subject with her students—*her* struggle and *their* struggle—with something represented by Biesta as unrepresentable; and how dissembling to posit this 'unrepresentable' space over the meaning and significance of teachers' lived struggles and contradictions as if the former had some kind of meaning in its own right. The unrepresentable, Biesta admits, cannot be a third text related to the two texts of teacher and student, yet in denying the aporia as *their* experience, not only *is* the relation posited as a third text, it is posited in such a way that it stands above the actual relation of teacher and student. It matters not that Biesta would protest that the space is not above the partners in education but between them. The point is that in granting primacy to the space over the experience of the subjects, it cannot be *their* space! As such, this postmodern theory of education has nothing of substance to offer the subjectivity of teachers at the moments of their most intractable difficulties.

But the philosophy of the teacher as we have presented it here in Part II, and I shall do again in more philosophical detail in Part III, can offer something more than a denial of subjectivity for teachers in regard to their aporetic experiences. It comprehends that the aporetic (external) struggle between teacher and student is also an aporetic (internal) struggle for the teacher. It is *their* struggle. To begin now to use language that can help to unpack this philosophy of the teacher, we can say that this one relationship of the external and the internal is the self-relation of education that is *in and for itself* when and because it is *for another*. We have already seen this beginning to emerge in Chapter 5, where contradictions and oppositions become, for Buber and Weil, spiritual and religious relations, and for Heidegger, spiritual and political relations. It still remains to us, however, to locate philosophers who can work with these contradictions and oppositions philosophically, and draw out from them philosophies of the teacher. This we shall do below in Part III. But to end Part II let us return finally to the thinker who began our study of the teacher, Gillian Rose. She has tried to articulate this philosophical education as a life being lived.

We saw in the Introduction to Part II that she found such philosophical qualities in one of her consultants. More generally, however, she asks, 'what do you need to become a philosopher?' (Rose, 1999, p. 42). In answer to this, she cites three qualities: first, 'endless curiosity about everything' (ibid.); second, 'the ability to pay attention' (ibid.); and third, an 'acceptance of pathlessness (*aporia*): that there may be no solutions to questions, only the clarification of their statement' (ibid.). Thus, she concludes, 'you discover that you are a philosopher: it is not something you ever *become*'; it is 'a passion' (ibid.).

Such a mind, fuelled by this philosophical passion, will not try to evade difficult or aporetic experiences. On the contrary, it will embrace the education and the learning that they commend. Rose is scathing about postmodern philosophers either who see reason and enlightenment as solely the province of the master, and so as merely totalitarian and domineering, or who, taking the servant's point of view, teach that this domination can and must be avoided. What both approaches miss or refuse is that reason already re-presents itself to us in experiences that are difficult and contradictory, or that, in Rose's term, are the representation of experience as a broken middle.[5] It is the teacher's job to re-present these re-presentations, even though they will, by definition, also be difficult and contradictory. No one can have these experiences on behalf of her students, and no one should stop the teacher having them in the misguided belief that freedom can be saved from itself.

Rose illustrates this in the following way:

> This decision by the intellectuals that reason itself has ruined modern life, and should be dethroned and banned in the name of its silenced others, is comparable to the decision to stop small children, girls and boys, from playing with guns, pugnacious video games, or any violent toys. This brutally sincere, enlightened probity, which thinks it will stop war and aggression, in effect aggravates their propensity. This decision evinces a loss of trust in the way that play (fairy stories, terrifying films) teaches the difference between fantasy and actuality. The child who is able to explore that border will feel safe in experiencing violent, inner, emotional conflict, and will acquire compassion for other people. The child who is locked away from aggressive experiment and play will be left terrified and paralysed by its emotions, unable to release or face them, for they may destroy the world and him or herself. The censor aggravates the syndrome she seeks to alleviate; she seeks to rub out in others the border which has been effaced inside herself (1995, pp. 117–118).

But for the teacher whose practice is philosophical, and who understands the gift she is entrusted with, there is meaning and significance not only in her struggles as a teacher but also in the way that she realises the truth of struggle in the education of others. This teaching, this vocation, is love, not only the love of the universal in and as the particular work of the teacher, but in and as the philosophy of the teacher itself.

Perhaps now I am going too far. Perhaps this call to the philosophy of the teacher has overreached itself. No matter. We must state the truth of this teacher even if it is thought to be too hard, or too unrealistic, or even too idealistic. In fact it is none of these, and it is already nearer to us than we realise. In our work the philosophy of the teacher is nearer to us than we are to our own selves, because it is the truth of the struggles of teachers. We all struggle between the universal that brought us to teaching and the particular ways that it is resisted. Between the universal and the particular, and in their struggle, we are the singular that holds that relationship in tension. This singular work that we perform is precisely the universality, the humanity that we share. Far from it being the case that we do not have these universal experiences, in fact they are all we have. The only equality to be found in the world is in suffering.

One does not have to be a teacher to lead this philosophical life. But, as was claimed earlier, the teacher is in the business of freedom. She is exposed to its contradictions because her practice always concerns the education—the freedom—of the student. If she does not doubt her own power and her authority then she is master. If she doubts them such that she eschews them altogether then she is only servant. But if she recognises her doubts to be the necessary negation of the illusion of her identity, her power and her authority, and teaches from within this experience, then she is master and servant, or, as we might call her, the philosophical teacher.[6] This teacher risks contingency as its own truth, and risks her contingency as her truth. This experience, this learning, repeated over and over again in the difficulty of having to be and not-be what we are, is our continuing education. It involves knowing and understanding that as teachers we are living a life of learning, always learning about ourselves, always learning the same thing but differently every time. How can such a life be lived? It can be lived by being recognised in the difficult experiences we have where the opposition between what we are and what we are not come together: in our power and powerlessness, in our independence and our dependence, in our being master and servant, in our being teacher and student. These meet above all in our arrogance in wanting to teach others and our humility in trying to do so.

NOTES

1. A phrase used of Franz Rosenzweig's teaching. See Oppenheim, 1985, p. 24.
2. See Tubbs, 2003b.
3. But, as teachers will know so well, the time for thinking is very limited. One headteacher who read this book in advance of its publication said that it had come too late for him! He no longer thought about teaching in the ways that he used to, or probably still should. Lack of time for thinking is, I think, part of the reason that so many new recruits leave the profession so soon after qualification. Teachers are not given time to think about what they do. Educators are steered away from their own education. Yet the philosophy of the teacher has shown us that those who educate others without educating themselves at the same time are only masters. The teacher who feels the need to continue learning so that she can better serve her students, yet who finds that there is neither time nor encouragement to do so, becomes resigned to a simple choice: continue teaching without learning, or get out. Many choose the latter.
4. The phrase Biesta uses here is from A. N. Whitehead.
5. I say more about this idea in Parts I and III of the book.
6. This is a dangerous term to employ here. It could be used against teachers as an abstract imposition and imperative of what they must be and do. But as we shall see in Part III below, it is the conjunction of philosophy and teacher that both disrupts the identity of the teacher and recognises learning about the teacher in this disruption. The philosophical teacher will be found in her work against abstract imposition, including against her own abstraction as the philosophical teacher.

Part III

Philosophy and the Teacher

UNIVERSITY OF WINCHESTER
LIBRARY

Introduction

Part III returns now to the more academic voice that was suspended at the end of Part I. There we introduced ways of viewing modernity and modern experience aporetically rather than deterministically. The challenge here lies in learning to comprehend the formation and re-formation of subjectivity in ways that recognise the social and political conditions of possibility but do not therein create new terrors or barbarisms or forms of domination. Such learning, we have argued, is the relation of subject and substance in speculative (philosophical) experience. Understood in this way, speculative experience is the actuality of contingency, actual in being neither overcome nor not-overcome by being known too well *or* too little.

Knowing too much *and* too little can also serve as a definition of the philosophical teacher who will emerge now in Part III. Yet—we have to ask here—which perspective within educational theorising has preserved for itself the philosophical resources that can articulate such an opposition? Which perspective is sufficiently grounded in the actuality of political experience to be able to re-present this opposition without positing its identity or non-identity? We saw above in Part I that major players in educational theorising do not leave themselves open to any philosophical understanding of their contradictions and oppositions. At times of greatest difficulty, their resolve leads them to new heights of ingenuity. But such ingenuity is the suppression, again, of the experiences in which consciousness can learn of itself as a learning consciousness.

Equally we saw, in Part II, how emancipatory perspectives know too much about the conditions of possibility, or about contingency. They posit the overcoming of these conditions as the overcoming of ideology by a consciousness that transforms them in knowing them. Postmodern perspectives know too little about these conditions, or about contingency. They posit the impossibility of a consciousness that can know its own determination in and for itself. In other words, they posit the totality of non-closure, yet eschew the possibility of that totality as being known in and by our own experiences. As we shall now see, in both cases the abstract forms of consciousness that they set themselves against are never recognised as determinative of, and repeated in, such positing. It is to the truth, and not just to the falsity, of abstract natural consciousness that we have now to look, in order to understand the domination of education within our own domination by the culture of modern abstract reason.

It may have been noticed that up to this point in our study the term 'philosophy of the teacher' has been aligned very sparingly with the educational perspectives on the teacher that have been examined. This is because, in failing to recognise the re-formation of their concepts and ideas by the consciousness that suggests them, these perspectives have generally failed also to make this experience of re-formation the substance of their philosophical work. This changed to a limited extent in Chapter 5 where Buber, Weil and Heidegger, in their different ways, preserve difficulty as the content of thinking and identity. The ideas of communion in Buber, of attention in Weil, and of Being in Heidegger all move towards the idea of spirit as the true, either transcendentally or ontologically. Yet even here these spiritual educators do not realise a philosophy of the teacher because they do not put spirit into relation with itself. When, in contrast, the experience of difficulty is allowed to become its own philosophical content, or where natural consciousness can learn about itself, from itself, without presuppositions being posited as resolutions to its contradictions, the aporia of spirit is made subject and substance. It is this education of natural consciousness by and through its negative experiences that forms the substance of the critique of educational theorising in Parts I and II. What is missing in Part II is an account of the ways in which these negations are educative and philosophical. Rose describes the relation of the speculative to the natural consciousness, in which it is both known and not known, as follows:

> a negative experience for natural consciousness is a positive result for us, for natural consciousness has been presented as phenomenal knowledge. Natural consciousness does not *know* itself to be knowledge, but it experiences the contradiction between its definition and its real existence. It thus contains its own criterion of awareness, the precondition of immanent change. But this change is only a change in perspective and results in further contradictions. Natural consciousness changes its definition of itself and of its existence, but this change is itself determined. It does not abolish the determination of consciousness by substance as such, a consciousness which persists as a natural consciousness in *relation* to the substance which determines it (Rose, 1981, p. 150).

This is the 'change of perspective' that non-speculative forms of theorising misrecognise either as an overcoming of natural consciousness (*praxis*), or as the impossibility of its being overcome (pluralism), or as the contradiction that can be avoided by refusing the totality of the domination of natural consciousness as such (post-structuralism).

Against such misrecognitions and further dominations, the re-presentation of this domination of modern, abstract reason as our experience, as our *philosophical* and *educational* experience, is now undertaken through the difficult and aporetic work of Hegel, Nietzsche and Kierkegaard. Here we shall explore ways in which these three philosophers, facing the re-presentations of freedom within unfreedom, do not retreat into mourning for the loss of freedoms but remain with philosophy as the working through of these inherently modern problems. At a time when many are seduced by the 'end of philosophy' into the search for new forms of ethical relations, Hegel, Nietzsche and Kierkegaard continue the struggle to know philosophy according to its own form and content—and, therein, in the relation of spirit to itself, as philosophy and education. It is here, within philosophies of the aporetic, that philosophies of the teacher can emerge through their own contradictions and oppositions.

Chapter 6
Hegel

INTRODUCTION

At the beginning of this chapter it is helpful, I think, to announce that we will be presenting an interpretation of Hegel that challenges some of the more common perceptions within educational theorising and philosophy of education regarding the nature of Hegel's philosophy. To be blunt, this philosophy is often dismissed as teleological and totalitarian. The argument runs as follows: as a teleological account of the history of Western reason, Hegel's philosophy works with the imperialist pre-judgement that all events and structures in Western history are stages in which reason gradually unfolds, until in post-Enlightenment Europe it culminates in Absolute Spirit. Thus, Hegel is seen as largely responsible for the idea of 'the end of history'—that is, that capitalist liberal democracy marks the very zenith of human rational, social and political achievement. There may still remain a bit of tinkering to be done around the edges, but to all intents and purposes the job is done.

The idea of Hegel's philosophy as totalitarian is drawn from this view of the end of history. What for Hegel were the achievements of reason are now, in fact, taken to be evidence of the terror of reason and its domination over other forms of thinking, identity and social organisation. Reason has colonised thinking as an imperialist power colonises other parts of the world (and maybe of ourselves). It suppresses, even obliterates, the voices of those it colonises, and imposes itself against the indigenous and the local. Only now, in post-foundational thinking, are these voices beginning to be heard again. Only now is the dominance and hegemony of reason being questioned and undermined, right down to its most basic building block: subjectivity and the *cogito*. Only now, thanks to the insights into contingency and historicism of the postmodernist and the post-structuralist, are we able to mount a critique of the sovereignty of the project of reason, a project that delivered so little of what it promised. In sum, what belonged to reason was honoured; what was different was outlawed.

This is the same story that we told in Chapter 4, only here we have placed the emphasis upon the pivotal role that Hegel's ideas play in this tale of woe. But this version of Hegel's philosophy, so widespread as to be almost unquestioned, even unquestionable, in educational theory and in the philosophy of education—this version is wrong, plain and simple. Let me meet assertion with counter-assertion.

First, Hegel's philosophy is teleological only in the sense that the present understands how the conflicts that have preceded it have been and continue to be formative to its own development. This *includes* the ways in which, at times, reason has been terroristic. This understanding of the present as the *relation to the past* is a dependency of relation that undermines all attempts to announce the end of history. Teleology does not end by knowing its formative and educative path to itself; this education continues *as* education, and therein refuses dogma, refuses any stability. Second, and following from this, Hegel's view of historical development is one characterised not by an endpoint, but by continuing development, understood now as its own educative development. This understanding is not a closure of history. It is a radical and undogmatic openness to the necessity of this education as its own contingency. The present in Hegel is the contingency of Time itself. Third, reason is a totality not in the sense that it colonises what is other, but in the sense that it imposes upon itself the necessity of understanding and respecting the complexities and the challenges posed by the very idea of the other. Indeed, with regard to post-foundational critiques that accuse reason of totalitarianism, there is the irony of all ironies. Where Hegel is prepared to yield to the truth of otherness as it is experienced, by yielding to the truth of the absolute contingency of this experience, post-foundational critics most often oppose this truth of contingency by presupposing the relation to the other as containing the identity of otherness. This presupposition *posits* otherness even before it is experienced; it posits it as incommensurability or exteriority. Domination over the other lies in the other's being posited. It is in Hegel that the other is recognised as an otherness within a relation of contingency that does not suppress that inevitable and necessary presupposition, and which, in fact, knows it to be the shape of otherness within particular and specific social relations.

These are all-too-brief responses to some of the most common misreadings—if indeed they are readings at all—of Hegel. But perhaps there is one misreading that, above all others, lends itself to such views. This concerns the term *Aufhebung* or, as it is commonly translated, sublation. It is a common fallacy that Hegel's philosophy is based around the triadic relationship of thesis–antithesis–synthesis. It is mostly overlooked that in Hegel any such movement changes the consciousness that experiences it. This change is the culture, the formation and re-formation, of the consciousness. Merely to observe this development and to comment upon its apparent logic from a vantage point, or as a voyeur, is both to presuppose and to misunderstand this culture of experience, and of subjectivity. Indeed, it is to eschew precisely the education that the sequence of the terms describes. In the mind of, let us say, a critic of Hegel, this formula is interpreted as one in which the synthesis overcomes the opposition of thesis and antithesis. Equally, in the same mind, a critique of this overcoming might be made on the grounds of the imperialism and domination outlined above. Overcoming and resolving oppositions is the terror imposed by reason over all oppositions or dualisms. The resulting standpoint may champion the views, on the one hand, that differences should not be overcome or, on the other, that overcoming falls to the way that the oppositions always exceed the illusory sovereignty of the synthesis that reason seeks to impose. The former might be called the pluralism of the postmodern, the latter the excess of the post-structural.

Hegel does not, however, have a philosophy based on the overcoming or resolution of opposing dualisms. As we saw earlier in Chapter 1, Hegel's philosophy is centred round the relations that serve as the conditions of the possibility for the thinking of objects. The sense of contingency found here is more radical, more penetrating and more significant than versions of contingency that seek only to assert relations of dependence. Such assertions are forced to presuppose the relation they wish to acknowledge. Or, put another way, the relation to the object is always made possible by, and is contingent upon, a prior relation to that object. This means not only that even assertions of contingency are contingent, but also that this realisation must in turn collapse under the weight of itself, even, or especially, when it is posited as difference or possibility, or as the relation, or as the impossibility of absolute thinking This insight into philosophy as the relation or as the relation of the relation does not, of course, belong exclusively to Hegel. On the contrary, it is the insight into the dialectic that gives form and content to Western philosophy from Plato to Derrida. What is significant about Hegel's contribution to this debate[1] is that his whole philosophy works not with the one relation or the other, but within the relation of both relations; that is, within the relation to the object and the relation to that relation. This is, we might say here, to work within the broken middle of the natural standpoint of thought's relation to an object and the philosophical standpoint of thought's relation to that relation. There is no overcoming here although there is a double negation; the negation of the object in relation to consciousness and the negation of that relation in relation to consciousness (now as its own object). Hegel's 'system' is a detailed exploration into the implications of each relation upon the other. It is not a system where mediation or negation are overcome, but rather one where critique is precisely the subject and substance of those implications. As an essentially educative experience, this broken middle cannot be resolved, for it precedes thinking as the latter's condition of possibility. But what it can learn from this impossibility of resolution is its own truth, a truth known in and as the form and content of the contradictory and inevitable conjunction of abstraction and mediation. It is the truth within the relation of contingency to itself.

Again there is here a most wonderful irony. It is the standpoints that seek to retrieve contingency from its closure and finality as they perceive it in Hegel, that, in fact, oppose the universal implications of contingency and, indeed, the necessity that contingency is universal. Hegel is the modern guardian of reason, which is 'the critical criterion [that] is forever without ground' (Rose, 1995, p. 119). The only way that overcoming could be introduced into this universality of contingency is abstractly, from a standpoint *posited* as contingent in its judgement upon (the open-endedness of) contingency. As we stated above in the Introduction to Part III, the evidence of this abstract and dogmatic standpoint lies precisely in the way that, where contingency is posited as understood too well, it is overcome (for example, as *praxis*) and, where it is posited as understood too little, it is not overcome (for example, as difference). This dualism falls within the universality of contingency. To judge Hegel's *Aufhebung* as overcoming or as not-overcoming is to suppress the relation to the object that makes the judgements possible. Overcoming and not-overcoming, to be blunt, are the abstraction of philosophical education from itself; this is, as we have argued above, the end of culture and the dialectic of nihilism.

Before exploring, albeit in a limited way, the way that Hegel's philosophy of contingency works itself out in, and as, the relation of (the relation of) philosophy and education, it will be helpful to explain systematically some of the key terms upon which this account depends.

1. The relation to the object as it precedes experience is our *natural consciousness*.
2. But as there is no such standpoint available to us prior to experience, natural consciousness *appears* to be the relation to an object; in fact it is an object already in relation to experience.
3. To miss the dynamics of this relation is to *misrecognise* the contingency of thought upon its prior form and content—that is, upon a prior form and content that is already thinking.
4. Our relation to the relation between consciousness and its object is our *philosophical consciousness*. As it negates the immediacy of the latter relation (between consciousness and its object), so it *posits* itself in that same relation to its object. Thus, the standpoint of our modern critical philosophical consciousness is the standpoint, also, of our natural consciousness. Our philosophical consciousness cannot escape this realisation as positing, and critique functions as a resistance to this even within it. Natural consciousness rises and falls in this circle of *negation* and *abstraction*.
5. This abstract philosophical consciousness is posited as the standpoint of *reflection*. But, unaware of its necessary and prior determination within the circle, this standpoint is *illusion*, or *illusory being* (*Schein*).
6. Illusion masks the political pre-determination *within modern property* relations of *freedom* as subjectivity by positing subjectivity as freedom. Our inner life owes its formation to a relation that is already the illusion of the inner life; or, a relation in which positing posits itself. As such, illusion carries the abstract freedom that subjectivity takes to be itself, unaware of its contingency upon and *re-presentation* of dominant (abstract) social relations.
7. Illusory being is, therefore, the re-presentation of the relation to the object that does not recognise that re-presentation as itself. This re-

presentation is both the domination and the critique of the domination of modern property relations.

8. When illusion is known, this is neither an overcoming nor a not-overcoming. It is a self-determination of consciousness within the circle of its own paradoxical contingency. This is the only sense in which the *re-cognition* of the misrecognition can be said to be a 'revolution'—that is, as its own continuing, self-turning wheel of philosophical education.

9. Thereafter, to know freedom is only ever to re-present the conditions for the lack of freedom. But it is also to know the education that freedom demands.

10. This is the real social and political significance of Hegel's philosophy of absolute contingency. Natural consciousness, the illusory ground of modern political freedom, is a subjectivity that cannot be overcome. It is how we know freedom and the negation of freedom, and our determination within their relation to each other. To elide subjectivity is to suppress the lack of freedom, which is, put differently, to suppress political experience *per se*. The recognition of misrecognition is the education *of* illusion *by* illusion. This is the substance and subjectivity of absolute contingency.

Hegel's philosophy here heralds a deeper sense of contingency than emancipatory or post-foundational viewpoints. Our education about illusion, within illusion, is determinative of substance and subjectivity in a way that those two standpoints deny to themselves. The point is often made that we should keep all the negations in Hegel's philosophy but decapitate from it its absolutist pretensions. This is again to suppress the political culture of subjectivity. As we shall see below, if the absolute cannot be known, then we have no stake in our philosophical critique of modern social relations, and subjectivity is relieved of its political import. It is, as Kierkegaard might say, as if those theorists who try to comprehend contingency are walking around 'like a man who is wearing his glasses and nevertheless looking for his glasses—that is, he is looking for something right in front of his nose, but does not look right in front of his nose and therefore never finds it' (Kierkegaard, 1989, p. 272).

Having now set out this interpretation of Hegel in advance, it behoves us to see how this contributes to the philosophy of the teacher as we are presenting it here. Parts I and II of our study of the philosophy of the teacher have employed speculative philosophy, and Rose's notion of the broken middle in particular, in two ways: as a means of critique of the elision of aporia within perspectives in the philosophy of education and educational theory; and as a way of theorising the contradiction of master and servant that arises in, and therein constitutes, some of the most persistent difficulties for the practising teacher. In addition, Parts I and II have begun to reveal ways in which familiar educational theorisations typically refuse such difficult experiences their own integrity, presupposing them as incapable of being substantial in and for themselves, or in and as our philosophical education.

Furthermore, we have seen how various attempts to explain or resolve the dilemmas presented in these experiences—*praxis*, difference and (political or spiritual) intersubjectivity—succeed only in suppressing again their philosophical and political significance. Chapter 1 in particular explored some of the ways in which the absolute is eschewed within educational theorising, an eschewal which, in different ways, seeks to avoid exposing itself to, or facing up to, the re-presentation of thinking the absolute as contradiction. Additionally, Chapter 2 argued in part that this denial of re-presentation can be seen as characteristic of what we called the end of culture. Culture is precisely the non-fixing of things, the maintaining of an openness to the political education that is carried in re-presentation. As far as post-foundational critiques in education are concerned, culture is denied—as philosophy, as education, and as their relation to each other. This denial therefore manifests itself as the end, the exhaustion, of metaphysics, and the end, the exhaustion, of modern reason. From within the philosophical subject and substance of the broken middle, however, such denials are formed in and by a despair that refuses to know itself. Such 'despairing rationalism without reason' (Rose, 1996, p. 7) marks the end of culture as a way of understanding the formation and re-formation of consciousness in modern social relations. It is, then, a fetishism of a despair that will not recognise its social and political determination, nor, therefore, the philosophical significance of such a refusal. The end of culture, in sum, threatens the absolute and total overcoming by abstraction of our political education.

It is against this background that Part III now offers interpretations of philosophies which do recognise the philosophical substance of aporetic experiences. In Nietzsche, Kierkegaard and first in Hegel, we will present the relation between philosophy and education in their work as precisely the formation and re-formation (the culture) of subjectivity and of substance that is lacking in educational theorising and in the philosophy of education. In particular, in the present chapter, we intend to explore the educational and philosophical significance of the Hegelian notion of illusion, sketched briefly above, in order to illustrate how illusion can retrieve from the end of culture a notion of learning as absolute. Within the hegemony of these post-foundational times, readers are asked to suspend their disbelief that such a thing could even be suggested. The argument will be made here that the notion of the absolute is absolutely necessary in any rigorous critique of modern social relations, and is itself formed in and by the relation therein of philosophy and education. As such, this chapter begins the re-thinking of the experiences discussed in Part I and in particular in Part II. We have witnessed for ourselves, as teachers, the attempts by educational theorists to overcome or not-overcome our experiences—of dualisms such as theory and practice, teacher and student, power and freedom; and we have observed the way these dualisms return to undermine the belief that these dilemmas have been overcome or not-overcome. Mindful of this circle we can now attempt to re-educate ourselves about the nature of this 'totality'. Within all the difficulties of Hegelian terminology, and within all the complexities of his thinking, Hegel nevertheless offers us an opportunity 'to know these oppositions in a wholly changed way' (Rose, 1981, p. 151).

The chapter is structured as follows: the first section, 'Hegel's Philosophy of Education', takes a short description by Hegel of his system and uses it to illustrate how it acts as a critique of perspectives outlined in Parts I and II above, and how it structures his own philosophy of education whilst the Head of the *Gymnasium* in Nuremberg. The second section maps the celebrated master–slave relationship onto the teacher–student relationship. Lastly, using some of the concepts explained a moment ago, the third and fourth sections—respectively 'Hegel's Education of Philosophy' and 'Freedom and the Teacher'—explore ways in which Hegel's philosophy of education is also an education for philosophy regarding its fundamentally educative character, and for the teacher.

HEGEL'S PHILOSOPHY OF EDUCATION

In his letter to Immanuel Niethammer[2] of 23 October 1812, Hegel outlined his philosophical system in the following terms.

> Philosophical content has in its method and soul three forms: it is, 1, abstract, 2, dialectical, and 3, speculative. It is abstract in so far as it takes place generally in the element of thought. Yet as merely abstract it becomes—in contrast to the dialectical and speculative forms—the so-called understanding which holds determinations fast and comes to know them in their fixed distinction. The dialectical is the movement and confusion of such fixed determinateness; it is negative reason. The speculative is positive reason, the spiritual, and it alone is really philosophical (Hegel, 1984b, p. 280).

This template of philosophical experience as philosophical education enables us to revisit the experiences of the teacher described in Part II to explore how, when taken together, they re-present this structure. The first element is the abstraction of the teacher who is master. The second element, with its emphasis on contingency, power, negation and deconstruction, is the dialectical. Obviously post-enlightenment theorists would resist this incorporation into anything resembling the dialectical. However, emancipatory *and* post-enlightenment pedagogies are included because both hold to the educational significance of doubt and uncertainty in their work. For Freire as for Ellsworth, critical education involves the critique of the shadows that hold the students prisoners to ideologies, be they political, textual or cognitive. Part II illustrates the common ground in critical education—that students need, in a sense, to be 'torn away from concrete representations' (ibid.).[3] But it also reveals the difficulty of the speculative, the spiritual or the positive form of reason. In the way that Part II above is presented, three different interpretations of (negative) critique are apparent. First, in critical pedagogy, critique was seen to be able to unify theory and practice, thought and being, and as such to produce positive interventions in the world as *praxis*. Second, post-enlightenment pedagogy was shown to eschew such unifications, and even the presupposition of oppositions, with a view to finding the positive affirmed in difference rather than resolution or reconciliation. Third, spiritual pedagogy tried to hold on to opposites without dominating them or refusing them, as encounter in Buber, attention in Weil and as questioning without interpretation in Heidegger. In each case there is the affirmation or denial of a third, but not the affirmation and the denial that constitutes philosophical experience.

It is now, however, that a philosophical critique can be made of all three of these responses. Each of them successfully undermines abstractions, not least of the identities of teachers as masters, yet they resist, in different ways, making the experience of the education of natural consciousness the education also of the experience. They resist philosophical learning; and they resist the truth that self-consciousness is known to participate 'in this antithesis as its own act' (Rose, 1981, p. 181). In critical, post-enlightenment and spiritual pedagogies this participation is never made content or concept. Thus, education is never recognised as necessarily philosophical, and philosophy is never recognised as necessarily educational. It is not so much that these approaches are 'wrong'; it is more that they fail to know the oppositions that they depend upon in any changed way. Philosophical difficulty—the site of our philosophical education—is suppressed by the imposition of resolutions of difficulty. These take form as 'third ways', or 'middles', not just as *praxis* or intersubjectivity, but also as difference and incommensurability which, even as the denial of such middles, repeat the illusory standpoint of thought and object. Impositions from outside, be they judgements of truth or untruth, of closed or open, are only required when the truth of learning is suspended. In such mis-recognitions of learning 'truth is thus defined as in itself, as outside any relation to consciousness' (p. 153). This represents the continuing domination of abstract social relations and objectified thinking. As a result, even the spiritual pedagogies impose spirit in the form of a third way against the philosophical experiences that the teacher has. The irony is that it is protestations *against* truth in the name of being open-ended that in fact fail to be open-ended, for, in finding third ways, they avoid making their own difficulties the content of their education. It is Hegel who goes that step further, being always open to experience as content, or being always open to learning about the truth of learning from learning. It is the third ways, even in the form of denials of such third ways, which close down this continuing and continual education.

It would also be wrong to see Hegel as having in some way solved the aporia of learning. Rather, learning is aporetic. Doing philosophy in this case is both true and incomplete. This is what Hegel tried to capture in his idea of the Concept. His own difficulties in trying to teach this philosophy, this learning of truth and truth of learning, are illustrated in his correspondence from the period that he was the Head of the Nuremberg *Gymnasium* (1808–1816). In trying to design a curriculum that would teach the structure of philosophical experience—the abstract, the dialectical and the speculative—he came up against the difficulties of teaching for such learning.[4]

Within the philosophy of the teacher as we are now presenting it and out of the experiences presented above in Part II, Hegel understood the demand that he be both master and slave. (I shall explore the structure of this relationship for the teacher in a moment.) As the master, Hegel had very definite views on what should be expected from the pupils. He discouraged duelling, fighting and smoking as well as political activity. In his school address of 1810 he stated that, 'from those who attend our school we expect quiet behaviour, the habit of continuous attention, respect and obedience to the teachers and proper and seemly conduct both towards these and towards their fellow pupils' (Mackenzie, 1909, p. 163). He also introduced military drill into the school day, as it helped students to learn quickly and 'to have the presence of mind, to carry out a command on the spot without previous reflection' (p. 165). He cited the pupils of Pythagoras as an example of such discipline, for 'Pythagoras demanded four years' silence of his followers' (Hegel, 1984b, p. 293). Surely, adds Hegel, 'the philosopher at least has the right to ask the reader to keep his own thoughts quiet until he has gone through the whole' (ibid.). Such comments as these, and the two that follow, give the impression of a dominating teacher, one who did not encourage his pupils to think for themselves nor express their own opinions: 'It has become the prejudice not only of philosophical study but also—and indeed even more extensively—of pedagogy that *thinking for oneself* is to be developed and practised in the first place as if the *subject matter were of no importance*' (p. 340). Four years earlier, Hegel had written to Niethammer that 'the unfortunate urge to educate the individual in thinking for himself and being self-productive has cast a shadow over truth' (p. 279).

However, (as servant) it seems he was much liked by his students and that his 'genuine enthusiasm for knowledge' was infectious (Mackenzie, 1909, p. 32). He could teach most subjects with ease, he encouraged wide reading, and took a personal interest in the students' reading material. He interviewed all students before they left the *Gymnasium*, whether they were proceeding to university or not. Moreover, his distaste for traditional didactic instruction is clear in his reproach of the District School Councillor, whose

> only concept of educating the young is the misery of endless inculcating, reprimanding, memorising—not even learning by heart but merely the misery of endless repetition, pressure and stupefaction, ceaseless spoon-feeding and stuffing. He cannot comprehend that in learning a young mind must in fact behave independently (Hegel, 1984b, p. 199).

The importance of the students' independence to Hegel is clearly revealed in his comments that teachers should not

> induce in children a feeling of subjection and bondage—to make them obey another's will even in unimportant matters—to demand absolute

obedience for obedience's sake, and by severity to obtain what really belongs alone to the feeling of love and reverence ... A society of students cannot be regarded as an assemblage of servants, nor should they have the appearance or behaviour of such. Education to independence demands that young people should be accustomed early to consult their own sense of propriety and their own reason (Mackenzie, 1909, p. 175).

If Hegel held necessarily ambivalent views on the independence of the student it was no more than a reflection of what would be required by pupils if they were to understand philosophy. As Hegel remarks, 'the process of coming to know a substantial philosophy is nothing else than learning' (Hegel, 1984b, p. 279). However, it appears that he had to learn how to teach this philosophy the hard way. He admits that starting the pupils with abstract logical exercises proved a failure. In a sense, he was risking the very kind of rote learning that he earlier criticised. He quickly abandoned this, choosing instead to begin with the abstractions that the pupils dealt with on a daily basis, in particular those found in law, morality and religion. The question 'where to begin' is crucial to understanding the difficulty that defines philosophy for Hegel. He understands that any beginning to thinking, 'precisely because it is the beginning, is imperfect' (p. 293). He means here that, since the thought of an object is already the mediation of that object, a beginning can never be made with the object itself. Every abstract beginning is negated for 'thinking is always the negation of what we have immediately before us' (Hegel, 1975, p. 17). In a sense then, Hegel was not required to teach how to mediate or negate an object, only to help the pupils recognise that they have already done this for themselves. In a remark that stands as an essential critique of critical, post-enlightenment and spiritual pedagogies, he notes that the dialectic can 'be taught more through the deficiency of this or that thought determination than according to its real nature' (Hegel, 1984b, p. 264). What would oppose this experiential learning (to borrow a phrase) would be if thought itself were 'reduced to a lifeless schema [or] a table of terms' (Hegel, 1977, p. 29). A textbook cannot contain 'the developments necessary' (1984b, p. 175) for the dialectic or the negative to be known by the student. As to the extent that the pupils comprehended the truth of their work to be philosophy itself, or learning in and for itself, Hegel is cautious. He notes that very few achieve this higher education, and so, he argued that the aim of philosophy in schools should not be to teach 'the absolute standpoint of philosophy' (p. 264). Needless to say this caution should not be applied to university education.

MASTER AND SLAVE, TEACHER AND STUDENT

We will now describe briefly one of the most contested areas of Hegel's writing, that of the relationship of the lord and the bondsman as it appears in the *Phenomenology of Spirit*, and relate this relationship to that of the teacher and the student.[5] Hegel uses the master–slave relationship as a template for understanding experience, or, as it has been explored above, for the truth that is learning. The Hegel scholar H. S. Harris states very clearly that the 'lord and bondsman are partners in *one* self-consciousness' (Harris, 1997, p. 15). In addition, the master–slave relationship is Hegel's template for understanding the determination of identity in, and by, prevailing property relations. I shall bring out the significance of this for teachers in a moment. First, a short description of the relationship as Hegel presents it.

The master, says Hegel, is 'the independent consciousness whose essential nature is to be for itself' (Hegel, 1977, p. 115). This master owns the slave in the same way that he owns all other 'things'. The master makes the slave do his work for him. In consequence, and not surprisingly, Hegel says of the relationship that it is 'one-sided and unequal' (p. 116). In this relationship the master enjoys a particular kind of status. He appears to be independent, a person in his own right, and, unlike the slave, not dependent upon anyone else to tell him what he must do. His life is one of independent pleasure.

It is not difficult to spot the problem with the master's so-called independence. He is, of course, dependent upon the slave for that independence. He needs someone else to do his work for him so that he can be this independent person. If the master needs the slave for his independence, then he is not independent at all. Thus Hegel says, 'the *truth* of the independent consciousness is accordingly the servile consciousness of the bondsman' (p. 117). Here, then, is the first way in which the master and the slave are in relation to each other. The slave is nothing to the master, yet the master is nothing without the slave.

From the slave's point of view, the situation looks a little different. Hegel points out that the slave has had two experiences here. The first is that he has experienced the pure fear of his being nothing in himself. He has 'trembled in every fibre of [his] being, and everything solid and stable has been shaken to its foundations' (ibid.). This experience, says Hegel, is his experience of death in the sense that the slave knows himself to have no life of his own, no firm ground on which to base any kind of identity; he is, in the eyes of the law, for the master, and for himself, literally nothing. We might say here that the life of the slave, because it belongs to someone else, is a living death, a life lived totally without being itself. In a difficult sentence, Hegel says that this 'absolute negativity' (ibid.) is a 'universal moment, the absolute melting away of everything stable' (ibid.). He is saying that implicitly the truth of the slave is negative, i.e. he has to live as *not-himself*, but still has to live.

The slave also has another characteristic, however. Not only is he implicitly negative; he is also explicitly negative for he lives out his own truth. Every time he works for the master he repeats his truth as negative. In his work, as in his 'identity', he is not-himself.

For Hegel something truly remarkable is happening here, something that has already been described above as the truth of learning. The slave is achieving something that the master cannot. The slave, in fear and in work, reproduces his own negative truth. As with consciousness, he participates in the act of his own negation. He can now come to know the oppositions between the master and slave in a wholly changed way, for he does what he is and is what he does. In contrast, this unity of theory and practice, or of thought and being, is denied to the master, for the contradiction of his independence only negates his self-certainty. It does not create his truth; it destroys it. So, whereas the master loses his truth, the slave gains his. Thus, says Hegel, 'through this rediscovery of himself by himself, the bondsman realises that it is precisely in his work wherein he seemed to have only an alienated existence that he acquires a mind of his own' (pp. 118–119).

The tables then are well and truly turned. It is the slave and not the master who has integrity, for he, and not the master, is true to himself. The slave is true to his identity in a way that escapes the master. The master's supposed self-identity is merely an hypocrisy because it negates itself. The slave, on the other hand, remains true to what he is.

This, however, is not the end of the story. It is all very well saying that the slave gains himself whilst the master loses himself. But what kind of gain is it that the slave achieves? Because he is true to himself, does he have some kind of independence in his slavery? He may well be the only one leading a life of truth, but how does it help him? What kind of independence is 'negativity'? He seems to have a mind of his own, and yet he is not 'free'.

The fact that the slave experiences the truth of himself, yet is not free, is the same truth of learning that is not closed. Both participate in their own negation, both require work on abstractions to do so, and both achieve minds of their own. They are both the same relation: learning as philosophy and the slave as himself. With philosophy, if this experience of itself changes nothing, then the experience has no educational significance. Yet it is precisely because we can know the experience, that the experience is *for us*, that already marks the development or the education. There is a very important point here in regard to all of the pedagogical models explored in Part II. The philosophical education that is borne within negative experience is not the production of a wholly new consciousness. That it is seen as such is often the presupposition behind notions of *praxis*, or difference, or intersubjectivity (spirit); i.e. that a new consciousness has overcome previous ideological or identitarian notions of subjectivity. This, as we saw above with illusion, is not the case. The consciousness that appears in variously distorted forms as our natural consciousness is the same consciousness that experiences itself as, and therein negates, those distortions. It is in the relation, the broken middle of the 'two' consciousnesses, that they are also, and still, the one consciousness. The slave does not overcome the master. The slave still works for the master. But, *contra* the influential reading of the master and slave relationship by Kojève that the future belongs to the slave/worker,[6] the future in fact belongs to the master and the slave. As master, the modern person is free only formally; and as slave the truth of this freedom is its incompleteness. Politics in this sense is learning and it is oppression. Not only is the modern person dependent for his mastery upon economic slaves in poorer parts of the world as well as in his own back yard, but also he is slave to the negation of that illusory mastery. The modern, as modern, is master and slave, having a mind of his own in relation to this unfreedom. The contradiction here is both the truth of the slave and his participation in its own act.

The same template can now be explored in and through the speculative relation of the teacher and the student. The experience in question is that described above in Part II. *Abstractly* the identity of the teacher is the master, and his work, on first view, appears to be 'teaching'. But on closer inspection it can be seen that in fact the work of education is performed by the student. Thus, the relationship is one-sided and unequal. The power and the authority lie within the identity of the teacher. He enjoys an independent status as the one who knows. The one who does not know is the student, and his identity is purely the lack of independence because of his lack of knowledge.

But of course the relationship is more complicated than it at first appears. From the teacher's point of view, his authority is the independence that his possession of knowledge (literally) buys for him.[7] However, there is a contradiction within the identity and independence of the teacher as master. His knowledge counts for nothing unless it can be 'taught'. There must be teaching if his identity as teacher is to hold secure, but this in turn means there must also be learning. At this stage, then, as with Hegel's master, the teacher is dependent for his identity upon the work of the student. Learning is what binds them together: the teacher has it; the student does not. But, just as the slave did the work of the master, freeing the master for his life of pleasure, so the student must do the work of the teacher in both senses—that is, because the student must obey and because the master is free (abstracted) from such work. As the master is the owner, so the teacher is the learned. The conclusion to be drawn here is that the truth of the independent teacher is accordingly the obedience and work of the student.[8]

However, the relationship has been viewed only from the one side, that of the master. We now need to view the relationship from the perspective of the slave, that is, the student. As with the slave, the student has two experiences here, which are the same experience. One is that he has experienced himself as unknowledgeable, as ignorant and without the property of the teacher, or in short, without education. His attending school or college, where he sits, when he learns, how he learns and how worthy his work is—all remind the student of his nothingness, his negative status, in terms of education or knowledge.[9] The person who arrives at the educational institution leaves behind him the knowledge and identities of home, family, friends and so on, and has to become the student, where, in terms of educational property, everything solid and stable in his identity is shaken to its foundations. It is a popular observation, at least in England, that as the student moves through the education system he is repeatedly told by one institution that what was learned in the previous one needs to be forgotten and will be of little use in the present one. It is also a common experience that a student can be made to look and feel stupid by teachers and lecturers. What else is the student's fear of being humiliated by his lack of knowledge, whether in front of others or alone, but the pure fear of being nothing in himself, of being property-less, within the educational relation?

As with the slave, there is another characteristic of the student in addition to the universal moment where everything stable melts away. Not only is the student implicitly nothing in educational (property) terms; he actually reproduces this nothingness in his work. In each lesson or lecture, in each essay and presentation, the student reveals his absolute dependence upon the teacher. In being asked to show a positive increase in educational property, he is being asked to repeat his status as lacking such property. In his work, as in his 'identity', the student is of negative status.

Something remarkable can be revealed, however, in terms of education within this double negation—in work as in being—of the student. The student is achieving something the master cannot. The student, in fear and in work, reproduces his own negative educational truth. He does what he is and is what he does. This unity of theory and practice, and of thought and being in education, is denied to the master, the teacher, for his negation by and dependence upon the student do not unite him and his work; they undermine and oppose it. But for the student, this rediscovery of himself consists in the realisation that it is precisely in his work, wherein he seemed to have only an alienated existence, that he acquires a mind of his own. There is an integrity here denied to the (abstract) teacher.

What kind of 'mind of his own' is it exactly that the student gains here? How can he be the truth of himself yet still be a student and still, therefore, be defined as the one without educational property? This is the same broken middle that has been seen in consciousness as the master and slave, and also in the truth of experience where consciousness participates in its own act of opposition. Hegel's philosophy carries no political import if the absolute cannot be known. Now we can add that education carries no significance if the truth of learning cannot be known. Indeed, this truth of learning can be known here, as the truth of the student who learns about himself, from himself, in his relation to the teacher. It is where we can experience the truth of education as learning. But this is not the truth of education that brings education to an end. It is not some sort of final closure. On the contrary, it is only realised in being brought about by oppositions in experience. This is why Part II of this book has the structure that it has. The truth of learning has to arise out of the contradictory experiences of the teacher. It is these experiences that, when unrecognised as of philosophical significance, demand resolutions of their dilemmas— *praxis*, undecideability and intersubjectivity—and therein close down their philosophical investigation. The philosophy of the teacher arises in these experiences and brings nothing to them from the outside. When the teacher participates in the thinking of these oppositions, these dilemmas, then she can come to know them differently, and to do so is to comprehend their truth in and as the philosophy of the teacher.

It would be wrong to interpret the teacher–student relation presented here as simply existing between two persons, the teacher and the student. We saw above that Harris is clear that the relationship is within the one consciousness. There are two complementary movements here. The teacher experiences the contradictions of her abstract identity in relation to her students. These experiences constitute Part II above. But the teacher becomes her own student when she is able to turn the experience of difficulty and aporia into philosophical content. In doing so, the truth of the student as learning in and for itself is the truth of the difficult experiences of the teacher who has become her own *philosophical* student of those experiences. It is when these experiences are not made philosophical content that philosophy of education and educational theory remain merely assertive and one-sided.[10] This amounts to refusing to the teacher the meaning of her difficulties.

When the teacher–student relation is the truth of the teacher become student to herself, then the relation in the one consciousness is the same as that described above. Her identity as master collapses into the doubts generated by teaching the students. But when these doubts remain unsuppressed and are able to become both content and activity, then the teacher is open to the truth of the student as her own truth, but always in the relationship to him.[11] Doubt is the identity of this content in that it is a pure nothingness, a despair. This is particularly true for teachers. I suspect there have been moments for all of us when we felt everything solid and stable melting away as we doubted our abilities, our effectiveness and therein ourselves. But doubt is also the activity, the work, that produces this fear and trembling of negation. In doubt there is the unity of theory and practice, for doubt *is* what it does and *does* what it is. It is not, however, a unification that ends the work; it is the unity of the work and its identity only in the experience of teaching, of being the teacher. Its essentially negative character assures that no closure is possible. If there is no dilemma, there is no philosophical education.

What does this mean then for the teacher? It means, first, that her dilemmas in theory and practice, and of theory and practice, are true—not only true because they are real, but true also because of their philosophical significance. It means, second, that in her philosophical work she can comprehend the truth of the learner. Her doubts are not to be suppressed or even resolved. They are to be thought about. In becoming philosophical content, they become her philosophical education. As this philosophical teacher she comes to know her dilemmas in a changed way. She comprehends the truth of learning within them—that in doubting her practice and herself she is both not-the-teacher and the work of the learner. It is in philosophy, in this philosophy of the teacher, that she undertakes this different and formative work. It is formative because she is both content and activity of this learning. She cannot remain unchanged, for in making doubt the content and activity of her own thinking she is already changed. She is neither master nor servant; she is both. Abstractly she is master, dialectically she is servant and speculatively she is the truth of their relation, as master and servant, in the philosophy of the teacher.

The question 'How does this change her practice?' is misleading. Changes of practice brought about by different methodologies may appear to make a difference. But they are seldom if ever truly different, at least politically and philosophically. What has changed is the teacher herself. Her work embodies its own truth. There is no telling how any teacher will bring the philosophy of the teacher into her work. But there will be a difference, all the difference in the world. She will now know the meaning and the significance of her work in all its joys and sorrows, difficulties and dilemmas. She will have found the truth of learning in her work and the truth of her work in learning. Her doubts will now have substance. *They* will make the difference. She is returned to herself as the teacher aware of significance and meaning in what she does. This is how and where the philosophy of the teacher retrieves for teaching its notions of vocation and service, and where the humanity of the work opposes any technical, bureaucratic or instrumental deformities. It returns the teacher to Luther's noble sentiment that there is no higher virtue than being a teacher whose life is devoted to the truth of learning by working for that truth in the learning of others.

HEGEL'S EDUCATION OF PHILOSOPHY

One way to approach Hegel's education of philosophy is through the structure and significance of illusion.[12] As we saw above, illusion in its Hegelian sense has its own logic, its own relation in thought, and can, therefore, retrieve its own educational and philosophical significance as spirit. Illusion here refers to the sphere of essence in the *Science of Logic* where essence presents itself as illusory being (*Schein*). In brief, illusion is present in the standpoint of reflection and for Hegel is positing, or presupposition. The one illusion has two characteristics. First, it is an immediacy, a non-essence, and counts for itself as nothing. Second, when this nothingness is known to itself it is reflection. The crucial point here is that, as with the slave above, the nothingness of positing and the activity of positing have their actuality in the subjectivity on behalf of whom, so it appears, the positing is carried out. We saw how, in Hegel's famous relation of master and slave, the master is the truth of the slave because the truth of the slave is nothingness in his work for the master. Equally, here, subjectivity is the truth of positing, or illusory being, because the truth of positing is also nothingness and work for that subjectivity. Illusory being cannot be avoided for it is already the 'beginning' of thinking. Thinking is posited and what is posited is thinking. Thus, as Gillian Rose says, 'reflection has presupposed what it claims it is positing' (Rose, 1981, p. 196).

This is significant for us in two ways. First it means that reflection is determinate within illusion and as such all beginnings in reflection are illusion. Second, the way that illusion is determinative of itself is, as we will see, the truth of the slave and its consequent political representation as the master. Thus, illusion is not only determinate, it knows its determinateness as illusion. This is the education of consciousness as subject and substance where education, here, means 'realised' both as achieved and as known. For Hegel, unless we work with illusion to comprehend the determinative truth of illusion's own re-presentation of itself in our critical thinking, our critique of illusion will remain an empty repetition of illusion, one without its own educational import. That illusion is determinative of subject and substance is the educational advantage that the speculative has over other forms of philosophising and is, as we saw above, the structure of experience and of philosophical education in the relationship of the master and the slave.

Illusion is also the positing that defines the character of the Hegelian system. Rose observes here,

> The *Phenomenology* is not a teleological development towards the reconciliation of all oppositions between consciousness and its objects, to the abolition of 'natural' consciousness as such, but a speculative presentation of the perpetual deformations of natural consciousness. The *Phenomenology* is the education of our abstract philosophical consciousness (Rose, 1981, p. 150)

—such that it might learn of itself, from itself. 'If the *Phenomenology* is successful it will educate philosophical consciousness to know these oppositions in a wholly changed way, by making it look and see into (intuit) their formation as the experiences of a natural consciousness' (p. 151). Therefore, and against readings of Hegel's system that judge it teleological but closed, and merely a dogmatic assertion of spirit as the true, we are offered a system of thought that is teleological, unresolved in its contradictions and able to recognise past, current and future deformations: a system where illusion learns the truth of itself within the social relations that embody it.

Why, then, if the system is only about mis-recognitions of the true, can Hegel produce a system? The answer is because there is systematic mis-recognition in natural consciousness of its relation to itself in experience. Illusion is both the presupposition and the work of that relation. So, because it is we who are having the experience that knows of re-cognition, or education, we are being educated in mis-recognition about mis-recognition. There is truth in illusion here, because we experience illusion through illusion. The criterion for such a judgement has not been imported from outside, even though on each occasion our experiences repeat the relation of inner and outer, and of true and false. The experience of negation is thought's own act upon itself. It can, therefore, judge its truth as its own object in a way denied to other objects.[13]

But, as also outlined above in Part I, I want to argue that this work, where natural consciousness, in Rose's words, 'experiences the contra-diction between its definition and its real existence' (p. 150), can be identified not just as a philosophical experience but as the work that is the broken middle of philosophy and education. The nature of the true in Hegel is not merely philosophy; it is philosophy *as* education and education *as* philosophy. This is because natural consciousness, in being negated, is not overcome; it is made aware of itself, and this change in its perspective is its philosophical education. All philosophy and social theory that heralds this change of perspective, this education, as either an overcoming of the illusions of natural consciousness or as a scepticism towards their ever being overcome, fails to recognise the educational and philosophical significance of natural consciousness's experience of itself.[14]

Retrieving education and learning as the core of the speculative experience not only opens up an absolute yet non-foundational reading of Hegel; it also retrieves the Hegelian system as an education of philosophy. As the truth of the slave and the student are retrieved in the integrity of their negative education, so the truth of Hegel's system as a whole can be read in the same way. Some of Hegel's frustrations at being misunderstood in his own lifetime are revealed early in his *Science of Logic*. He states

> I have been only too often and too vehemently attacked by opponents who were incapable of making the simple reflection that their opinions and objections contain categories which are presuppositions and which themselves need to be criticised first before they are employed. Ignorance in this matter reaches incredible lengths (Hegel, 1969, pp. 40–41).

There are three observations made by Rose that help us here to address the most fundamental of these presuppositions and that go to the core of any coherent reading of Hegel's education of philosophy. These observations are: that the foundations of the state and religion are identical; that 'social relations contain illusion' (Rose, 1981, p. 81); and that the absolute can be known. I shall very briefly explain each of these in turn.

In his lectures on the philosophy of religion Hegel put forward the view that 'religion and the foundation of the state are one and the same' (Hegel, 1984a, p. 452). It is the case, he argues elsewhere, that the state and its laws 'are nothing else than religion manifesting itself in the relations of the actual world' (Hegel, 1956, p. 417). Such propositions at first sight strike one as empirically wrong. How can religion, the subjective disposition regarding truth, become the foundation of a legal relation? How can love be the foundation of law? It seems more to be the case that they are incommensurable with each other, one subjectively and freely given, the other objectively and heteronomously demanded.

So what does Hegel mean by his claim about religion and the state? Rose argues that this proposition, as with many of Hegel's most difficult statements, requires reading speculatively, that is, according to the broken middle of its being experienced, and not merely as an abstract assertion. To read a proposition speculatively, she says, 'means that the identity that is affirmed between subject and predicate is seen equally to affirm a lack of identity between subject and predicate. This reading implies an identity different from the merely formal one of the ordinary proposition' (Rose, 1981, pp. 48–49). Read in this way, the statement about the common foundation of state and religion becomes a statement that contains our experience of our lack of freedom. In Rose's view of the speculative proposition it is precisely the lack of freedom and autonomy that religion represents. To affirm the identity of state and religion as an experience, therefore, is, for Hegel, to know 'this divorce in the idea of the absolute [the lack of freedom] as the state and as religion' (p. 93).

Rose's second observation concerns the role played by illusion in thinking in general and in philosophy in particular. As we will see in a moment there is illusion in social relations for Hegel and Rose in that our natural consciousness takes its relation to the object as the standpoint of reflection. As argued above, even hermeneutics, along with critical and post-enlightenment philosophies, contains illusion in this way. They may well be alive to the contingency and historicism of reflection but it is this observation, this positing of the relation, that is then precluded from being its own philosophical content. The refusal of illusion as self-determinative is the continued domination of modern, abstract, rational consciousness. Style, perhaps irony, is often called upon to register that awareness of illusion deconstructs even the critique of illusion. However, perspectives that claim to be *post* the illusions of natural consciousness are in fact denials—unphilosophical denials—of the domination of illusion. Illusion remains unrecognised philosophically when it is not pursued as constitutive of abstract consciousness, as the critique of abstract consciousness and as the abstract philosophical doctrine that can be recorded of these relations.

It is here, in the self-determination of illusion, that Adorno, for example, cannot follow Hegel. For Adorno,

Hegel's philosophy contains a moment by which that philosophy, despite having made the principle of determinate negation its vital nerve, passes over into affirmation and therefore into ideology: the belief that negation, by being pushed far enough and by reflecting itself, is one with positivity. That ... is precisely and strictly the point at which I refuse to follow Hegel ... for if I said that the negation of the negation is the positive, that idea would contain within itself a thesis of the philosophy of identity and could only be carried through if I had already assumed the unity of subject and object which is supposed to emerge at the end (Adorno, 2000, p. 144).

Hegel's response can be taken from the Introduction to the *Phenomenology*:

Should we not be concerned as to whether this fear of error is not just the error itself? Indeed, this fear takes something—a great deal in fact—for granted ... To be specific it takes for granted certain ideas about cognition as an instrument and as a medium, and assumes that there is a difference between ourselves and this cognition. Above all, it presupposes that the Absolute stands on one side and cognition on the other, independent and separated from it ... or in other words, it presupposes that cognition which, since it is excluded from the Absolute, is surely outside of the truth as well, is nevertheless true, an assumption whereby what calls itself fear of error reveals itself rather as fear of the truth (Hegel, 1977, 47, emphasis removed).

Adorno's 'fear of the truth' (ibid.), then, prevents him from pursuing the educational and philosophical implications of knowing illusion. Adorno is well-known for his melancholic view that reification is total and that it is, therefore, hard to see how even critique itself can any longer be effective. With Horkheimer he famously observed that 'even the best-intentioned reformer ... strengthens the very power of the established order he is trying to break' (Adorno and Horkheimer, 1979, p. xiv). Yet even though Adorno finds positivity in the idea that negative dialectics is able to 'crash through' (Adorno, 1973, p. 17) the illusions of identity thinking, he still does not follow the path of despair to the point where it can articulate itself as an education, or as philosophy. It is in illusion, Rose reminds us, where natural consciousness experiences the contradiction between itself and its self-consciousness, that it can find the criterion of this education in itself. Knowing this criterion brings education and philosophy together, but not, as Rose says, as the 'reconciliation of all oppositions' (Rose, 1981, p. 150).

This leads to Rose's third point, that the absolute can be known in philosophy as social critique. Within the illusions of the modern abstract culture of *Verstand*—that is, of abstract rational consciousness—this is tantamount to a theoretical blasphemy. Nevertheless, it is the very fact that illusion knows itself that contains the criterion by which truth can be judged. The following quotation from Rose presents her interpretation of how it is that, amidst all the dualisms and mis-recognitions that illusion provides,

> once the shapes of consciousness have been experienced, one thing can be stated. It can be stated that the absolute or substance is negative, which means that it is determined as the knowing and acting self-consciousness which does not know itself to be substance, but which knows itself by denying or negating substance, and is certain of itself in opposition to its objects. This is not an abstract statement about the absolute, but an observation to which we have now attained, by looking at the experiences of a consciousness which knows itself as an antithesis, as negative, and thus 'participates' in this antithesis as its own act (p. 181).

This participation can be understood as thinking knowing itself through its own work, or as the relation of activity and result, or of education and philosophy. What Hegel draws attention to is that there is a notion of truth here that does not have to assert itself dogmatically against prevailing conceptions of the true, for such assertion is already part of the philosophical experience in question. Critiques of the Hegelian absolute depend upon the presupposition of the categories that they have to employ. As Hegel remarked above, such critiques become purely arbitrary, selecting those presuppositions that suit their case and rejecting others. Thus, whilst spirit repeats political and religious mis-recognition as its own determination, the critiques repeat the very oppositions that form the absolute, but without the re-formation of the critique that the political and religious preconditions ensure. The difference can be summed up in the different recognitions of subjectivity. Spirit is subjectivity become political and religious substance, whilst the critiques of the absolute reject subjectivity as merely a posited identity, as illusory. It is spirit however that is the truth of the illusion, for spirit knows illusion as its own self-determination. Rejecting illusion, or even trying to embrace it as myth, merely dominates our abstract philosophical education, from one side of the relation (the overcoming of illusion—that is, the principle of *praxis*) or the other (non-overcoming—that is, the principle of difference).

Within Hegelianism the ambivalence of this philosophical education in and as spirit is illustrated by the way the relation is itself often reproduced only one-sidedly. For example, in a right-wing reading of Hegel, the absolute can be imposed as the truth of existing law over and against illusion; and in a left-wing reading, the absolute can be critiqued as the illusion of existing law. In both cases the substance of illusion is suppressed beneath the posited relation of theory and practice. Hegel's triadic philosophy, however, takes this experience of the broken relation as substantive, and as such, it re-presents the relation of theory and practice not only as a critique of each position, but also as a critique of their critiques of each other. The right-wing and left-wing readings are themselves the re-presentation of the abstract oppositions of philosophy and education. The former, philosophy without education, reinforces the idea of philosophy as at its end in the sense that it is teleologically completed; the latter, education without philosophy, repeats the aspiration to change the world without recognising the way in which philosophy itself is re-formed in the process. Neither allow for the culture, for the formation and re-formation of consciousness in their work.

FREEDOM AND THE TEACHER

We are now in a position to assess the political and philosophical import for the teacher of Hegel's philosophy of education and education of philosophy as it has been presented here. This will be a difficult task for we are being asked to think about the way that contradiction and dichotomy are the truth of thinking, and that education is the truth of that truth. Furthermore, we will see how freedom, experienced in the aporia of the former, is present in the latter.

When Rose says that 'Hegel's philosophy has no social import if the absolute cannot be thought' (Rose, 1981, p. 204) she is not saying that truth lies outside of the political experiences in which we fail to think truth. It must be the case that we can think the absolute, else all philosophy—taken as the realisation of thought's own work in and by itself—is not *our* thinking. If coming to think something new about previous conceptions is not our thinking, then philosophy has no educational significance at all. It is hard to imagine even those philosophers who are vehemently opposed to the absolute also arguing that the philosophical case they make for such claims has no educational import. Such writers may not hold with the absolute, but by producing philosophical work they are already claimed by a notion of philosophy that knows such work as its being thought, and as being at least assumed to be transformative. When attention is being given to the ways in which our thinking is distorted, suppressed, wrongly conceived and so on, and when arguments are made for the educational importance of deconstruction, critique and other anti-foundationalist shibboleths, these are in essence arguments for philosophy *as* education. Moreover, even within the critiques and deconstructions of the subject as thinking agent, there is still posited the assumption that such thinking is work and has formative significance for us.

The political significance of the relation of philosophy and education lies in the concept of work or transformative activity. The ambivalence of re-presentation is that in it we think the truth and fail to think the truth; we know of relation but also we are relation. As philosophical experience, this aporia is the truth of our political education in regard to our social determination. What makes this assertion true rather than merely assertion has to do with the illusions that are carried in each historical period by the notion of transformative activity or work.

Rose argues that for Hegel 'a society's relation to nature, to transformative activity determines its political and property relations, its concept of law, and its subjective or natural consciousness' (p. 204). In Ancient Greece, for example, work represented a relation to nature characterised by ethical life as custom. Here, the individual 'sees the whole of himself in the totality of his productions' (p. 129). Now, whereas here the individual knew work as his own, for he knew the totality of ethical life as his own, in Roman law this unity was broken into objective law and subjective will. This separation also characterises modern social relations. The result is that freedom, once known in the custom of immediate ethical life, can now be known only in the opposition between individual and law. This opposition is actual as private property for private property is not one's own work, it is work performed by others and appropriated by persons. Work is now the re-presentation of freedom based in self-interest and the priority of the private person over the social (and indeed global) totality. Thus, freedom is in the aporia of universal property law that enshrines the freedom of each person as freedom from every other person. Asking which came first, that is, work or law, or which caused the other, misses the significance of illusion here. As illusory being posits itself in reflection and in the relation of subject to object, so, freedom posits itself in the relation of work and law. 'A change in relation to nature is in itself a change in the political relation' (p. 138).

In relations of private property, then, freedom is the decay of communal relations, the strengthening of private interest and, as we saw earlier in Chapter 2, the beginning of a subjective inwardness that laments this decay and, at times, reproduces that relation as political intrigue and as Fascism. There is a great deal at stake here. The (political) relation to nature becomes the determination of political freedom. All freedom in this sense is 'natural law', for all law represents the relation to and the work upon nature. Natural law is itself a positing, an illusion of freedom. It is in the experience of freedom as illusion or as positing, then, that freedom is self-determinative; not merely abstractly, as it must be, but also as the relation to nature that is philosophical consciousness. This is not a reconciliation of the community and the person. It is, rather, an education about the unfree conditions in which freedom appears. Thus, freedom is essentially an educational undertaking, one in which the relation of work or transformative activity to nature is both illusory *and* actual. The 'and' here[15] is our representation of real political relations and their philosophical critique. Even, or especially, in the political re-presentation of freedom as the broken middle of subjectivity and substance, this experience is *our* experience, and it is our experience of the truth of social and political relations as they are reproduced as subjectivity itself. Rose notes here that 'recognising our transformative or productive activity has a special claim as a mode of acknowledging actuality that transcends the dichotomies between theoretical and practical reason, between positing and posited. Transformative activity acknowledges actuality in the act and does not oppose act to non-act' (p. 204). This 'special claim' is our philosophical education, for the lack of identity between law and work, or between metaphysics and ethics, or even between God and Caesar, 'gives rise to experience, to a re-cognition that sees what the act did not immediately see' (pp. 204–205). If this is not the case, then there is no political education, and it marks the end of culture within a totality of act without law, ethics without metaphysics and Caesar without God. If we cannot recognise in our subjectivity the mis-recognition that *is* subjectivity, then political education, the truth of thinking and the thinking of truth are at an end.

This relation of work to nature, realised as subjective formation and reformation, is precisely the notion of culture that we argued earlier is missing from educational theory and philosophy of education. Culture is the philosophical work of illusion known to itself. But the philosophy of education has little idea of itself as a culture because it recognises no speculative experience able to know how it is reformed in its being known as formed. Here, there lies a potential advantage within the philosophy of education denied to philosophy in general. The former is the relation of culture but its moments are held in stasis by the inability, the refusal, of the philosophy of education to recognise its mis-recognition within modernity. Philosophy in general has to find its educational subject and substance within the domination of abstract philosophical consciousness (*Verstand*). Philosophy of education carries the illusions of *Verstand* up front, as it were, and keeps the speculative truth of education and philosophy in view. But still it has not recognised itself as re-formed by property relations in such a way as to be the truth of the experience of modernity. Why this resistance? Cruelly, it is because the philosophy of education and educational theory derive from modern experience no concept of the formation and re-formation of (the relation that is) philosophy and education. Much is written *about* education; much less is written about the illusions that dominate the relation of philosophy and education; and even less is written about this relation as culture.

To draw this chapter to a close I want to relate these thoughts more directly to the teacher–student relationship. The significance of the master–slave relation is nothing less than the re-presentation of freedom in unfree social relations. The master–slave relation is how freedom is known, by itself, where its actuality is unfreedom. Freedom, here, is our political education. But in the teacher–student relation our political education is also our education regarding freedom. Since the truth of the master–slave relation in its re-presentation of freedom is education, it is not surprising that the teacher–student relation bears the weight of being the re-presentation of education itself. In other words, the philosophy of the teacher can maintain a transparency of the truth of the experience of freedom, a transparency of which the modern master–slave relation is deprived. In modernity the latter has taken the form and content of formal equality and freedom. There are no legal slaves—although there are many visible and many more invisible slaves. Formal freedom is the freedom of the master and the suppression of the slave; their relation is rendered opaque. But in the teacher–student relation, the truth of that merely formal equality cannot survive the dialectic of education that attacks it. The classroom is not defined by formal equality. Neither is the philosophy of the teacher able to define itself without the negative work of the productive activity of the student or learning. Even when domination is masked by formal legal relations, the educational relation is not.

The aporia of education that Parts I and II have traced, then, is known now to be a political experience, just as the teacher is now also seen as a determination of that experience. This political experience is the site of our experience of ourselves within existing property law, where relation to nature is also the definition of subjectivity. The teacher *must* take his place as part of that experience for the student.[16] For the teacher, however, as for the student, '"subjective meaning" can only re-present actuality, it cannot present it' (Rose, 1981, p. 213). A beginning cannot be made with the thought of contingency (myth); only with the contingency of the thought of contingency (myth and enlightenment). 'Thus,' says Rose, 'the inversion of actuality in the media of re-presentation should be the point of departure' (ibid.). The teacher, in other words, must teach, must be the teacher, for as such he is this re-presentation. To refuse the teacher as being this point of departure is to refuse our experience of freedom and the absolute in all its difficulties. It is to deny the student the truth of his own experience and is, in itself, potentially a new form of terror and domination over actuality.

What does this mean in and for the philosophy of the teacher? First, it means that any talk of overcoming domination in the classroom carries illusions. This covers all of the pedagogies outlined above in Chapter 4, which sought to overcome domination or political reality in some way. Second, these illusions are far more powerful forms of political education even than the mastery of the teacher. The domination of the teacher, exemplified in Chapter 3, is a direct political experience. The failure by teachers to re-present political reality refuses the student their own subjectivity for it refuses a validity to the latter's discrimination between illusion and actuality. In short, it refuses them their formative and re-formative political experiences. Intrigue, in Benjamin's sense, charac-terises this teacher who therein creates new tyrannies over the students within the broken relation between the hypertrophy of his inner life and the decay of the universal. They, the students, will have to look elsewhere for the recognition of their political experience of this intrigue. Third, it means that those classrooms and seminars that take illusion to be political education give a re-presentation of the truth of freedom as education that, whilst acknowledging the prior determination of social relations, do so without suppressing either of its political moments, that of the teacher or that of the student. This means, as we have seen, that teachers must risk the re-presentation of the political reality of the classroom and of the teacher–student relationship and have faith in the power of education to ensure that these illusions become formative political experiences. The point here is not that teachers can go into their classrooms and seminars and 'pretend' to be teachers until the students can critique their identities. Rather, it is the case that teachers can remain true to the (untruth of the) formation of their subjectivity in and by social relations by refusing their own abstract suppression of philosophical and political education, both theirs and their students'. The reduction of the teacher to the pretence of 'the facilitator' is just such political intrigue. It is, says Rose, to risk 'recreating a terror, or reinforcing lawlessness, or strengthening bourgeois law in its universality and arbitrariness' (1981, p. 219). The whole point is that we *are* teachers: we are partly exactly what we appear to be, a domination. But it is by remaining teachers that we can work for the re-formation of the experience of education as a whole. The teacher–student relationship carries truths within it that will become educational if the ambivalence that they re-present is not itself dominated. For those who work in education it is of added significance to know the true as this learning. Nothing is closed down; learning will continue; and indeed, it will find itself in all the struggles that learning commends. There is always learning; there is always the true; but, alas, there is not always the courage, the philosophical *character*, in education or in philosophy, to pursue the true in the ambivalence of modern freedom, or, in other words, to keep learning.

NOTES

1. And, I would argue, to Kant, Nietzsche and Kierkegaard; see Tubbs, 2004.
2. Niethammer was the man responsible for the reorganisation of the Bavarian education system at the time that Hegel was in charge of the Nuremberg *Gymnasium*.
3. With younger children Hegel remarks that 'this stage is more difficult than the abstract; and is at once the stage in which the young, eager for material content and sustenance, are least interested' (Hegel, 1984b, p. 281). For teachers coming to the negation and/or deconstruction of their own taken-for-granted assumptions and identities, however, one can anticipate greater curiosity, at least in pursuing the pathway of despair that such critique stretches out before them. I shall return in a moment to a discussion of this education as it applies specifically to teachers.

4. Yet he also makes clear the benefits for him of doing so. Of his years in Jena, during which he wrote the *Phenomenology*, he says he was 'bound to the letter of my notebook' (Hegel, 1984b, p. 331). But, in contrast, of his time as a school teacher he remarks that it 'has helped me gain a freedom in my lecturing that probably can be attained nowhere better than in such a position. It is', he continues, 'an equally good way of attaining clarity' (ibid.), even more advantageous to clarity than having 'a university professorship' (p. 332).

5. I have to note a change of terminology here. Throughout the book we have referred to the master and the servant. Yet Hegel's bondsman is very clearly a slave. I have not yet employed the term 'slave' within the philosophy of the teacher because it could so obviously be rejected by teachers as inappropriate to their position. The term 'servant' carries greater spiritual connotations of service to others and the consequent struggles with power, identity and authority. Nevertheless, whether as servant or slave, it is still the case that the teacher has no self-certainty within the negative experience of herself as master.

6. See Kojève, 1969, p. 52.

7. Remember that the teacher with no knowledge at all, Socrates, did not get paid.

8. Such a model may look as if it falsely separates the teacher from learning. The point, however, is that the identity of the teacher is precisely the abstraction of learning. We have seen this in Part II, not just where the teacher is master, but also where the teacher is servant. It is the contradiction here for the teacher in terms of learning and teaching that is the substance of the teacher's speculative, aporetic experience of her work and identity.

9. One might say here, that this is only nothingness in terms of the knowledge that passes for education, or curriculum knowledge. But we are dealing with the concept of the teacher here and thus are exploring the components of the experience that is constructed by 'education' between teachers and students. There are many examples of 'sociologies' that explore the particular ways by which the identity of the students is constructed. But the educational import of such sociologies will remain suppressed without the idea of sociology as culture—which is, then, philosophy.

10. See Chapter 1 above.

11. Thus, the philosophy of the teacher could never countenance a life in higher education that did not involve teaching.

12. It is more usual to undertake such an exploration through the more familiar notions of spirit, or recognition, or logic. But, in the reading of Hegel being presented here, the formation and re-formation of illusion in and by itself underpins the triadic structures of those notions.

13. But that can, thereafter, educate us about the notion of an object and of objectivity *per se*.

14. Elsewhere I have explored this as 'philosophy's higher education' (Tubbs, 2004). For present purposes, however, it can be stated as follows. Spirit that participates in its own act as the broken middle of a separation and a unity—*this can be called learning*.

15. This question of the import of 'and' is taken up again in Chapter 7, and in Tubbs, 2004, Chapter 6.

16. Or else posit for himself an alternative form of law altogether as, for example, Heidegger does. When Hegel says in his letter of 1812 that knowledge or science is 'a treasure of hard-won, ready-prepared, formed content … [and that] the teacher possesses this treasure, [and that] he pre-thinks it [whilst] the pupils re-think it' (Hegel, 1984b, p. 280), this looks like an unpalatable domination of the slave by the master. One could then turn to Heidegger's comments to find a pedagogical relationship in which the truth of the student remains 'without interpretation' (Krell, 1993, p. 375). Michael Bonnett has taken up this theme. He finds in Heidegger a teacher–student relation that is 'a genuinely creative, because genuinely open, encounter', one wherein the teacher has 'to attend to the withdrawn (the as yet *un*thought, the incipient) that alone draws thought forward' (Peters, 2002, p. 240). This poetic relationship, as he calls it, would be 'highly reciprocal and based on *trust*, which preserves both the integrity of the learner and of the material' (ibid.). The differences between this view and that found in Hegel's letter, however, serve as exemplars of the differences between Heideggerian and Hegelian higher education as a whole. The actuality of Hegel's teacher means that he is already in relation to the student as other, and in relation to himself as student. The teacher is other, but the other is not the teacher. It is precisely because he cannot think for or on behalf of the student that his mastery is negated and collapses. It is in this negation and collapse that the student and the teacher gain minds of their own. This is the humility and necessary vulnerability of 'pre-thinking', for pre-thinking is only the re-cognition of the teacher's own necessary negation by the other. But Heidegger's teacher

only has the pretence of learning from the student because Heidegger refuses the actuality of property relations. In the call to the subject of the question by the teacher, and, in the approach of the student, heeding the question, to the teacher, the question is deprived of its own object. Each withdraws from that which also withdraws. This is what might be called the dialectic of nihilism. The teacher never actually becomes the owner, and the student never actually becomes the property-less. This is not the result of any successful overcoming of universal equivalence by *Dasein*. This is due solely to the fact that the abstractions that pre-determine the teacher–student relation are denied by Heidegger in such a way that neither actually experiences the totality of these property relations. And to fail, or to be prevented from experiencing oneself in property relations, is to be prevented from the experience of the other, and of otherness in general. Where the Hegelian philosophy of the teacher takes its 'starting point in the contingent' (Hegel, 1969, p. 549), in the limits that prevailing law impose, the Heideggerian philosophy of the teacher posits a starting point in Being and beyond the reception of the law. It is, as Rose says, 'Yahweh without Torah' (Rose, 1984, p. 80). Indeed, the Heideggerian teacher only finds law in the error of metaphysics and theory. Eschewing the difficulties of universal political experience, rather than seeing oneself as determined within them, is the characteristic of fascism that rises above the state of emergency of present relations via a myth of past or future relations. Heidegger's concept of education, and of the teacher–student relationship in particular, turns the inequalities and despair of real class relations into a myth of authentic purity. Heidegger turns to the law of the individuality of the *Führer*, rather than the law, the broken middle, of actual modern, property-based social relations. He thus embodies a philosopher of the teacher as the intriguer whose political machinations of 1933, events that are so well documented, are rationalised according to a mythical representation of spiritual authenticity that re-presents the loss of metaphysics as a state of Being. Heidegger's philosophy of the teacher, if it is to teach anything, must teach us how the refusal of the absolute in real relations leaves the way open for myth, for intrigue, and for a way of life that is potentially at one with death-heads and destruction.

Chapter 7
Nietzsche, Zarathustra and Deleuze

INTRODUCTION

Gilles Deleuze confronts many of the concepts and ways of philosophising that have come to characterise philosophy. In doing so, he demands attention to the changes in thinking that he commends. This makes a straightforward description of his ideas deliberately troubling. Brian Massumi, writing recently about Deleuze, has also to confront his writing about writing about Deleuze. Half-way through his article Massumi confesses:

> my deadline is months past. My word-limit is fast approaching. And still no 'results', by the standard I set for myself beforehand: reader-friendliness; coverage; comparative breadth; no false leads and loose ends; a demonstration of my 'expertise' that met these goals yet didn't betray 'my' philosophy ... (Massumi, 1998, p. 568).

He comments further on the pain and joy that living with Deleuze's philosophy demands for him:

> My stomach anticipated this failure with a wrenching I felt for weeks before sitting down to write. An excruciating ache in my jaws bears witness to the grinding tension that wracks my body when I try to write as a 'Deleuzian' 'about' Deleuze ... I enjoy this, intensely. I enjoy this, to exhaustion. I would leave my home and my job and move to the other end of the earth to have more time to luxuriate in this feeling (ibid.).

The paradox here, for Massumi, is that whilst becoming Deleuzian is 'liberating the blockage in oneself' (ibid.), which in turn 'is to surrender to openness' (ibid.), nevertheless he is still forced into 'dissection for ... academic debate' (p. 559), something that offends what Massumi himself calls Deleuze's 'pedagogy of the concept' (p. 568).

Mindful of such difficulties, I need to perform my own dissection of Deleuze's philosophy as I think it pertains to the teacher, and most notably to Nietzsche's Zarathustra as teacher. This chapter, then, first describes some of the ideas in Deleuze, notably that of imperceptibility, that are needed to understand what kind of a philosophical teacher his philosophy suggests, if any. These ideas are then read against themselves, through Zarathustra and Nietzsche, before returning to a different conception of the imperceptible. I will make two criticisms of Deleuze: first, that his rhizomatic scheme has to employ the very kind of speculative education that it eschews; and second, that Nietzsche and Zarathustra sustain a very different kind of imperceptibility to that posited by Deleuze.

THE SCHEMA OF THE RHIZOME

I understand the *multiplicity identified to be the man Deleuze* to be arguing that subjectivity is not what it appears to be. None of us are how we appear to be, either to ourselves or to others. There are processes at work, operating behind our backs as it were, which cannot be seen in the same way as other objects. And yet, in order to come to know these hidden movements, it is not necessary to guess at or hope for any kind of *a priori* transcendental conceptions which would offer the possibility for knowing these movements and giving them meaning. In this sense, one can, perhaps surprisingly, proceed empirically, for coming to know these movements requires only that they be seen as happening. They do not need to be classified; all that is required is that one comes to know them.

On the other hand, to *know* subjectivity is to have been given a face. Deleuze argues that such subjectivities

> are always pinned against the wall of dominant significations, we are always sunk in the hole of our subjectivity, the black hole of our Ego which is more dear to us than anything. A wall on which are inscribed all the objective determinations which fix us, put us into a grille, identify us and make us recognised, a hole where we deposit—together with our consciousness—our feelings, our passions, our little secrets (Deleuze, 2002, p. 45).

We have to 'unmake the face' (ibid.). But how can we liberate ourselves from this black hole of identity, from the face? How can we get 'past the wall while avoiding bouncing back on it, behind, or being crushed?' (p. 46). Would not this escape leave us 'imperceptible?' Indeed, even though this unmaking of the face would be carried out in the open, it is, says Deleuze, 'we who have become a secret, it is we who are hidden'. It is the case that 'when you no longer have anything to hide', this is when 'no one can grasp you' for you have become imperceptible (ibid.). They do not know who you are without the face.

What is this imperceptibility? What is it, this secret, wherein one has, says Deleuze, become 'identical' (ibid.), which wears no face, and that is not a subject but is a secret precisely because it no longer has anything to hide? This is the question we will now explore.

But where can one begin this questioning? Not in the face-to-face, for the face is an answer to a different question; it answers the question 'Who are you?', but our question is 'Where to begin?'. But, Deleuze would suggest, is not the question the becoming of the question? Are we not already in the middle of what can be termed the question-becoming? The hyphen here is essential to Deleuze in constructing his distinctive philosophy. It links former identities, or faces, to a process of becoming wherein they can be called multiplicities. This will be explored further in a moment. For Deleuze, we are always 'in the middle of something' (pp. 28, 113). At first it may not be obvious that this is the case, for there is machinery at work, or powers at work, which need 'to overcode the whole body and head with a face' (p. 18). For example, there is the binary machinery of segmentation. These machines are lines of power that form us within dualisms—man/woman, child/adult, black/white and so on. In addition, as it shapes our lives into these defined segments, so the different segments collide and cut across each other, offering further binary choices that were not present on the first line. Power as segmentation here does not overcome dualism, for even its 'choices' are binary. In addition, lines of segmentation determine their own codes, but they are all overcoded by the power of the state apparatus which 'organises the dominant utterances and the established order of a society, the dominant languages and knowledge, conformist actions and feelings, [and] the segments which prevail over the others' (p. 129). Finally, the rigidity of the lines of segmentation organises the formation of subjects within them.

Segmentation, then, is anything but imperceptibility. It is along these lines of power that we are identifiable and identified. The harmonisation of the form of the segment is, says Deleuze, 'the education of the subject' (p. 130) into who he or she is. But if we find ourselves between lines of segmentation, for example, between family and work, or between child and adult, or between black and white, and then find ourselves between other segments such as Afro-Caribbean and British, or father and teacher, or pupil and adolescent, what are these 'betweens'? For Deleuze, they are different forms of powers. They deterritorialise the boundaries of the segments, and are experienced by us as betweens. These fluxes shake the territories of segments; they cross thresholds but do not cross into other segments. Where the binary machine fixed the subject for identification, here, in the between, there is only movement or becoming.

It is important to note here that, for Deleuze, the flux of betweens is not part of the segments. It is independent of them. As such, 'losing' one's subjectivity to imperceptibility is not a lack or a loss of identity, not a negation. This is one of the most significant elements in Deleuzian philosophy which, for Deleuze, distinguishes it from Hegel and the whole paradigm of negativity within consciousness. It would only be a loss if overcoding was taken as subjectivity. But the deterritorialisation of such a concept of subjectivity comes from outside. It is to be known, therefore, not only differently but *as the difference itself*. We might say here that the different from being is becoming. Becoming is not known in relation to being; it is known as different from being and as difference *per se*. In Deleuze's terms, it is a plane of immanence 'proceeding by thresholds, constituting becomings, blocs of becoming, marking continuums of intensity, combinations of fluxes' (p. 130). Furthermore, these molecular lines, as they are called by Deleuze, make the 'fluxes of deterritorialisation shoot between the segments' (p. 131). They are only 'relationships of speed and slowness' (p. 130). They are fluxes that do not belong to the binaries or to the segments. Deterritorialisation is not a matter of synthesis

> but of a third which always comes from elsewhere and disturbs the binarity of the two . . . It is not a matter of adding a new segment on to the preceding segments on the line . . . but of tracing another line in the middle of the segmentary line, in the middle of the segments, which carries them off according to the variable speeds and slownesses in a movement of flight or of flux (p. 131).

This line of flight is the third line of power. It is the line of gravity for it carries us across segments and thresholds, and it is the line of velocity for it registers as intensity, be it slow or fast. Together the three lines constitute all becomings. But those people who only have segment and flux, only territory and threshold, are still perceptible. They are in a middle but still related to the binaries. Here, deterritorialisation is an unhappy consciousness. For Deleuze, only those who learn to fly and to travel to unknown destinations, only they are the joy of the becoming, and are imperceptible.

Let us try this again, slightly differently. The question asked was: where we might begin to know ourselves without faces? The answer, seen above, is along the lines of segmentation, flux and flight. However, Deleuze sees that it is more likely that one will not seek the answer to this question from within the intersecting of lines and flights. It is more likely that one will try to start at beginnings which do not in fact exist. For Deleuze there is no beginning, for even the idea of a beginning is a middle. Philosophy, he argues, when it has thought in terms of beginnings and ends, has employed the tree model of philosophy. The French, he says, 'think in terms of trees too much' (p. 39). A tree can begin by putting down roots. The roots enable it to grow. The tree, therefore, is a whole from start to finish. Grass, however, is the deterritorialised tree. Grass grows in the middle of paving stones. It is unrelated to the paving stones, yet it marks their territory by growing through their thresholds. Trees have tops and roots but grass 'grows from the middle' (p. 23). 'Grass has its lines of flight, and does not take root' (p. 39). Thought, therefore, is like grass. It grows between segments but is unrelated to them. It grows through fissures and cracks but does not put down roots. Quoting Henry Miller, Deleuze states, 'grass only exists between the great non-cultivated spaces. It fills in the voids. It grows between—among the other things' (p. 30). Philosophy that is tree-bound in its structure crushes the grass with its binary machines and its segments. One has to 'set about opposing the rhizome to trees. And trees are not a metaphor at all, but an image of thought, a functioning, a whole apparatus that is planted in thought in order to make it go in a straight line and produce the famous correct ideas' (p. 25). Grass is experimentation, for in the middle there is not an average, or any kind of amelioration. The intensity of the middle is its line of flight and its speed. Its movement 'does not go from one point to another—rather it happens between two levels as in a difference of potential' (p. 31). The intensity that is this difference 'produces a phenomenon, releases or ejects it, sends it into space' (ibid.). Thus absolute speed and flight has content not as the reconciliation of dualism but as a multiplicity or an assemblage. Like grass it is a clump but without roots, existing only in the middle. This multiplicity is an assemblage of lines and flights. It is nomadic. It is grass and speed.

Philosophy must then face the deterritorialisation of its face. Multiplicities are ideas; to know multiplicities as ideas is to grow through the spaces left by trees and to fly between and across thresholds. There is no *a priori* here to act as a root for this rhizomatic thinking. In the middle, 'concepts are exactly like sounds, colours, or images, they are intensities which suit you or not, which are acceptable or aren't acceptable' (p. 4). This is not a matter of identity but of style, not of probabilities but of chance combinations. This is not the overcoming of dualisms, or even the recognition of each in the other. It is primarily desire and the encounter of desire with proper names, where the encounter is effect but not subject or person. In the becoming-effect of middles and flights, 'it is not one term which becomes the other, but each encounters the other, a single becoming which is not common to the two, since they have nothing to do with one another, but which is between the two' (pp. 6–7). Deleuze has us call this encounter a double capture, one not realising couples but expressing nuptials between two reigns. As such, there is woman-becoming, man-becoming, revolution-becoming, where '"what" each becomes changes no less than "that which" becomes' (p. 2), in an asymmetrical and a-parallel evolution. 'Nuptials without couples' (p. 8); 'becomings without history' (p. viii); 'individuation without subject' (ibid.); thought 'without image' (p. 24).

Where, we might ask now, are philosophy's intensities, flights, assemblages, multiplicities and chances? Deleuze argues that they are in the AND that is between elements or segments.[1] 'Even if there are only two terms, there is an AND between the two, which is neither the one nor the other, nor the one which becomes the other, but which constitutes the multiplicity' (pp. 34–35). Moreover, this AND, which carries on *ad infinitum*, is the stuttering in one's own language; it is that from within which is the flight, the speed and the repetition of chance and combination. For Deleuze, then, this stammering is the opening of experimentation, of life lived in the middle without roots, without representation, but with grass and speed.

Rhizomatic thinking encompasses *desire* and *style*. Desire is immanent in thinking. Its objectivity is flux (p. 78). It is the manufacture of the unconscious, for it gets it flowing. Psychoanalysis, says Deleuze, beats down the connections and assemblages of desire, for it treats each instance as the structure of the whole. In fact, desire is the 'raw material to experiment with'. It is not 'internal to a subject, any more than it tends towards an object; it is strictly immanent to a plane which it does not pre-exist, to a plane which must be constructed, where particles are emitted and fluxes combine' (p. 89). In other words, desire is where 'someone is deprived of the power of saying "I"' (ibid.). But this is not a negation or a lack of something; the grass does not lack the paving stones that it grows through. Grass, or that which grows in the middle, does not grow because it lacks something; it grows as its own positive plane of desire, albeit in the cracks which appear in social organisation. Desire is already intensity, but 'you haven't got it' (p. 90) if you do not know how to construct it in assemblages and fluxes. 'It is created all alone, but know how to see it . . . You have to create it, know how to create it, take the right directions, at your risk and peril' (p. 91). Deleuze's mentor, Zarathustra, might say: 'not lack I tell you, but will to power'; or Deleuze: not identity but 'hecceity'— that is, events and intensities of affects, of combinations of movements and fluxes, and which are 'always in-between' (p. 93). 'Do you realise', Deleuze asks, 'how simple a desire is? Sleeping is a desire. Walking is a desire. Listening to music, or making music, or writing, are desires. A spring, a winter, are desires. Old age is a desire. Even death. Desire never needs interpreting, it is it which experiments' (p. 95).

But if desire is released from 'lack', does this not assume a state of nature? Deleuze has anticipated this question. 'We say quite the opposite: desire only exists when assembled or machined' (p. 96). Nevertheless, is not the existence of suffering evidence of a lack? Again no, because even suffering is a becoming; even suffering is desire. How then should one treat suffering? As another 'in-between', which is again the affirmation of chance and one multiplicity among an infinity of multiplicities. Suffering without image is affirmative of one's own becoming-suffering whilst, in the more traditional philosophical sense, suffering with image, with representation, is both the lack or negation of a fixed segment or territory, and it is not becoming-suffering but only resentment and bitterness at one's lot, measured against an ideal and fixed image of what ought to be.

Desire, for Deleuze, is, therefore, not separate from its assemblage for it *is* the assemblage. It is not spontaneous; it is made on the plane which makes it possible. Desire is not about drives but about assembly and the creation of itself in assemblage. How then do we live the imperceptible? How do we live as desire and in positivity rather than in the melancholic sadness of the priests who know desire only as a lack?

Here Zarathustra is Deleuze's exemplar. To live in the middle 'all that is important is that each group or individual should construct the plane of immanence on which they lead their life and carry on their business. Without these conditions you obviously do lack something, but you lack precisely the conditions which make a desire possible' (p. 96). In constructing this plane of immanence one is in the movement of becoming, for becomings 'are acts which can only be contained in a life and expressed in a style' (p. 3). Style is, therefore, 'a right to desire' (p. 147).

This stylising of life as becoming is what Deleuze intends by the idea of living as imperceptible or as without the face by which one is pinned to the wall of identity. It is where one becomes identical only to a secret. We are to think of Kierkegaard and the knight of faith in *Fear and Trembling*. This knight, observes Deleuze, is interested only in movement. He is in this sense one step on from the knight of infinite resignation. The latter is resigned to the impossibility of a unification between the infinite and the finite. The former, on the other hand, the knight of faith, has taken the leap from resignation to faith. This leap, however, does not distinguish the knight of faith from the crowd. Quite the contrary:

> he does not make himself obvious, he resembles rather a bourgeois, a tax-collector, a tradesman, he dances with so much precision that they say he is only walking or even staying still, he blends into the wall but the wall has become alive ... There is now only an abstract line, a pure movement which is difficult to discover, he never begins, he takes things by the middle, he is always in the middle ... (p. 127).[2]

The imperceptible man is the becoming-man, as he is the becoming- of all his fluxes. Here life in the middle is style; style is the between of social segments; style is the grass between the paving stones; and style is rhizomatic, without roots; style is multiplicity and style is becoming-imperceptible. It is the unfacing of the person who can affirm desire as his own becoming.

Here is not just a stoicism regarding life's hardships and struggles; here in addition is their affirmation. 'What affects are you capable of? Experiment ...' (p. 61). It is 'not easy' (p. 62) to be a free man for all around there are vampires, tyrants and priests, 'captors of souls' (p. 61), who 'have a stake in transmitting sad affects to us' (ibid.). They do not rest until they have transmitted to us 'their neurosis and their anxiety, their beloved castration [and their] resentment against life' (p. 62). But the soul, for Deleuze, demands that we experiment, that we become-experiment so that one may become 'the child of one's own events' (p. 65). And should one be injured, for example, on the battlefield, then one affirms 'my wound existed before me, I was born to embody it! *Amor fati*, to want the event'; indeed, for Deleuze, it means to extract from actions the 'immaculate part' that goes beyond mere accomplishment, even to 'a love of life which can say yes to death' (ibid.). The new categorical imperative will be 'give way to rhizomatic movements' (p. 67). Here is the post-structural multiplicity that, as subject, is become-deterritorialised. Here, as Deleuze tells us in *Nietzsche and Philosophy*, is Zarathustra, for whom 'I will' is 'I am'.

DIFFERENCE AND REPETITION *CONTRA* HEGEL

In *Nietzsche and Philosophy*, Deleuze claims that there can be 'no possible compromise between Hegel and Nietzsche' (Deleuze, 1983, p. 195). Later, in *Difference and Repetition*, he affirms his philosophy of affirmation as part of 'a generalized anti-Hegelianism' that includes ontology, structuralism and the discovery of 'fields of a power peculiar to repetition ... [in] the unconscious, language and art' (Deleuze, 1994, p. xix). Central to this thesis are his observations that

> difference and repetition have taken the place of the identical and the negative, of identity and contradiction. For difference implies the negative,

and allows itself to lead to contradiction, only to the extent that its subordination to the identical is maintained. The primacy of identity, however conceived, defines the world of representation (ibid.).

Deleuze stakes himself in the claim that 'modern thought is born from the failure of representation, of the loss of identities' and of the collapse of representation into simulacra. Identity is only simulated, 'produced as an optical "effect" by the more profound game of difference and repetition' (ibid.). The continued subjection of difference to the identity, or to the concept of the same, 'seems' (p. 262) to mean that difference only becomes thinkable 'when tamed' by the four 'iron collars of representation', namely: identity, opposition, analogy and resemblance (ibid.). Even, or especially, in Hegel where difference is pushed 'to the limit' (p. 263), the path is 'a dead end' (ibid.) which ultimately brings it back to identity—the very condition upon which the examination of difference was allowed to proceed. Thus, representation is 'a site of transcendental illusion' (p. 265) which takes four interrelated forms of the subordination of difference: under the identity of the concept, under resemblance, under the negative and under the analogy of judgement. If Hegel is the high point of the history of a 'long perversion' (p. 164), then 'something completely new begins with Kierkegaard and Nietzsche', a 'theatre within philosophy' in which the ultimately static concept of mediation is replaced by 'movement' which can affect the mind 'outside of all representations'. Finding such 'immediate acts' is, therefore, for Kierkegaard and Nietzsche 'a question of making movement itself a work, without interposition; of substituting direct signs for mediate representations; of inventing vibrations, whirlings, gravitations, dances or leaps which directly touch the mind'. In doing so, they created simultaneously a 'theatre of the future and a new philosophy' (p. 8).

Leading directly from his presentation of affirmation in *Nietzsche and Philosophy*, Deleuze reaffirms in *Difference and Repetition* that 'representation fails to capture the affirmed world of difference' (p. 55). 'Representation has only a single centre, a unique and receding perspective, and in consequence a false depth. It mediates everything, but mobilises and moves nothing' (pp. 55–56). Hegelian movement can only represent 'the universal' to 'everyone' (p. 52). But 'there is always an unrepresented singularity who does not recognise precisely because it is not everyone or the universal'. This singularity, who is spoken for does not follow the Hegelian process of synthesis. Rather this 'sensitive conscience'

> subsists in its immediacy, in its difference which itself constitutes the true movement. Difference is the true content of the thesis, the persistence of the thesis. The negative and negativity do not even capture the phenomenon of difference, only the phantom or the epiphenomenon. The whole of Phenomenology is an epiphenomenology (ibid.).

Where representation offers only the indeterminate or negation, the philosophy of difference affirms itself in the refusal of these pseudo-alternatives. The affirmation of difference is its own essence. This is unlike the yes-saying that agrees to bear difference in order to cleanse it of its negativity. Such asceticism suffers in order to 'deliver difference up to the identical' (p. 53). On the contrary, the affirmation of difference is to deny 'everything which can be denied and must be denied' (p. 55). It is Nietzsche's new categorical imperative: deny everything 'which cannot pass the test of eternal return'. Those who do not 'believe' in eternal return will affirm for themselves the epiphenomenon of abstract knowledge. But for those who can deny negative representation, those who can affirm difference in itself, this will ensure that the negative 'consumes itself at the mobile centre of eternal return. For if eternal return is a circle, then difference is at the centre and the same is only on the periphery: it is a constantly decentred, continually tortuous circle which revolves only around the unequal'. Affirmation has difference as its object, and, therefore, affirmation is multiple. It is difference in itself. Negation is also difference 'but seen from below'. When we put or leave affirmation in the undetermined, we also put 'determination in the negative'. Negation, therefore, is only 'the shadow of the more profound genetic element—of that power or "will" which engenders the affirmation and the difference of affirmation'. Or, put more simply, negation is a form of *ressentiment* against power, for rather than affirming difference, it offers only epiphenomena as reality. 'Those who bear the negative know not what they do: they take the shadow for reality, they encourage phantoms, they uncouple consequences from premisses . . .' (ibid.).

Is this idea, which 'knows nothing of negation' (p. 207), in fact, the beautiful soul, or, 'differences, nothing but differences, in a peaceful coexistence in the idea of social places and functions'? Deleuze says 'the name of Marx is sufficient to save it from this danger'. Why? Because unlike Hegel, Marx, says Deleuze, knows the real movement of production to be *differenciation*—the division of labour—in a social multiplicity.[3] Hegel, however, knows difference only as 'opposition, contradiction and alienation' (ibid.). The beautiful soul cannot form out of the power of differenciation for difference is affirmation, not merely melancholy. When difference then becomes the object of a corresponding affirmation, it releases 'a power of aggression and selection which destroys the beautiful soul' (p. xx). In this sense the negative is the shadow of a problem, and as such always 'represents' problems to consciousness as opposition. The negative here is difference without affirmation. Seen as 'the wrath of the social idea', however, revolution is affirmation as 'the social power of difference' (p. 208). Thus, says Deleuze, to be aware of negativity as shadow is already to know a second determination, that 'the negative is the objective field of the false problem [and is] the fetish in person'. He concludes: 'practical struggle never proceeds by way of the negative but by way of difference and its power of affirmation' (ibid.).

The negative, as such, is illusion, or the shadow of problems, but not their imperative, their intensity or their differenciation. *Contra* the negative, then, affirmation, understood as the affirmation of difference, is produced by the positivity of problems understood as differential positings; multiple affirmation is produced by problematic multiplicity. It is of the essence of affirmation to be in itself multiple and to affirm difference. As for the negative, this is only the shadow cast upon the affirmations produced by a problem (p. 267).

We will return to Deleuze's position on Kierkegaard in a moment. What is now required is to put this Deleuzian account of will to power and eternal return in opposition to a very different interpretation of Nietzsche.

HEGEL'S ZARATHUSTRA

I want now, breaking with this idiom, to retrieve the speculative significance of Nietzsche's Zarathustra against Deleuze's reading in *Nietzsche and Philosophy* (1983).[4] I think it is correct to say that Deleuze sees Zarathustra as the imperceptible man of desire, and opposed to the man of *ressentiment* of the *Genealogy of Morals*. *Ressentiment*, he argues, acts to hinder and delay action. Its acts are designed to bring about the cessation of action. When reaction prevails over action, nihilism is to be found, a will to nothingness. It marks the triumph of non-act as value. Nietzsche calls this the slave revolt in (and as) morality. But for Deleuze, Nietzsche's Zarathustra marks a transvaluation of all such values wherein a new freedom is released, a new way of feeling, thinking and above all being (1983, p. 71). This transvaluation is brought about through the completion of nihilism. If we know that will to power as negation or nihilism is only one form of will to power, only 'one of its qualities' (p. 172), then we are already thinking will to power differently. This marks a transvaluation from the knowledge of values to the value of knowledge, where will to power 'teaches us that it is known to us in only one form' (ibid.). Thus, we learn of will to power as intensity, multiplicity and desire. The man who achieves this transvaluation is, therefore, the man who can unface himself and live in 'the eternal joy of becoming' (p. 174). Only his 'no' affirms itself through the denial of negation, segment and identification. The reason this 'no' is not Hegel's negative lies, for Deleuze, in eternal return. There is no return of the negative; rather, it is 'the returning itself that constitutes being' (p. 48). Deleuze, therefore, concludes that

> Nietzsche's speculative teaching is as follows: becoming, multiplicity and chance do not contain any negation; difference is pure affirmation; return is the being of difference excluding the whole of the negative ... Nietzsche's practical teaching is that difference is happy; that multi-plicity, becoming and chance are adequate objects of joy by themselves and that only joy returns ... The death of God needs time finally to find its essence and become a more joyful event ... This time is the cycle of the eternal return (p. 190).

This theory and practice for Deleuze is Nietzsche's Zarathustra-becoming.

What price then Hegel's Zarathustra? This brings us to our first criticism of Deleuze. The contested territory between Hegel and Deleuze for

Nietzsche's 'speculative' teaching is the middle. For Deleuze the joy of becoming is always in the middle. For Hegel the middle is always broken and known in experience. For Deleuze becoming is not negation but desire. For Hegel experience is the negation of desire because in experience is mediation *as* knowing. Where Deleuze affirms the middle, Hegel affirms and negates the broken middle. But, at this stage, it is appropriate to ask, what is *our* philosophical experience of their difference? How are *we* educated by and within the broken middle of such a dispute between Hegel and Deleuze? In Deleuze's terms we can experience it as the affirmation not only of *their* difference but also as the becoming of our difference from them. Here, as the grass between them, our education is where will to power 'teaches' (p. 172) us to think. In denying the denial that Deleuze sees as Hegel's negative, we instead free ourselves from the resentful 'yes' to all that is negative. In saying 'no' even to no itself, we are affirmed as difference.

But in order to differentiate difference from Hegel's broken middle in this way, Deleuze is dependent upon a speculative concept of philosophy as education, the very type of concept that he criticises. This education is carried within the transvaluation of values and the overcoming of the negative that Deleuze argues for. There *is* a philosophy of education in Deleuze, but not, as I will argue, one which comprehends the philosophical and educational (speculative) relation between philosophy AND education. In *Difference and Repetition* he argues that learning is knowledge which allows it (knowledge) to be grasped positively (Deleuze, 1994, p. 64). Indeed, what Deleuze seems to be claiming here for learning is that it is an opening or a gap 'which relates being and the question to one another' (ibid.). The truth of learning here, in itself, is as an 'apprenticeship' (p. 164) which has two aspects, both of which are different from knowledge. The first is that the apprentice explores ideas 'according to what one understands of a problem' (p. 165) whereas 'knowledge designates only the generality of concepts or the calm possession of a rule enabling solutions' (p. 164). The second is that the apprentice elevates the faculties into experiment and communication through and as multiplicities. It is the learning where culture is 'an involuntary adventure, the movement of learning which links a sensibility, a memory and a thought' (pp. 165–166). This is in contrast to learning as a method which presupposes 'the innate right of knowledge to represent the entire transcendental realm' (p. 166) and which therein 'regulates the collaboration of all the faculties' (p. 165).

Deleuze is critical of the model of apprenticeship found in Hegel. The philosopher has an apprentice, says Deleuze, in the way that a scientific researcher might have a lab rat in a maze. The former carries away the results, the knowledge, 'in order to discover its transcendental principles' (p. 166). Deleuze states 'even in Hegel, the extraordinary apprenticeship which we find in the *Phenomenology* remains subordinated, with regard to its result no less than its principle, to the ideal of knowledge in the form of absolute knowledge' (ibid.).

For a thinker who opposes eternal return to the dialectical reproduction of the same, however, for whom learning takes place 'not in the relation between a representation and an action ... but in the relation between a sign and a response' (p. 22), Deleuze's critique of Hegel is *precisely* a reproduction of the same. It is a reproduction of the same abstract concept of truth and of education, used without thought to its presupposition, that Hegel bemoaned nearly two hundred years ago, and that we highlighted in the preceding chapter. The charge is that in Hegel philosophical education is subordinated to a preconceived totality of concepts. Yet to read Hegel in this way requires that Deleuze subordinate Hegelian philosophy to a preconceived totality of one concept in particular, that of education. The concept of education that Deleuze is presupposing here is that learning is essentially open-ended. However, and this is the whole point, this idea of education is not open-ended enough to learn about itself—to have itself as form and content, to have itself as experience, to have its own truth according to itself as it participates in its own act. It becomes, therefore, another example of the suppression of education and philosophy because it is based upon a presupposition of that relation. The whole structure of Deleuzian philosophy that has been outlined above stands upon the presupposition of learning as difference, but it lacks the necessary corollary of the experience of learning as difference from itself. Every multiplicity, every plane of immanence, every pure difference is claimed as will to power teaching us to think. Yet how are we to know this as a teaching, and as a learning, if education *per se* is denied its own relation of difference and repetition? This goes to the very heart of the contested terrain between Deleuze and Hegel. Deleuze can claim the middle, the between, the AND, because it is posited as the unity (learning) that is pure difference. Hegel cannot claim the middle because in Hegel the relation, the broken middle, is the true, and the true made object to itself in and as philosophical education, whilst for Deleuze the relation is known without being known, that is, as the between. It is this positing, this prejudice of the formal equivalence as the end of culture that was marked out as characteristic of the bourgeois notion of culture in Part I above. It is this positing which enables Deleuze to occupy the becoming-middle ground without the loss of the middle to the relation that joins and separates them. In short, Deleuze can have the middle because he does not have a philosophical notion of the middle as its own education, or as the broken middle, in and as philosophy. I contest, therefore, that Deleuze is limited to a very interesting and detailed hermeneutical analysis of the relation of the middle in the ontological difference that is the question and the problematic. He fails, however, to let this hermeneutic be open to itself as its own truth, and fails thereby to have a philosophy of the middle at all. In consequence, and in comparison to the speculative conception of philosophy and education, we have in Deleuze merely learning without learning, education without education, and philosophy without philosophy.

THE WAR ON REPRESENTATION IN THE PHILOSOPHY OF EDUCATION

I will make this same critique now but related this time to a contribution from within the philosophy of education; namely a recent essay by Gordon Bearn invoking the University of Beauty, a sympathetic but largely Deleuzian critique of Lyotard's notion of the sublime.[5] Lyotard knew, says Bearn, that Universities were 'already becoming centres designed to improve the performance of the system by the delivery and discovery of information' (Bearn, 2000, p. 231). He knew that this would put restraints on the forms of knowledge, of teaching, and of research, for only that which contributed to the efficient management of 'the system' (ibid.) would be deemed acceptable. Bearn notes that efficiency, under the guise of 'development' (p. 253), is behind the drive for greater use of the Internet and distance learning, the demand for greater independent learning by students, and the demand for greater flexibility in teaching methodologies. The drive for performativity lies behind each of these so-called innovations.

But Bearn is critical of Lyotard's response to such institutional performativity. Lyotard, he argues, paints a 'melancholic grey' (p. 232) over the possibilities of resistance to such performativity. This is, he continues, because, where genres of discourse mask the differend that lies in the gap between phrases (where one such link, for example, would be that of the discourse of performativity), there is no way to retrieve the differend without the repetition of the exclusion, again, of the differend. Lyotard, says Bearn, turns here to a Kantian notion of the sublime. Here the experience of the sublime will register both the limits of the system and that which exceeds them: 'In this way he hoped at one and the same time to acknowledge the inevitability of the system's power and the ethical importance of what escapes, if only for a moment, the system's grasp' (p. 236).

Here Bearn argues that Lyotard was wrong to turn to a University of the Sublime rather than a University of Beauty. Lyotard searches for a way to witness the differend, the links between phrases, without employing genres of discourse that will occlude the differend. How, in other words, can we think without representation? Against the presentation (or is it re-presentation?) of the sublime in Kant as a No to a representation of the infinite followed by a Yes as the sublime (re-)presentation of the infinite as the excess of any representation, Bearn finds in Lyotard a No followed by a second No, a double negation. Where the Yes in Kant is reason's idea of the infinite beyond its being cognised, 'Lyotard's story never finds its Yes' (p. 240). This is, says Bearn, because Lyotard fails to affirm life as 'linking ... in all its forms' (ibid.). The first negation is of representation; the second negation is of desire itself. The blank, the abyss between phrases, the differend, is, therefore, defined only negatively as not this thought and not this living self. The nihilism of representation becomes in Lyotard nihilism *per se*: not-known and not-now. His response, says Bearn, is religious. The holy is invoked to 'plug the holes' (p. 242) that the nihilism of double negation has realised.[6]

Bearn employs a Deleuzian form of affirmation to re-phrase Lyotard's negative, even nihilistic, un-phrasing. Before exploring a little how Bearn does this, it is instructive to note why he does it. On the one hand, in response to Lyotard's double negation, he asks, 'why should we settle for this? Is this not a failure of philosophical imagination?' (ibid.). On the other hand, he states that Lyotard's negation 'needs to be supplemented by a positive affirmative account of what is beyond representation' (p. 243). Why? Why the need for the affirmative? Why is representation seen as a failure? Assertions such as this, so often overlooked as commanding consensus, in fact reveal the misrecognition of philosophy within the culture of modern abstract reason, mis-recognition which is then imposed as a *sollen* (an ought). They are, in effect, misunderstandings of our abstract philosophical consciousness. As we have seen above in Parts I and II, and now in Part III, the philosophy of education appears unable and unwilling to recognise its own contingency within the culture of abstraction that it sets itself against. Who is the 'we' in Bearn's question? Why does the negative need supplementing? The mistaken assumption is the same in both questions. The 'we' who do not have to settle for negation is the 'we' that is abstracted from the determination of its thought within modern social and political culture. This need and failure is not, therefore, a critique of our technical, instrumental and performative forms of theory and practice; it is a repetition of them without philosophical education. From within Hegelian rather than Deleuzian speculative philosophy, this repetition, realised as abstraction, is negative for the abstract consciousness that sees its perspective on itself changed. But for this consciousness that knows the change to itself as education, no supplement is required; nor is this merely a failure. Bluntly, the dissatisfaction with the education of our abstract philosophical conscious-ness and the call for supplementary affirmations amount to the point of view of abstraction itself. This is precisely how, for our purposes here, Deleuzian post-structuralism reproduces philosophy as further abstract domination. Its desire for affirmation—let us say, for a genuinely lived life which is not dominated by *ressentiment*—is the denial of its philosophical education in the name of affirmation.

In the war being waged on representation here, as elsewhere in educational theorising, Bearn argues for a genealogical transformation. 'When you approach the other side of representation,' he says, 'with your feet squarely planted on this side, then nihilism and holiness will be your only options' (p. 242).[7] Let us turn this around. When you approach the other side of nihilism and holiness with your feet squarely planted on this side, failure and need will be your only options. The natural consciousness rejects the true before it seeks it, and it then seeks it only within the terms of that rejection. The rejection is the domination of abstract philosophical consciousness. Beauty is not the freedom from this domination; it is the freedom of its representation as our education—a freedom only available as the education of natural consciousness where representation represents itself, for example in Kant's third Critique, as both aesthetic and teleological, as beauty and the sublime, and as both formation and finality.[8]

Much is made by Deleuze of the AND that links such relations. But there are two notions of 'and' at stake here, not surprisingly given that the real disagreement between the two forms of the speculative precisely concerns the nature of the middle. Indeed, it is not just a disagreement about the 'and' of judgement in Kant and the Deleuzian AND of the rhizome; it also concerns, in itself, the representation of the relation between post-structuralism and modernity. This opens up for us another way in which to illustrate the reproduction of abstract culture within Deleuzian philosophy of education, concerning this time the suppression of spirit—the third partner in the work between infinite and finite, or between truth and representation. In commenting on a draft of this chapter, John Drummond has emphasised most strongly that the rhizome and the tree are not alternatives to each other. Their relation is to be seen as one of interaction, not opposition. In the same vein Paul Standish has argued that, with reference to Bearn's account, 'the witnessing of the sublime could exist alongside the exuberance of beauteous intensity and be part of the same student's experience' (Blake *et al.*, 2003, p. 221). Rhizomes do not rule out trees. Rather, the rhizome is the moment of experimentation, of flight, in relation to the concrete practices of the arboreal. This same view can be found in Bearn. He is not saying that the University of Beauty is an alternative to the institution of performativity; rather that the Deleuzian teacher can work within the latter to release swarms of multiplicities, that lie suppressed under its technical and managerial discourse:

> The primary idea will be intensity, intensity achieved through pointless investigations ... [I]t is through achieving pointlessness that one breaks through the frame of representation releasing swarms of intensities, and it is this experience which is the source of breakthroughs which may sometimes actually even increase performativity but which, even if they do not, teach students what real thinking is like: not calculating within a representational frame, but experiencing the joy and ecstasy of breaking through (Bearn, 2000, p. 247).[9]

The safeguards against lapsing into dualisms are, then, in place: not *either* rhizomes *or* trees, but rhizomes AND trees; intensities AND representations; groundlessness AND discourse; Yes AND No. They coexist; the one is always interacting with the other. The rhizomatic teacher does not overcome trees; she is not rhizomatic all the time, nor, therefore, does the rhizome in any sense overcome the trees. The affirmation is not instead of the No; it is the No known affirmatively, not as lack but as possibility.

As we will now see, however, the more poststructuralists protest that the accusation that they are returning to dualisms misses the subtlety of their argument, the more this refusal and denial negates the education they seek to protect. This safeguarding against an oppositional dualism between, say, rhizomes AND trees, betrays itself. As we saw above, for Deleuze the rhizome is between segments. The rhizomatic is the AND. It is the multiplicity between segments; it is the thought without image; the affirmation of difference and repetition. What happens, then, in the relation not between two segments but in rhizome AND tree, that is, when the pair are coupled as coexistent and interacting with each other? Has the multiplicity not become the segment (as Lyotard mourned) wherein another multiplicity comes, or is it between multiplicity AND non-multiplicity? This is not just a sophistic observation, for it goes to the very 'centre' of the different speculative philosophies that are at stake here.

For Bearn, from Lyotard's point of view, this process by which each multiplicity becomes segment for another multiplicity is the melancholic grey where there is only failure, a failure heralded by a 'need' for the holy. From Bearn's perspective this process is precisely the repetition of difference. It illustrates how each return is different and thus affirmative of itself even if the affirmation becomes the relation to another segment. The affirmation out of dualism is affirmed, again, by the AND, the middle. Whereas for Lyotard the differend was negated by its incorporation into dualism by representation, for Bearn such incorporation only explodes again into the joy and ecstasy of being off balance: precisely differ-ence AND repetition, repetition AND difference. The third, here, the immediacy of the rhizome, comes between segments even if one of the segments is the representation of immediacy itself. This is the crux of the Deleuzian argument against dualism and against negation; it is his argument for imperceptibility.

But Deleuze, and by implication Bearn, have misunderstood Hegel, the negative, the logic of representation and abstraction. First, as we saw a moment ago, in order to argue for immediacy as teaching us how to think, a notion of the middle as education, or as transformation/transvaluation, is presupposed. The criticism made there of Deleuze stands now as a critique of Bearn's Deleuzianism. If the middle is education—teaching us 'what real thinking is like' (Bearn, 2000, p. 247)—then the middle is being presupposed as the identity or the perceptibility of learning.

Second, the assertions of AND against dualism or the binary of either/or also enables us to illustrate the arguments rehearsed above regarding the claims to the middle of Deleuze and Hegel. There is a logic of education from within education which, when played out as the rhizome, realises the complicity of the middle rather than its joys and ecstasies. Perhaps it can be put like this. Rhizomatic difference is the middle, the AND, between segments. But when it is argued that in Deleuze's speculative philosophy there must be rhizomes AND trees, is this the same AND as in the previous sentence? If it is the same AND, then the return of difference has made no difference. If it is a different AND, then the rhizome is not the first AND, which implies that it was not the middle at all. This means, somewhat bluntly for those wishing to retain the middles as without representation, that education requires, by the logic of itself as difference and repetition, that it be represented as the relation of rhizome and tree. The question then is 'what is it to learn of education as rhizome AND territory? But it is not in Deleuze, nor in Bearn, that this question is asked, nor this relation represented, for it is this relation that is affirmed as non-relation. The affirmation is represented, however, in the AND of rhizome and tree. Precisely, the affirmation negates itself because it *is* an education. Being taught that the middle means rhizome and tree, education is re-presenting itself. Its negative moment is not a refusal of affirmation; it is the substance of affirmation. In Hegel, the third partner who affirms this misrecognition, this domination of abstraction, is, as we saw above, spirit. In Lyotard, it is the recognition of this mis-recognition which is the third partner, the holy. But in Bearn, as in Deleuze, it is the third partner that is consistently suppressed by the presupposition of education *as* difference, but not itself *of* difference. It is this suppression that then takes form as the 'need' for affirmation, and as the 'failure' of philosophy.

At root, then, AND, or the middle, is affirmed in its own work where we, the philosophical observer, can see for ourselves how in this work the middle, to be true to itself as education, must become—has already become—its own object. For us to know this representation is for us to know ourselves as the broken relation of philosophy and education. It is how we know of abstraction, including our own. As observers we know the truth of the relation between philosophy and education, not as failure, or as affirmation but as our education regarding the truth of that relation, as of all dualism and all representation. This truth is spirit when we approach both sides of representation, affirmation and failure, from the broken middle that is the AND. Indeed, this truth is spirit, or it is not known at all. In Deleuze the AND is the Last Man of *ressentiment*, refusing to be the relation of affirmation and failure. (We will return to this theme in a moment.) In Hegel, as in Nietzsche and Kierkegaard, however, that 'and' is the ambivalence of philosophy and education, and it is known as such.[10]

We can take this critique to the very core of Deleuze's theorising, that is, to Nietzsche's Zarathustra. I shall make three related points here, which will bring this chapter on Nietzsche to a close. First, I shall describe Zarathustra's own educational journey through the four books of Zarathustra. Second, I shall relate this to Nietzsche's own journey through his publications from *The Birth of Tragedy* in 1872 to *The Genealogy of Morals* in 1887. Third, I shall argue the case that Zarathustra is neither Overman nor imperceptible.

NIETZSCHE'S ZARATHUSTRA

Through the four books, Zarathustra repeatedly learns the same lesson. But because it is learned repeatedly it is also learned differently. In the Prologue, in teaching of the Overman, Zarathustra teaches that God is dead. But his teaching is not comprehended by the crowd that has assembled. 'They do not understand me,' he laments. 'I am not the mouth for these ears' (Nietzsche, 1982, p. 128). This failure to teach is repeated in each of the following four books of *Thus Spake Zarathustra*.

In Book 1 his disciples reward their master with a gift of a staff on which 'a serpent coiled around the sun' (p. 186).[11] At the end of Book 1 Zarathustra realises that they have come to believe what he has taught them, but only abstractly. They have not done what the teaching requires.

Thus he demands of his disciples that they leave him. He urges them to resist their teacher, else they might believe him at the cost of their own education; 'resist Zarathustra! And even better: be ashamed of him! Perhaps he deceived you' (p. 190). I taught you yourselves he says, yet 'you had not yet sought yourselves'. In short, 'one repays a teacher badly if one always remains nothing but a pupil'. Zarathustra's second failure ends, then, with him saying, 'I bid you lose me and find yourselves; and only when you have all denied me will I return to you' (ibid.).

At the end of Book 2 Zarathustra learns again of his failure to be the teacher, but here he is learning more about the nature of that failure. When the hunchback asks him why he speaks 'otherwise to his pupils than to himself' (p. 254), this is a recognition that Zarathustra is learning for himself in new ways about the nature of being the teacher of the Overman. In Book 2 Zarathustra has learnt the hard lesson of nature as will to power, as 'that which must always overcome itself' (p. 227). His will to power has been to teach so that all that blocks the way to the Overman may be overcome. Yet the reason why nature triumphs over the teacher, and the reason why Zarathustra fails as this teacher, is that nature, will to power, must overcome itself. The more successfully he teaches his disciples, the less he himself is overcome. As we saw in Part II above, it is the fate of the enlightened teacher always to dominate in his students that which should only obey itself. Zarathustra learns this lesson as the eternal return in the teacher/student relationship of obeying and commanding. 'He who cannot obey himself is commanded' (p. 226). But even the commander must obey nature and must also be overcome. The teacher who is commander must also obey. At this point Zarathustra knows that the teacher must command and be commanded, but he does not as yet know how this is to be done. 'What persuades the living to obey and command and to practise obedience even when it commands?' (ibid.). To learn this lesson Zarathustra has to return again to his solitude. Without voice, he hears: 'your fruit is ripe, but you are not ripe for your fruit' (p. 259).

Book 3 sees failure being understood differently again. Here it is the most abysmal thought—eternal return—that is Zarathustra's education. Since the circle of will to power that he is obeying and commanding is universal, it is the nature of all life. *Ressentiment* and revenge are the attitudes that seek to deny will to power. 'The will cannot will backwards; and that he cannot break time and time's covetousness, that is the will's loneliest melancholy' (p. 251). Everything is will to power, and there is no going back. Every event is a victory of will to power, but since nature is that which must overcome itself, even this victory must be overcome. As revenge, this is 'the will's gnashing of teeth', a self-hatred at what it is. But the secret of will to power is that eternal return is the truth not only of all commanding and obeying; it is also the truth of the *ressentiment* that would overcome or deny will to power. The bitterness at the fact that the will cannot will backwards turns into the joy that even as *ressentiment* will to power is nature's truth. Every 'it was' is now understood as 'thus I willed it' (ibid.). The truth of will to power is eternal return. Here

Zarathustra believes he has finally understood his failures as a teacher of the Overman. He *had* to fail. This is the truth of the teacher. Now, however, he can will this failure repeatedly, for that is the truth of will to power. At the end of Book 3 we find Zarathustra celebrating this truth in the song of the yes-sayer and amen, the 'thus I willed it' song. 'How should I not lust after eternity and after the nuptial ring of rings?' he asks. 'I love you O eternity' (p. 341). With these words of affirmation for the circle Book 3 comes to an end.

However, Zarathustra's greatest success is also, as it must be, his greatest failure. Just as he taught his disciples to 'seek yourselves', so now he must take his own advice and 'become who you are' (p. 351). Sitting on his mountain, alone for years, the Zarathustra of Book 4 is troubled. 'My happiness is heavy' (p. 349), he says, for just as in the Prologue Zarathustra again has much he must share with mankind. Only this time he waits for them to come to him. But meanwhile, in the absence of teaching, the truth of his teaching as commanding and obeying is lost. The celebration of eternal return alone on the mountain has become a caricature of itself, eternal return as stasis. The final lesson that Zarathustra learns about his failures as a teacher are the lessons which in the end drive him back down the mountain to enjoy the eternal return of the success and failure of his work. Even on the mountain, joined as he is by the higher men, even there his teaching fails for the best that his guests can do is to will eternal return 'for Zarathustra's sake' (p. 430). This time Zarathustra does not retreat in the face of failure. This time he comprehends failure as the truth of the teacher, the truth of will to power that is the truth of eternal return. This time he knows: 'all eternal joy longs for failures. For all joy wants itself, hence it also wants agony' (p. 436). The broken middle of joy and pain is eternal return as will to power and will to power as eternal return. It is, therefore, also the truth of the relation between teacher and student when the teacher becomes his own student and says: 'was that education? Well then, once more'. Now Zarathustra leaves the mountain, again, but this time not concerned with teaching the Overman, but rather in the work that must be done between the teacher and his students.

ZARATHUSTRA'S NIETZSCHE

There is a corresponding philosophical education in Nietzsche's own development. For Nietzsche, 'the law-giver himself eventually receives the call; *patere legem, quam ipse tulisti*' [submit to the law you yourself propose] (Nietzsche, 1968, p. 597). In *The Birth of Tragedy* will to power is present in the tragic, in the 'primordially One' (p. 132) and in the 'glorious consummation' (p. 47) of Apollo and Dionysus. The Dionysian cannot overcome the Apollinian for the Dionysian is forced to work in the world of images, of concepts and of representations. Equally the Apollinian cannot overcome the Dionysian for every representation will be destroyed by the will that created it. As the nature of commanding and obeying, the desire for peace is also the eternal desire for war. It is, says

Nietzsche, 'an eternal phenomenon: the insatiable will always finds a way to detain its creatures in life and compel them to live on, by means of an illusion spread over things' (p. 109). The illusion is within even the law of overcoming.

In the essay 'On the Uses and Disadvantages of History for Life' (1874), the moment of eternal return is captured in the cows in the field whose memory is not long enough even to know of itself. As such, they remain in eternally forgetful silence. Nietzsche then compares the historical man of memory to the unhistorical man of forgetting. Here the attitude of will to power to itself is apparent. The man of memory never acts because he is always contemplating the implications of past acts. His memory ensures he always puts off action until a clearer picture of the whole emerges, which it never does. The eternity is paralysing to the present. The man of forgetting, however, 'forgets most things so as to do one thing' (Nietzsche, 1983, p. 64). This eternity is conducive of the present. Both men are will to power. The memory man is *ressentiment* against 'it was'. The forgetful man is will to power as 'thus I willed it'. But only together and apart in their broken middle are they the comprehension of the eternal return of will to power. At this stage, however, Nietzsche is writing of this as yet unknown idea as required 'in equal measure' (p. 63). This equality is not overcoming, it is tension. Only by means of a division, says Nietzsche, is an individual or a nation 'just as able to forget at the right time as to remember at the right time' (ibid.).

In the essay 'Schopenhauer as Educator' (1874) Nietzsche finds in Schopenhauer a teacher who serves life. This teacher is untimely because he represents an ideal that is suppressed by culture, and particularly in education:

> The sciences, pursued without any restraint and in a spirit of the blindest *laissez-faire*, are shattering and dissolving all firmly held belief; the educated classes and states are being swept along by a hugely contemptible money economy ... Everything, contemporary art and science included, serves the coming barbarism (1983, p. 148).

In this essay it is thinking which is will to power. In thinking nature presses towards man 'as towards something that stands high above us' (p. 158). In this way, the 'ideal educates' (p. 156). Schopenhauer embodies this ideal, for in him education as will to power is able to say 'this is the picture of all life, and learn from it the meaning of your own life' (p. 141). Eternal return here is still the 'tragic contemplation' (ibid.) of the teacher in whom the ideal still educates.

Between the 1874 essays and the *Genealogy of Morals* of 1887 come Nietzsche's books of aphorisms, *Human-All-Too-Human*, *Daybreak* and *The Gay Science*. The education of Nietzsche into the truth of will to power as eternal return is announced abstractly in the end of Book 4 of *The Gay Science*, and worked through speculatively as the broken middle of Zarathustra's education as teacher and student. As Nietzsche himself states: 'within my writings my Zarathustra stands by itself' (Nietzsche,

1979, p. 35). After Zarathustra Nietzsche says he turned from the yes-saying which culminated in Zarathustra to the no-saying that is 'the revaluation of existing values themselves' (p. 112). If Zarathustra is Nietzsche's education regarding the whole that is eternal return and will to power, it is an education towards which he was developing in his work up to Zarathustra, and it is an education that he repeats in the work after Zarathustra. Nietzsche can adopt a less aphoristic, more academic style because now he is his own work. There is an objectivity in the critique of values that was not claimed in earlier works. This objectivity is Zarathustra. It is the objectivity of the broken middle—not an abstract objectivity that merely asserts, but a speculative objectivity which knows failure in assertion and, therefore, joy in this eternal return of will to power. What Nietzsche says in the history essay is true for him, becomes him, only in and after Zarathustra, namely, that being is never itself, it is only 'an un-interrupted has-been, a thing that lives by negating, consuming and contradicting itself' (Nietzsche, 1983, p. 61). In Zara-thustra, and in Nietzsche post-Zarathustra, it is 'the redeeming man of great love and contempt' (Nietzsche, 1968, p. 532) who can teach now not merely subjectively but in the (re-evaluated notion of) objectivity of his own commanding and obeying.

In his critiques of morality and of *ressentiment*, particularly in the *Genealogy of Morals*, a reading of Zarathustra is also necessary. Here Nietzsche presents the broken middle of commanding and obeying, or of will to power, as the relation of master and slave. The questions that underpin *The Genealogy* are: 'under what conditions did man devise [the] value judgements good and evil? and what value do they themselves possess?' (p. 453). Nietzsche's answer is well rehearsed. In questioning the value of these values, which act as the foundation of all value judgements, Nietzsche finds their genealogy to lie in the attitudes associated with victory and defeat. That is to say, he finds the value of all values grounded in relations of power and more specifically in the ways in which will to power resolves itself into human character traits and attitudes. What is valued as good represents the character of the noble, but the noble is only he who has established himself above another. Equally, what is valued as bad is that which is ignoble, or merely that which is defined as less than or different from those who enjoy themselves as the Archimedean point of all values.

Nietzsche describes a slave revolt in morality which has several phases. First, in an act of spiritual revenge, the good are recast as evil, and good itself is seen to lie in the sufferers rather than the oppressors. This is the first inversion of values, and is itself political in that it represents the revolt of the vanquished. What is significant about this inversion of values is that it does not conquer its oppressors by physical force and subdue them as they have subdued others. Rather, the battle is fought out from the position of the vanquished. The war is now to redefine strength, ego, and will as bad, and to acknowledge the denial of power, victory and war as truly good. Here, says Nietzsche, it is the attitude of the oppressed that becomes creative, which is wholly different in character from the creative will of the noble. With the latter, good is affirmative of self and of will. With the former, good is the suppression of self and of will. It is not, says Nietzsche, that the denial of will *is* good, even though current moral sensibilities still hold to this. It is that this definition of good arises out of a spirit of *ressentiment* against those who have enjoyed the creative power of their will over others. This becomes morality grounded in *ressentiment*, and creates values which reproduce this attitude:

> The slave revolt in humanity begins when *ressentiment* itself becomes creative and gives birth to values ... While every noble morality develops from a triumphant affirmation of itself, slave morality from the outset says No to what is 'outside', what is 'different', what is 'not itself'; and *this* No is its creative deed (p. 472).

This is characteristic of the ascetic for whom overcoming 'love and luxury of refinement ... was the dominating instinct whose demands prevailed against those of all the other instincts' (pp. 544–545). But Nietzsche describes the significance of the philosophical education of the ascetic. As slave he seeks to overcome his will. But this is precisely an inversion of will to power. When the ascetic realises this, it inspires a *ressentiment* and finally nihilism. It is nihilism because the ascetic knows, now, that he is *all* will to power. His final denial is equally ambivalent. In denying himself redemption he is never stronger or more wilful. His nihilism is that of the Last Man. What he denies now is not will to power itself but its truth as eternal return. This is the education that Zarathustra achieves over the ascetic, and it is why Nietzsche concludes that

> as the will to truth thus gains self-consciousness—there can be no doubt of that—morality will gradually perish now: this is the great spectacle in a hundred acts reserved for the next two centuries in Europe—the most terrible, most questionable, and perhaps also the most hopeful of all spectacles (p. 597).

This self-consciousness, for Deleuze, is the transmutation into 'a new way of thinking, feeling and above all being' (Deleuze, 1983, p. 71). For Nietzsche, this self-consciousness, which is 'the will to truth become ... conscious of itself as a problem' (Nietzsche, 1968, p. 597), has the potential to produce the 'man of the future' (p. 532). Such a man will 'redeem us not only from the hitherto reigning ideal but also from that which was bound to grow out of it, the great nausea, the will to nothingness, nihilism; this bell-stroke of noon and of great decision that liberates the will once again', (ibid.). I shall conclude this discussion of Nietzsche, however, by arguing now that Deleuze and Nietzsche do not have the same teacher in mind.

ZARATHUSTRA'S MISS MARPLE

For Deleuze, nihilism is defeated by itself. We saw above that, in knowing will to power as *ressentiment* to be only one of its forms, this knowing of will to power for Deleuze is thinking 'in a form distinct from that in which we know it' (Deleuze, 1983, p. 173). Herein lies the philosophy of education of Deleuze that we have explored above. Knowledge, he argued, is merely the result of thinking but learning is its movement; it is the between which grows out of the relation of segments or faculties. Learning, then, is becoming for Deleuze. With such a notion of learning he can assert that the '*ratio* in terms of which the will to power is known is not the *ratio* in terms of which it exists' (p. 175). This statement is pivotal not only for Deleuze's interpretation of Zarathustra but for his whole philosophical project. It rests on a distinction between knowledge as result and learning as difference, that is, of the difference between difference and result. Here the merely reactive power of *ressentiment* is transformed into an affirmative and creative power of the excess of knowledge. Becoming and excess are the same thinking—not the *ratio cognoscendi* of will to power but the *ratio essendi* of will to power. Thus, for Deleuze, 'destruction becomes active to the extent that the negative is transmuted and converted into affirmative power: the "eternal joy of becoming"' (p. 174).

> Nihilism reaches its completion by passing through the Last Man, but going beyond him to the man who wants to perish. In the man who wants to perish, to be overcome, negation has broken everything which still held it back, it has defeated itself, it has become of affirming, a power which is already superhuman, a power which announces and prepares the Overman (p. 175).

Whilst Hegel's negative says yes to all denials, Deleuze's Zarathustra knows to say no even to that (yes to) denial. Here is the transvaluation of value. What is at stake between Hegel and Deleuze, then, not least within the philosophy of education, is the educational significance of negation. Deleuze sees in Hegel a repetition of the same, of negation. As such, nothing happens. For Deleuze, however, 'the negative becomes a power of affirming: it is subordinated to affirmation and passes into the service of an excess of life' (p. 176). 'Only affirmation produces what the negative announces' (ibid.).

One thing is clear here. Deleuze and Hegel are both speculative thinkers trying to ascertain what is learned in the adventures of the negative. They meet, in a sense, at the point of the negation of the negation. Here Hegel argues for a determinate negation, and a negative that becomes positive in its own work and its relation to knowledge—the truth of the slave to the master. Deleuze argues for an education regarding a transformation of value where the 'power' and 'autonomy' (ibid.) of the negative are converted into affirmation. In these respective educations, Hegel realises the philosopher whilst Deleuze finds the Overman, where the scholar is replaced by the legislator (p. 173).

Which of these different notions of philosophical education is correct? Which of them provides a criterion by which any such judgement could be made? If we use Nietzschean terms to explore this, then the question becomes 'which of these speculative enquiries is true to will to power and its eternal return?' Deleuze claims for Nietzsche the discovery of 'the negativity of the positive' (p. 180), where negations here 'form part of the powers of affirming' and overcome Hegel's 'positivity of the negative' (ibid.). For Deleuze, eternal return is the return of that which differs. For Hegel, eternal return is *of* the negative but *as* the concept. Deleuze argues that eternal return as a physical doctrine of being is the 'new formulation of the speculative synthesis' (p. 68), where conformity to a law of identity is now overcome by the principle of selection in difference and repetition that constitutes will to power. In addition, 'as an ethical thought the eternal return is the new formulation of the practical synthesis: whatever you will, will it in such a way that you also will its eternal return' (ibid.). But what can be willed eternally? Only difference itself or, as we have seen it above, the no-saying to all negativity, all reaction. Only in thinking, in the 'thought of the eternal return' (p. 69), is willing also creativity. 'Only the eternal return makes the nihilistic will whole and complete' (ibid.). Zarathustra, for Deleuze, is such a completion, and it would be, we may suppose, the rhizomatic teacher-becoming.

I want to bring this discussion of Deleuze to an end by making three related criticisms of his Nietzscheanism: first, that Deleuze does not overcome *ressentiment*; second, that he resembles the Last Man, the ascetic; and third, that the rhizomatic teacher-becoming represents nihilism in the suppression of the meaning of modern political experience. Finally, out of these criticisms comes a different kind of Nietzschean teacher.

First, then, the speculative synthesis as Deleuze understands it is, I would argue, only another form of un-reformed *ressentiment*. If the slave revolt is the representation of will to power as morality, then the rhizome is the representation of will to power as affirmation. It is not a thought without image; on the contrary, a thought without image is a moral value masquerading as a transformed value. It is where will to power is asserted, again, against its own law that it must overcome itself. The middle is not a new value. It is an old value dressed in post-structural garb. The fact that the middle is eternally overcome, and that thought is eternally returned from the middle to its aporetic structure by its own law, is suppressed by Deleuze's concept of the middle. Indeed, epistemological *ressentiment* is as strong a force as moral *ressentiment*. Where the latter is reactive, the former, in contrast, identifies itself as act, as will. Yet its 'no' to nihilism is rhetorical; it is not actual. A 'no' to nihilism is not a transvaluation; it is the return of *ressentiment* this time against its representation of itself. The determinate negation in Hegel contains the truth of *ressentiment*, that it is total and cannot be overcome without repeating itself, and, therefore, is never overcome. But *ressentiment* is not only negative; it is true to itself in negation. The 'yes' to the negative is the truth of *ressentiment*, recognised but not overcome. Deleuze's 'no' to the negative is a *ressentiment* against the truth of *ressentiment*. The whole idea of *ressentiment* overcome must include the negation of itself *as ressentiment*.

We can begin to see the implications of Deleuze's *ressentiment* against *ressentiment* by comparing it to the *Trauerspiel*, which was explored earlier in Chapter 2. There, Benjamin argued that Baroque allegory re-presented a theological situation through a myth which masked this re-presentation. Post-Luther, the desertion of God from the acts of men realised an unhappy consciousness divided against itself by a loss of meaning both inwardly and outwardly. The former re-presented rejection from the world as rejection of the world (asceticism), whilst the latter re-presented rejection of the world as rejection from the world (political intrigue). We argued above that allegory became the re-presentation of culture as myth without enlightenment regarding the social and spiritual conditions of its own possibility. Baroque allegory did not see itself formed by its relation to the absolute, nor its being re-formed as a repetition of that relation.

Reason can do better than this. As culture it can realise just such repetitions and re-formations. The absolute here becomes the most important concept in the critique of the abstract domination of culture, for it knows its truth as its own work, but equally not as its resolution. The absolute is the only concept able to do this, to speak the truth as *ressentiment* without a denial that further terrorises its culture, its re-presentation or its education. But the kind of post-structuralism found in Deleuze returns again to the suppression of the culture of reason and is, therefore, also the suppression of our philosophical education regarding domination. Post-structuralism in the manner of Deleuze's imperceptible middles also re-presents the relation of state and religion without acknowledgement of such. In the desertion of the absolute from the formal person of civil society, post-structuralism asserts the myth of the ruin and collapse of subjectivity. This 'no' to the substance of subjectivity is the modern form of philosophical asceticism. Knowing that he is all desire, this ascetic refuses himself philosophical substance as subject. It is a denial in the tradition of the slave revolt, one made in *ressentiment*, as a moral value against the self being known in the tradition of the slave revolt. It is, at its most resentful, the nihilism of the ascetic made into the myth of the decline and ruin of the self. It refuses any relation to the relation of self and the world, because it refuses our education as the re-presentation of the relation (in all its difficulty); a refusal from which it then asserts the transformation, or education, from *ressentiment* to the joy of experiment and the imperceptible. The middle in Deleuze is just such a *ressentiment* against abstraction or against modern social and political relations—a freedom from duality by positing the ruin of subjectivity as without substance. But duality here is not overcome; it is merely denied. There is only the domination of abstract philosophical consciousness. There is no Overman—only the ascetic who, in denying himself, claims will to power as his own positivity and who, in doing so, repeats the culture of reason that is supposed to have been overcome. There is no Overman in Nietzsche who survives or overcomes this culture, or who transforms it. But there is a teacher in Nietzsche who can learn of *ressentiment* as the true, and can recognise therein the relation of philosophy and education in which the absolute is realised, or re-presented as representation. This teacher can affirm the eternal return of will to power precisely because he cannot affirm it. The culture of the eternal return of will to power, its formation and re-formation, is not overcoming. Nietzsche affirms the positive in the negative but not the negative in the positive. The former recognises values, the latter only repeats them. Here, in the former, the 'no' to 'no' is affirmed philosophically as education, but it is not overcome. Nietzsche's political recognition of the dominance of the culture of abstract reason is to be found here, in the paradox of overcoming not-overcoming, and in the philosophical education that knows itself as this circle.

There is a further implication here for Deleuze. It is because he posits difference as the identity of the middle that he can claim, as we saw, that the subject can unmake the face, can be liberated from the wall of identity by merging into it, and can become imperceptible. But imperceptibility is also an idea whose genealogy is *ressentiment* against abstraction, or against dominant social and political relations. This domination ensures that we are always in part exactly as we appear to be: formal, bourgeois persons defined in and by modern property relations. Our abstract philosophical consciousness is dominant and is that against which any notion of the imperceptible must be re-presented. Imperceptibility as thought without image is in actuality imperceptibility as thought without politics, without determination.

Suppressing the political, then, imperceptibility in Deleuze appears as independent of the dualism of abstraction and experience. His middles are *between* but not *of* the segments. There are immense dangers in eliding the political in this way. It opens the line to the intriguer who re-presents political difficulty in a myth of being without truth. It matters not whether myth is baroque or post-structural, for the dissemblance of abstraction without mediation, and of ethics without metaphysics, is the path again to terror and tyranny where 'anything can be made to stand for anything else . . . because nothing is absolute' (Jarvis, 1998, p. 10).

As such, there can be no sustainable concept of the teacher in Deleuze's philosophy because there is no one for whom the experience of difference is allowed to speak for itself and re-present this broken middle as philosophical education. Learning in Deleuze, in being claimed as learning, is not left open to its relation to being known, nor, therefore, to the social relations which determine it. It is in the relation of being known that learning can participate in its own act. How can the teacher participate in her own act of learning if she is granted immunity from the very relation—difference—that generates the learning? She has to be different even from learning in order to participate in the circle of possibility and necessity that Deleuze might call—but does not—becoming-learning. And in order to be different from learning she has to be the subject whose natural consciousness has learning as an object.

What, then, are the implications for the teacher of this critique of the construction of the imperceptible in Deleuze? As we saw above, towards the end of *Dialogues*, Deleuze likens the imperceptible to the knight of faith in Kierkegaard. They share, he says, an interest in movement that 'is always in the middle—in the middle of two other lines' (Deleuze and Parnet, 2002, p. 127). Movement unmakes the face; movement is the process of becoming; it is multiplicities; it is, in essence, the idea by which Deleuze distinguishes his thought from territorialisation, identity and negativity. And yet, the choice here of the knight of faith by Deleuze to re-present movement stands opposed to itself in a way that compromises, and must compromise, such movement.

We will explore the knights of faith and infinite resignation in the next chapter. Here we can say that Deleuze is wrong to see his idea of the imperceptible in the Kierkegaardian knight of faith. In Nietzschean terms, the knights, between them, obey the law of nature of commanding and obeying. They know will to power in resignation, and they know eternal return in faith. They know the truth of the relation in the same way as Zarathustra does, as the experience of the broken middle of philosophy and education. The knight of faith is absolutely not the same rhizomatic movement as Deleuze's grass between the paving stones. Quite the contrary: as with trees, the knights also have roots that speak of the true relation of their philosophical education. Weil says: 'it is the light falling continually from heaven which alone gives a tree the energy to send powerful roots deep into the earth. The tree is really rooted in the sky' (Miles, 1986, p. 86). And Rose repeats this quotation, both in her discussion of Weil (Rose, 1993, p. 218) and in her posthumous work *Paradiso*. She writes

> What courage is summoned by this icon of the visible and the invisible. To be a tree. To be suspended in the empyrean, with no security, no identity, no community. Yet only this willingness to be suspended in the sky, to be without support, enables us to draw on the divine source and sustenance which makes it possible to put down roots. It is not the prior fixity of established roots that qualify us to drink greedily out of the sky. The sky is universal—it is the silky canopy that moves with us wherever we go. And we feel lost, we are in the abyss; and the sky has become dark and occluded, we need to pull up those roots for the channel of grace is run dry. We need to venture again the courage of suspense, not knowing who we are, in order to rediscover our infinite capacity for self-creation and response to our fellow self-creators. Orthodoxy embraces exile (Rose, 1999, p. 63).

The movement that Deleuze claims as moving in such a way that it can paint 'grey on grey (Deleuze, 2002, p. 127), or, like the Pink Panther, paint the world 'in his own colour' (ibid.), is not the movement of education—neither political education regarding the forms of law that pre-determine the form and content of movement, nor its philosophical re-presentation. Deleuze's Pink Panther is the movement of Zarathustra at the end of Book 3, dancing the ring of rings, but it is not the story of Zarathustra as a whole, or of Nietzsche's own development. In its post-structuralist form this movement is a dialectic of nihilism—dialectic because its disavowal of relation is relation, and nihilistic because both relations are disavowed. As such, post-structuralism is a response to and a representation of the modern aporia of law and reason, but it is one in which these conditions of its own possibility are repeatedly denied. Even this repetition is repeatedly denied as re-presentation. At worst, the rhizomatic teacher-becoming is the dissembler whose roots are not in education. He is the relation of thought and being that takes upon himself immunity from prosecution in the court of modern abstract reason. Those who lack roots have neither depth nor dependency; they are between the relation of teacher and student but not of the relation. They have no notion of education grounded in the real educational relations that they re-present. They mistake the aporia of subjectivity for the decline of subjectivity *per se*. They are, again, the aestheticisation of the political, which, as we saw in Chapter 2, can be the godless spirituality in which evil thrives, and this time with the increased potency that imperceptibility brings with it.

There is, however, a different model of imperceptibility and the knights of faith and resignation that can be offered to teachers here. The example, from Rose, is Agatha Christie's Miss Jane Marple. The sleuth is much more the knight of faith that Kierkegaard intends. In Miss Marple we can recognise the recollection of the woman with the mind like a bacon slicer; she knows that she does not know; and we can recognise the repetition of this ignorance in her ordinary appearance as 'a proper, fussy, inquisitive old lady' (Rose, 1993, p. 222).[12] Her success 'in establishing justice invariably depends on her being able to pass unnoticed whilst noticing everything herself' (ibid.). The infinite, known as not known, *is* known here as 'the paradox of existence' (Kierkegaard, 1983, p. 47). Miss Marple carries truth within the duality that masks it. Her ambivalence commends 'something transcendent' (Rose, 1999, p. 18) for in her 'identity' truth sees everything whilst itself being unseen. Such work, says Rose, moves 'beyond the preoccupation with endless loss [the post-structural dissembler] to the silence of grace' (p. 17). This relation of resignation, faith and the transcendent means that Miss Marple 'remains the most observant intelligence and the most spiritually free in all manner of woeful situations' (Rose, 1993, p. 222). The third partner is always present in the abstraction, and its recollection and repetition, that Miss Marple is and knows herself to be.

This presents quite a contrast for the teacher here: the Deleuzian rhizomatic teacher and the Marplesque and Zarathustrian teacher. The latter commends being master and servant, teacher and student so that the truth of education can exist without new forms of suppression or violence. The former is just such suppression masked by the deceit of relation masquerading as non-relation. In modern social relations, where abstraction is dominant, the teacher must be partly exactly as she appears to be—a teacher in all its ordinariness—in order to teach, unnoticed, for education. As justice in its aporetic form encompasses the truth of Miss Marple's broken middle, so, education in its aporetic form can encompass the truth of the teacher. Both require faith, but faith to be knowing and unknowing, powerful and powerless, natural and philosophical consciousness, and commander and obeyer. This is the truth of Zarathustra, as of Nietzsche, and it is the truth of the relation of philosophy and education as it is re-presented in Nietzsche's work. Like Zarathustra one must learn to teach and become a teacher in order, then, to teach to learn. There is a grace in the teacher whose faith is in the whole of education, a whole of which she is its eternal return and its will to power.

NOTES

1. I am keeping to Deleuze's use of upper case for the term 'AND'.
2. We return to the knight of faith at the end of this chapter and again in the concluding chapter.
3. In *Difference and Repetition* Deleuze defines 'differentiation' as 'the determination of the virtual content into an idea' (p. 207), and 'differenciation' as the 'actualisation of that virtuality into species and distinguished parts' (ibid.). I have not in this chapter explored the relation between the virtual and the actual in Deleuze, nor, therefore, the two sides of his transcendental empiricism. My remarks below about the coexistence of multiplicity AND segment give an example of the kind of critique that would be offered if I had done so.
4. I have attempted this in greater detail in Tubbs, 2004, Chapter 5.
5. This is also to read Lyotard's later work against that of his middle period, specifically *Libidinal Economy*.
6. Lyotard is due a certain sympathy here. The moment he acknowledges the third partner in philosophical work, the absolute, or philosophy itself, he is dumped by those who have courted him.
7. Precisely the philosophical perspective—nihilism and holiness—of Zarathustra in Book VI of *Thus Spake Zarathustra*. This is explained in the following sections of the current chapter.
8. I defend such a reading of Kant in Tubbs, 2004, Chapter 1.
9. Or, as stated elsewhere within the philosophy of education, 'you should work within the system, but work carefully at its weak spots' (Blake *et al.*, 2000, p. 117).
10. I defend this view of 'and' in the final chapter of Tubbs, 2004. There I argue that 'and' is the presence of social and political relations within relation itself, which requires, therefore, to be recognised as both domination 'and' philosophy's higher education.
11. The image conjured up here is of an uroboros—the snake or dragon that swallows its own tail as an emblem of infinity or wholeness. In *The Birth of Tragedy* Nietzsche notes that 'logic coils up ... and finally bites its own tail' (Nietzsche, 1968, p. 98).
12. Recollection and repetition are used here as Kierkegaardian terms. Their educational import is explained more fully in the final chapter below.

Chapter 8
Kierkegaard

INTRODUCTION

In a footnote to Chapter II, Book II of the *Concluding Unscientific Postscript*, Kierkegaard, or Johannes Climacus as he signs himself for this volume, makes a dialectical remark that represents Kierkegaard's direct and indirect relationship to Hegel and his direct and indirect means of communicating the truth of that relationship.

> The frivolity with which systematists concede that Hegel has perhaps not been successful in introducing movement everywhere in logic, about as when a huckster thinks that a couple of oranges more or less is nothing to worry about when the purchase is a large one—this farcical complaisance is naturally an expression of contempt for Hegel, which not even his most violent antagonist has permitted himself (Kierkegaard, 1968, p. 99f).

But Kierkegaard concludes this footnote with the following insightful remark: 'Let admirers of Hegel keep to themselves the privilege of making him out to be a bungler; an opponent will always know how to hold him in honour, as one who has willed something great, though without having achieved it' (p. 100f). Read carefully, Kierkegaard is assigning to Hegel's supporters the usual critique of Hegel as having a system that is closed and finished, even though there may be one or two loose ends that still need to be tied up in order to finish it off. Behind Kierkegaard's wit here lies the insight that it is the claims of these supporters for the system that are in fact the real misunderstandings of the system. Kierkegaard is unforgiving and relentless in his critique of these 'Hegelians'. To those who argue for the system as complete, even despite a few minor alterations that might be necessary, Kierkegaard asks when *will* it be finished? Perhaps 'by next Sunday' (p. 97). And he adds: 'I shall be as willing as the next man to fall down in worship before the System, if only I can manage to set eyes on it' (pp. 97–98). He continues:

> once or twice I have been on the verge of bending the knee. But at the last moment, when I already had my handkerchief spread on the ground, to avoid soiling my trousers, and I made a trusting appeal to one of the initiated who stood by: 'Tell me now sincerely, is it entirely finished; for

if so I will kneel down before it, even at the risk of ruining a pair of trousers . . .'—I always received the same answer: 'No, it is not yet quite finished.' And so there was another postponement—of the System and of my homage (p. 98).

Why, then, asks Kierkegaard, call it a system at all? If it is not finished, why is it offered as such? 'A fragment of a system is nonsense' (ibid.).[1]

The relation of Kierkegaard to Hegel is not, I think, an attempt by the former to rescue the truth from the system, but rather a way of re-presenting the asymmetry of the relation—within the system and in relation to it—as the true. One example of the complexity of this difficult relation that Kierkegaard must keep open to Hegel is in his own direct and indirect communication about him within the *Postscript*. At first sight Kierkegaard seems to provide ample evidence of his opposition to Hegel and to Hegelianism. The *Postscript* is littered with biting and withering criticisms of the Hegelian system. In addition, the issue of direct and indirect communication is central to understanding not only Kierkegaard's critique of Hegelians, but also his style of writing. In the *Postscript* he attacks Hegel(ians) for their direct communication of the system. In a long footnote Kierkegaard writes that Hegel is supposed 'to have died with the words upon his lips, that there was only one man who had understood him, and he had misunderstood him' (1968, p. 65f). Why, then, asks Kierkegaard, did Hegel write in such a direct fashion? If he had sought to be understood, why did he write 'the entire series of seventeen volumes [as] direct communication?' (p. 66f). In this way, Hegel had 'absolutely nothing in common with Socrates' (ibid.).

This footnote requires careful reading. Kierkegaard is communicating directly that Hegel communicated directly. Yet for Kierkegaard this direct communication is equally inappropriate as the form for his critique of Hegel. The danger here is that Kierkegaard will be understood and, therein, not understood at all. Kierkegaard employs direct communication to *induce* misunderstanding. He notes, for example, in the *Postscript*, that approval of his work will corrupt its 'dialectical precision' (Kierkegaard, 1968, p. 14). It is better, therefore that the work remain imperceptible. 'Better well hanged than ill wed' he states, as the motto to the *Fragments*. Indeed, for the truths of double reflection that Kierkegaard is working with, direct communication is the most indirect form of communication possible. Thus he honours Hegel, for the latter's direct communication, as we saw above regarding the philosophical structure of the speculative proposition, is equally indirect. For both Hegel and Kierkegaard the movement of thought is the truth of thought, and Kierkegaard plays this brilliantly with bluff and counter-bluff through the *Postscript*, as throughout all his texts. His pseudonyms are the clearest example of the way that the direct and the indirect are related and separated in his communications.[2]

In addition, Kierkegaard further teases Hegelians over the issue of 'beginning', a question also raised at the beginning of Hegel's *Science of Logic* that asks 'With What Must Science Begin?' If, as Hegelians claim, the system begins with the immediate, then surely, says Kierkegaard, such a conclusion can only be reached through reflection? This perfectly represents what Hegel is arguing *in* the system, *for* the system, and *as* the system. Any beginning, 'precisely because it is the beginning, is imperfect' (Hegel, 1984b, p. 293). Since 'thinking is always the negation of what we have immediately before us' (Hegel, 1975, p. 17), then it is impossible to begin with the beginning. Furthermore, the 'Hegelians' might offer a systematic answer that a beginning is made with nothing. But this would not be true for Hegel.[3] On the contrary, and as we have seen above many times now, a beginning is always made with the abstract, which is also immediately mediated. If there is a beginning, it is in the broken middle of the beginning where immediacy and mediation are in the relation of their relation and separation.

This question of beginning is one of the ways in which Hegel and Kierkegaard share a philosophy of the teacher. It is in the misrecognition of the beginning that, as we saw earlier, critical, post-Enlightenment and spiritual pedagogies suppress philosophical education by refusing thought's relation to itself as subject and substance. In their judgements that education can overcome its illusions, be this for emancipation, pluralism or forms of intersubjectivity or spirit, a mistake is made regarding the beginning. Self-consciousness is always reflective *and* abstract. 'There is nothing', says Hegel, 'nothing in heaven or in nature or mind or anywhere else which does not equally contain both immediacy and mediation' (Hegel, 1969, p. 68), and this is known philosophically and aporetically as the third partner in the relation. If the abstract is overcome, then middles are posited that suppress the difficulty, the inequality, of the beginning. Readers of Kierkegaard need to take account of the considerable efforts that the latter goes to in order to reveal why indirect communication must always oppose itself. It is Kierkegaard who knows the significance of being Hegel's opponent rather than his supporter. It is by ensuring the abstract in Hegel, as the abstract teacher of the system, that the system is the truth of the teacher. Kierkegaard honours the abstract in Hegel in a way that 'Hegelians' often do not. Throughout the *Postscript* when Kierkegaard says that Hegel has failed to achieve the movement of the existing subjectivity of the system, it is precisely this recognition of failure that recognises the movement in the system.

THE ETHICAL AND THE ABSOLUTE

It is as commonplace to oppose Hegel and Kierkegaard as it is to oppose Hegel and Nietzsche. In a recent article in the *Journal of Philosophy of Education*, however, Ian McPherson has argued for a greater level of complexity within their commonly stereotyped relation. Against abstract readings of Kierkegaard as ascetic, individualist, existentialist and even as analyst/therapist, McPherson argues for a reading of Kierkegaard that is based within his ambivalent relationship to Hegel. On the one hand, McPherson claims that communication in Kierkegaard is influenced by

Hegel's ethic of recognition, which, he says, has been 'brilliantly retrieved' (McPherson, 2001, p. 158) by Robert R. Williams (1997), whose account lends itself to an interpretation of Kierkegaard based on communication as 'interpretive exchange' (McPherson, 2001, p. 159).[4] On the other hand, McPherson argues that Kierkegaard saw in Hegel 'an impatient grasping for an intellectual totality' (p. 158), which results in the latter losing 'himself and his followers in his system [and] that his system substitutes itself for human life and Christian life' (p. 162). As such, Kierkegaard's campaign against Hegel is 'a prophetic "no" to intellectual and educational idolatry' (p. 163).[5]

McPherson argues that communication in Kierkegaard is an interpretive exchange between different ways of being and different capacities. If direct communication is more product than process then indirect communication is more process than product. The former lends itself to closure and to the 'what' of communication; the latter to development, to the 'communication of a capacity or capacities' (p. 164) and to the 'how' or means of communication. There are significant educational implications here for McPherson. First, both the 'how' and the 'what' of communication can mean self-involvement or inwardness. They can both contribute to the truth of subjectivity. Second, indirect communication has a particular relevance for teachers because the communication of the 'how' aims to help others 'to develop for themselves the capacities they need' (p. 167). Thus indirect communication lends itself to the asymmetry of the teacher–student relation where the relevant abilities 'are less equally shared' (p. 166). It is in the nature of indirect communication to respect the privacy of the other, to inspire in him concern and unrest, but leaving him with the impulse to go his own way.[6] In addition, McPherson pursues this difference and asymmetry in the relation between the finite and the infinite. For example, the indirect communication of Kierkegaard's pseudonyms can be both a non-interfering device to leave the reader to go his own way, or a recognition of the unequal relation between human and divine communication. This inequality, says McPherson, is the absurd paradox in Kierkegaard between God and man, and requires 'indirect communication, via interpretive exchange' (p. 169), in order to ensure that the relation is kept open. Beginning to take responsibility in this way is, he says, the leap from the aesthetic to the ethical and finally to the religious. It is not just the 'what' of God that is communicated in religion, but more importantly the 'how' of that communication. As the 'what' can be reduced to idolatry, so the 'how' keeps open the asymmetry of the relation between God and man. For McPherson, 'religiousness A' in Kierkegaard is the paradox of this asymmetry whilst 'religiousness B' is the transformation of the asymmetrical relation into the truth of God. Thus, 'the relatively modest paradox of type A is trumped by the absolute paradox of type B' (p. 172).

There is much of interest here to the philosophy of the teacher. McPherson's retrieval of Kierkegaard's difficult relation to Hegel opens up Kierkegaard's work to the wider speculative tradition of which it is a seminal contribution, and contradicts many of the more common ideas on Kierkegaard that misread this. Of greater significance is the observation of the asymmetry in the relation of teacher to student and of God to man. In his notion of indirect communication, at least as it is related by him to the teacher and his pupil, McPherson acknowledges this imbalance as the substance of the relation.

The speculative import of this latter relation is, however, threatened by McPherson's reading of Hegel and in particular by the concept of the 'ethics of recognition' (p. 158) that he takes from Williams. There is not space here to engage fully with Williams' thesis. Of immediate concern, however, is his claim that 'recognition is a general concept of intersubjectivity' (Williams, 1997, p. 10). Williams argues that the master–slave relation is merely a 'first phase of unequal recognition that *must* and *can* be transcended ... Genuine recognition is fundamentally reciprocal and involves the mutual mediation of freedom' (ibid.). It is a gross error, he continues, to equate 'recognition with the struggle between master and slave' (ibid.).[7]

Such a notion of mutual recognition as ethical relation, however, sits unhappily with McPherson's argument. I shall make three brief points in relation to this. First, the notion of interpretive exchange that McPherson posits wherein 'each self recognises itself in the other, and the other in the self' (2001, p. 172) suppresses the very inequality that indirect communication expresses. Second, the master–slave relation is the template of recognition in that it plays out the continuing recognition of misrecognition; as spirit it is a recognition that can only repeat the asymmetry of this relation. Third, the idea of reciprocity or mutuality in recognition, because it is *not* the current form and content of spirit, becomes for Williams, as for McPherson, a *sollen* (an ought). It repeats the domination of social relations because this domination is excluded from its representation in spirit. Overall, the notion of interpretive exchange conflates paradox or the absurd into intersubjectivity. This is to fail to read Kierkegaard speculatively at his most difficult point, namely, the relation between the ethical and the absolute. Ironically, then, it is actually McPherson's misreading of Hegel that then sees the reduction of the absolute in Kierkegaard to the ethical.[8]

There are implications here for Kierkegaard's philosophy of the teacher, and we will explore this in more detail in a moment. In brief, however, if McPherson's notion of indirect communication is ultimately a unity of the 'how' and the 'what' in the mutual dependence in communication of each with the other, then it cannot be appropriate for the communication of teacher and student, for it would have to assert the mutual over the different shapes of struggle that McPherson acknowledges within the inequality between teacher and student. Similarly, if indirect communication *is* appropriate to the teacher and student relation, then it cannot also be posited as mutual exchange between persons. The unity of the 'how' and the 'what' that McPherson finds in religiousness B, in its transcendence of religiousness A—the sublime in the pedestrian—does acknowledge difficulty as philosophical content. But it does not then represent its inequality to itself as subject and substance. This leaves McPherson's interpretation of Kierkegaard, of Hegel, of spirit, and of the absolute without the asymmetry of the relation that they re-present. Mutuality becomes a middle that is posited over and against the broken middle, a relation that is the condition of its (mutuality's) own (negative) possibility.

In a way, this is to read McPherson against himself. He follows Kierkegaard's systematic and abstract account of the relation of inwardness to itself in the *Concluding Unscientific Postscript*. Here, the relation of the person to the ethical is the experience of inequality that, as the third partner, is religion. Further, the relation between religiousness A (inequality) and religiousness B (the inequality of religion itself) is again a triadic relation. Precisely where McPherson needs to refuse this relation of religion to itself—to refuse it a middle—he turns indirect communication into the balanced relation of mutual dependence and exchange. The absolute in Kierkegaard, as in Hegel, is inequality known to itself as torn halves of a relation that does not add up to itself. It is the absolute known in the torn halves of relations of process and product, direct and indirect communication, immediacy and mediation, and, in Kierkegaard in particular, here, as religiousness A and B. The third partner is the re-presentation of this asymmetry; and is why the master–slave relation carries all such relations within it. Intersubjectivity, mutual recognition and interpretive exchange are, therefore, only so many suppressions of the absolute that they fail to re-present absolutely. This is why religiousness B in McPherson's reading becomes the transcendence of religiousness A. He is able to say that 'this divine self-communication is . . . absolutely beyond all of us, and beyond each part of each of us' (McPherson, 2001, p. 172) only because he has posited the self-communication of the divine as unable to be expressed in the finite. Yet de Silentio *speaks* in *Fear and Trembling*; Climacus climbs the heights that his philosophical texts decry, and Kierkegaard, who can do nothing, nevertheless works for his soul in his *Upbuilding Discourses*.[9] As we have seen throughout our study of the philosophy of the teacher, failing to know the absolute in the finite, as it is shaped in and by social and political relations, is a failure to recognise those relations as they are present in our thinking and our not thinking the absolute. It is not inequality, power and paradox that are overcome by mutuality and interpretive exchange; on the contrary, it is the illusions of the latter that re-present the former as our knowing of the absolute. In short, intersubjectivity robs Kierkegaard of the inequality of the absolute, and thus ensures that his work, as he would say, does not move beyond the Socratic. So, in order to retrieve the insights that McPherson draws out for the teacher–student relation in indirect communication, we must look instead to the *Philosophical Fragments* where the truth of that inequality is explored. I shall return to this in a moment.

SUBJECTIVITY'S SUBJECTIVITY

I shall begin this exploration of Kierkegaard's philosophy of the teacher where Part II above 'ended', namely with the issue of Socrates' midwifery. In 1841, Kierkegaard wrote his PhD thesis on Socrates and criticised several aspects of the latter's negative pedagogy.[10] First, he noted that Socrates could only truly be a servant of the student's own philosophical development through irony. Socrates says he knows nothing; he says he has nothing to teach; he says he is not a teacher. At best teaching that one has nothing to teach is housed within the opposition of direct and indirect communication; the truth of which can only be ironic for Socrates.

Second, and perhaps more importantly, Kierkegaard argues that by remaining with the ironic, Socrates and his students are never able to learn the full implications of this opposition in terms of educational development. There is, as it were, a higher education that they make possible but never attain. This is because, says Kierkegaard, Socrates is content to ask questions without any interest in the answer. As far as Socrates is concerned, all answers are equivalent, for what he is actually trying to do is to show the inadequacy of all answers and to introduce the students to doubt through their own thinking. Socrates aims only 'to suck out the apparent content by means of the question and thereby to leave an emptiness behind' (Kierkegaard, 1989, p. 36) Or, even more graphically, Kierkegaard says, 'he [Socrates] placed individuals under his dialectical vacuum pump, pumped away the atmospheric air they were accustomed to breathing, and left them standing there. For them, everything was now lost ...' (p. 178).

As the teacher who fills his students with content is the master, so the teacher who drains them of content is also the master. Indeed, Kierkegaard goes further, calling Socrates a seducer because he excited a passion to learn that he did not fulfil, abandoning the beloved as soon as the passion was aroused. He thus engendered passion without satisfaction, questioning without answers and negativity without the positive. This might sound acceptable in the sense that this teacher is serving the student's development by refusing to inculcate pre-given answers into them. But perhaps it is even worse than the positive and dominating master in the enlightenment model, for this teacher pulls the rug out from under the feet of the students and leaves them with nothing—indeed, it leaves them looking down and staring into an abyss that threatens nihilism.

Kierkegaard also notes, however, that this was about as far as Socrates could go. A different philosophy of the teacher was required after Socrates in order to understand how this negative master could also be enough of a master to provide the student with something positive, something substantial, which could be the source of further growth and development. It is as the philosopher Johannes Climacus that Kierkegaard reasons as to how this substance is to be realised. Climacus is the pseudonym of Kierkegaard's philosophical doubt and is in many ways the closest of Kierkegaard's incarnations to Hegel. As Climacus, Kierkegaard describes himself as in love with thinking (1985, p. 118). As a boy, he had enjoyed listening to his father engage in argument over dinner where he displayed the ability to turn the case of his opponent against him (as Socrates had done). His father embodied a Socratic spirit, listening to the arguments of his guests before 'in an instant, everything was turned upside down; the explicable was made inexplicable, the certain doubtful, the opposite was made obvious' (p. 122).

In his private moments Kierkegaard admits to the joy of trying to think something through, finding faults in his own arguments, seeing the whole thing collapse and then beginning again. Like his namesake John Climacus and his ladder of divine ascent (see Climacus, 1982), his joy is to climb, step by step, to higher thoughts. Even more joyful was to make the same movement, up and down, down and up, to try to ensure that the movement and the result were perfect to each other and complete. 'His soul was anxious lest one single coherent thought slip out, for then the whole thing would collapse' (p. 119), but he learned early on that joy *and* anxiety coexist in thinking.

Whilst for Kierkegaard—still telling this story through the identity of Johannes Climacus—his 'whole life was thinking' (p. 123), nevertheless even as a university student it had not occurred to him to be a philosopher. Whilst the latter sought answers, the former was in love only with the process. Indeed, as his reading proceeded, he began to learn that the results that philosophers offered were often characterised by dissemblance. Titles did not fulfil their promise and lacked the 'rigorous dialectical movement' (p. 130) that he loved. In addition, he noticed how alert he was at the beginning of lectures, but 'how dejected at the end, since he perceived that not a single word had been said ... although it gave the appearance of saying something' (p. 165). Everything must be doubted, and everything must begin with doubt, but in fact Kierkegaard observed how they employed doubt only selectively. He was forced to think through for himself the totality of doubt and its contradictions. In an insight that is central to understanding Kierkegaardian thinking and education, he notes that if one begins to doubt, then it must be because somehow doubt has already existed.

> He thought through the thesis again and again, tried to forget what he had thought in order to begin again, but, lo and behold, he always arrived at the same point. Yet he could not abandon the thesis; it seemed as if a mysterious power held him to it, as if something were whispering to him: something is hiding behind this misunderstanding (p. 139).

How, he asks himself, does the question of truth arise? He concludes that it must be by way of untruth, because the moment he asks about truth, he has already admitted the presence of truth as a lack, as not-known, or in its untruth. In the question of truth, consciousness is brought into relation with something else, and what makes this relation possible is untruth (p. 167). Within the speculative logic of this dialectic he reasons that immediacy is always cancelled by mediation and that as such, mediation can only presuppose immediacy. So, he asks, what is immediacy? Immediacy is 'reality' (ibid.), whilst mediacy is the expression of reality. In their relation there is always a contradiction, for what is expressed is never its expression. 'The moment I make a statement about reality, contradiction is present, for what I say is ideality' (p. 168). He extends this logic of doubt and untruth to consciousness and its 'beginning'. In the contradiction of ideality and reality is the coming into existence of consciousness. He says, 'reflection is the possibility of the relation; consciousness is the relation, the first form of which is contradiction' (p. 169). But if consciousness is itself *of* this relation then a further relation exists between consciousness and itself, the relation of knowing that relation. As for Hegel, so for Kierkegaard, whilst categories of reflection are always 'dichotomous' because they make possible the relation or the dualism, the categories of consciousness are 'trichotomous'.[11] This is because only in the latter is doubt possible as the relation to, or of, the relation: 'Consciousness is mind, and it is remarkable that when one is divided in the world of mind, there are three, never two ... If there were nothing but dichotomies, doubt would not exist, for the possibility of doubt resides precisely in the third, which places the two in relation to each other' (ibid.).

This is significant in the whole of Kierkegaard's works. It is where spirit in Kierkegaard separates itself from spirit as it appeared in Chapter 5 above with Buber, Weil and Heidegger. Spirit in Kierkegaard is the relation of the relation, or the relation become philosophical content. This realises a substance that of necessity eluded Socrates. When Socrates taught for the negative experience of our knowing nothing, nothing positive was learned. But now, because the mind can relate itself to itself as both the work and the actuality, a great deal can be learned that is of enormous significance. The difference from Socrates is this. Whereas Socrates brought doubt and knowledge together and left only doubt, Kierkegaard reasons that the work is our *own* thinking, and that the work is how we come to know ourselves. We have learned something about ourselves that Socrates did not, something that Kierkegaard calls 'subjectivity's subjectivity' (Kierkegaard, 1989, p. 242). Where philosophical content becomes both the subject and the substance of thought, as here, then our education, our learning from experience, participates in its own act and we come to know the opposition of subject and substance in new ways. We are, as it were, servant to ourselves as master.

What, then, are the implications of subjectivity's subjectivity for the teacher? I want to answer this question in two related ways: first, briefly, around the relation of the teacher to the eternal through recollection and repetition, and in the light of its importance for the pedagogy of direct and indirect communication; and second, by relating this philosophy of the teacher to Kierkegaard's *Upbuilding Discourses* and to the philosophical character that this upbuilding education, this formation and re-formation, demands.

RECOLLECTION AND REPETITION

Subjectivity's subjectivity complicates the teacher–student relationship for many reasons, but for two in particular. First, if the thinker can now become his own master and student, what part can a teacher play in what appears to be an internal process? We have addressed this question throughout the book for at its centre stands the dilemma for the teacher of the relation of freedom and authority in education. Second, might it be the case that the teacher has to become his own student before he should even consider teaching others to question? If you have not understood the full significance of being a question for yourself, what right do you have to make others do it?[12]

We will consider both questions. What contribution can a teacher make if learning through questioning must occur *in the mind of the student*? Any input from the teacher will distract from, even perhaps resolve, the difficulty that is the work. The teacher who understands this paradox of questioning and doubt now recognises his own contradiction in trying to be the teacher who encourages questioning and doubt. We know from Socrates that it can be a most dangerous, even terrifying enterprise to engage in, as it can leave the student distraught and despairing, and seemingly with nothing. Yet it is also the case that without the teacher there is no certainty that the student will come to have doubt as the object of her thinking. This is not to say that the student will not doubt; she does this all the time. It is to say, however, that she may not come to understand the ways in which doubt becomes content as philosophical experience, nor, therefore, its formative educational significance and the part it plays in her own self-identity and its continual negation. Here the task for the teacher is not only to hear these questions and doubts but also to recognise their substantial formative import. We have seen how, for example, Buber and Weil sought to influence and attend to this import. But unlike Hegel, Nietzsche and now Kierkegaard, they did not recognise the speculative form and content of doubt and could not, therefore, fully develop a philosophy of the teacher.

Here then we approach Kierkegaard's philosophy of the teacher. As we will see now, the teacher knows that the truth of a student's own development through thinking is not the teacher's to give. When the student understands doubt, it is because the doubts are his own, the work is his own and what he realises about himself is that he is at the same time both master and servant of this work. Kierkegaard is able to give this learning, this education, philosophical form and content, and to comprehend this we must employ two further Kierkegaardian terms, repetition and recollection.

For Kierkegaard, the truth of education through questioning cannot be introduced into a student. It must already be there, implicitly and potentially, waiting to be recognised by the student. This is why Socrates is a midwife. He only delivers what is the conception of the student herself. Kierkegaard's philosophy of the teacher demands that the teacher also understands that although the moment of delivery is here and now, its very nature is something eternal, something that exists before and after the moment of each delivery. A teacher, therefore, cannot teach the truth of the moment, for that would be to become the master of the eternal. But she can teach the untruth of the moment, i.e. that untruth has always been the condition of the student. Untruth is realised by the learner when what he *recollects* from his (new state of) knowing is that he now knows that 'previously' he did not know. Indeed, it was 'his own fault' (Kierkegaard, 1985, p. 15) that he did not know. In this new state of knowing that he was in untruth, he is nevertheless still in untruth, for now all he knows is that he did not know, and by knowing that he did not know, he is removed from or 'excluded from the truth, even more than when he was ignorant of being untruth' (p. 14). The moment, the teacher, is the truth of that untruth. It can be brought about by the teacher but precisely at the moment when the teacher becomes redundant. She has been the keeper of the truth of the student's doubt, but now that the gift has been received by the student from himself, the keeper's job is done. Kierkegaard is clear. The teacher can 'save' the student from himself, 'deliver' him from his own self-captivity and 'reconcile' the student to knowing himself through the contradiction of his own doubting, his own thinking and his own work. The student becomes 'a new person' (p. 18). The teacher has been 'the occasion for the pupil to understand himself' (p. 24).

What exactly does it mean for the teacher to be the moment or the occasion of truth and untruth? Her part in this recollection is in effect determined in and by *repetition*. Climacus understands consciousness to be reality and ideality, and understands consciousness of this relation to be the third partner or subjectivity's subjectivity. In this respect, the third partner is already presupposed in any experience; experience is, therefore, always a repetition of what it has not yet realised but what must be presupposed if there is to be any experience at all. Without repetition, without the third partner, there is, as Kierkegaard keeps repeating throughout his analysis of the teacher in *Philosophical Fragments*, only the (empty repetition of the) Socratic. Repetition is not merely reflective, for the latter is only a duality. Repetition is speculative because it repeats precisely the impossibility of a beginning that can be known only as unknown. Recollection is of repetition, and repetition is of recollection. The teacher is implicated in this relation as its actuality. She has not provided the condition for learning, that is, she has not been able to begin with doubt. Nor has she been able to be the whole circle of learning, the whole of recollection and repetition. The vocation of the teacher here is to be the love that gives recollection and repetition its actual moment, its subjectivity and its inequality with itself.

Since the eternal alone is the beginning and the end that are presupposed but known as untruth, and since the eternal has love within and not without, then this actuality of learning is love being made known. Love is what moves the eternal 'to make his appearance' (p. 24) says Kierkegaard, for only love can find equality or unity in what is unequal. In this philosophy of education, and its import for the philosophy of the teacher, it is love that is eternity fulfilled in time as the moment, and love that is the moment 'swallowed by recollection into its eternity' (p. 25).[13] Kierkegaard says of the teacher as this moment, or this occasion, that 'the moment emerges precisely in the relation of the eternal resolution to the unequal occasion. If this is not the case then we return to the Socratic and do not have the god or the eternal resolution or the moment' (ibid.). Or, let us say, the teacher emerges precisely in the relation of the eternal to the finite. If this were not the case, then learning and teaching would have no substance and subjectivity of their own; there could be no philosophy of the teacher for there could be no occasion of inequality.

In *Philosophical Fragments* Kierkegaard argues that recollection is the ancient form of repetition, lacking, as it were, subjectivity's subjectivity. Viewed merely Socratically, recollection does not have the significance of an historical point of departure, a third partner between knowing and object. Thus Socrates is a midwife but not a teacher. But recollection as the eternal relation of the duplexity of consciousness, or as repetition, becomes a moment 'in time [that] must have [a] decisive significance' (p. 13) for it is when the previously unknown and nonexistent eternal 'came into existence' (ibid.). The decisive significance of this historical point of departure, where recollection is repetition, or is subjectivity's subjectivity, is also the philosophy of the teacher in Kierkegaard: the moment of decisive educational significance, but not the significance itself. The lover and the beloved, God and his children, are known to each other in the inequality of time and the moment. This 'unhappiness is the result not of the lovers' being unable to have each other but of their being unable to understand each other' (p. 25). This equality in inequality is the vocation of Kierkegaard's philosophical teacher.

If we want to locate this third partner within a philosophical pedagogy, we can return to Kierkegaard's notion of indirect communication. In the *Postscript* he notes a crucial difference between thinking that is objective and thinking that is subjective. In line with the demand that there needs to be a 'form of communication suitable to each' (Kierkegaard, 1968, p. 68), Kierkegaard discusses what those forms might be. Objective knowledge is what is final, complete, and known as a result. As such, it can be copied and learned by rote. It 'imparts itself without further ado, and, at the most, takes refuge in assurances respecting its own truth, in recommendations as to its trustworthiness, and in promises that all men will at some time accept it—it is so certain' (p. 70). Indeed, such certainty, says Kierkegaard, may even be for 'the sake of the teacher, who feels the need of the security and dependability afforded by being in a majority' (p. 71).

The case with subjective knowledge is, however, entirely different. We have seen throughout this study of the philosophy of the teacher that the goal of the teacher to attend to the student thinking for himself repeats the aporetic (and unequal) relation of freedom and authority. We have also seen the irony that the more successful the teacher is in teaching someone to think for herself, the greater is the danger that the student merely re-thinks what she has been told by the teacher. Kierkegaard notes a similar problem with regard to teaching all forms of knowledge and thinking that are subjective and have their truth as activity inwardly and not outwardly. First, their characteristics differ. Objective knowledge is abstract and certain,[14] whereas subjective knowledge is always in the process of becoming, or being generated inwardly by experience. Their modes of communication are, therefore, very different. Objective knowledge can be taught directly since the subjective dispositions of teacher and taught do not affect its veracity. With subjective knowledge, however, the situation is the opposite. By definition, such knowledge is not directly transferable from one person to another. Therefore—the second point—Kierkegaard refers to the communication of subjective knowledge as containing 'a double reflection' (p. 68). 'The reflection of inwardness gives to the subjective thinker a double reflection. In thinking, he thinks the universal; but as existing in this thought and as assimilating it in his inwardness, he becomes more and more subjectively isolated' (ibid.).

Kierkegaard cites a few examples to illustrate this conundrum of communication. For example, suppose someone wanted to communicate that Truth is inwardness, that in the God-relationship each must know the truth of God inwardly. Suppose, says Kierkegaard, this teacher was 'a philanthropic soul who simply had to proclaim this to all and sundry; suppose he hit upon the excellent short cut of communicating it in a direct form through the newspapers, thus winning masses of adherents' (p. 72). His problem, of course, would be that adherents to or disciples of the message 'think for yourselves' act contrary to the truth that they espouse.[15] Indeed, Kierkegaard goes as far as to say that the truth of subjective inwardness when it attracts disciples gets bellowed out by 'town criers of inwardness' (p. 71). Such a man is 'quite a remarkable species of animal' (pp. 71–72) for he fails to see the contradiction of being a disciple of the truth of someone else's inwardness.[16] What is at stake here is the nature of the negative. The double reflection of inwardness is both the thinking of the universal and the relationship of the subject to that universal. Through the latter he becomes conscious of the negative, for truth is only as it appears for him—that is to say, it is subjective, and thus precisely its universality is negated in being known. If this, then, is the truth of the content—that it can only be known negatively—it is this truth that has to be taught. Yet it cannot be taught directly as if it were positive knowledge. So Kierkegaard says that in his relation to his knowledge, the subjective thinker is 'as negative as he is positive; for his positiveness consists in the continuous realisation of the inwardness through which he becomes conscious of the negative' (p. 78). Those disciples who then try to teach the truth of negative knowledge are like town criers trying to 'advertise, prescribe and offer for sale their beatific negative wisdom'. They are, however, 'deceived' for whilst the genuine subjective thinker of the truth of the inward 'constantly keeps the wound of the negative open', the town criers 'let the wound heal over and become positive' (ibid.).

The difference between the teacher who knows the truth of inwardness and the teacher who mis-recognises its negativity and its difficulty lies, then, in their respective modes of communication, or in their methods of teaching. The teachers who are town criers are vain because they believe that 'some other human being needs their help' (p. 73), and they hold that their interventions 'must have results' (p. 79). As such, they communicate directly the kind of knowledge that 'does not lend itself to direct utterance' (p. 73). Subjective knowledge, which is essentially negative and always in process of becoming, 'cannot', says Kierkegaard, 'be directly communicated'. Thus, 'when anyone proposes to communicate such truth directly, he proves his stupidity; and if anyone else demands this of him, he too shows that he is stupid' (ibid.).

It is easy to see here how the difference between objective and subjective knowledge that Kierkegaard describes leads to the conclusion that indirect communication avoids or perhaps overcomes the abstraction of direct communication. But this is not the truth of Kierkegaard's observations here. To teach the negative indirectly requires abstraction because the negative will be realised in the deficiencies of that abstraction. To teach the negative directly is also abstraction, for the negative is not direct. Therefore the teacher, in order to take the negative seriously, must take its abstraction seriously enough to recognise the essential part it too plays in education. Kierkegaard is not offering the teacher a choice here between *either* direct *or* indirect pedagogies in teaching for the moment or for the occasion of learning. Seen as a choice, the negative is again abstracted, this time from itself as the relation of the relation of direct and indirect communication. When Kierkegaard's dualisms are not read speculatively, their triadic truth in and as the education of self-consciousness is suppressed. This is true, in one way or another, of each of the perspectives in philosophy of education and educational theory explored above in Parts I and II. To take education seriously the teacher has to take its abstraction seriously and, indeed, teach abstraction, and be abstraction. Only in this risk is the third partner, the work, free to be itself within the conditions of its possibility. Kierkegaard offers a pedagogy of both direct and indirect communication, as we saw above, as love and as the inequality of the true as it exists. The inequality of teacher and student in the philosophy of the teacher is not optional. It is precisely where the educational substance of the relationship is to be found. The same is the case in recollection and repetition. The teacher must teach for recollection, and then be negated in repetition. It is an inequality that teaches abstractly for its own (educational) truth.

We can further understand this in terms of the master and the servant. Kierkegaard is not saying that the teacher must not try to teach the students to think for themselves. Rather, as with Hegel's and Nietzsche's philosophies of the teacher, it is the truth of the teacher to do so. There is a great deal at stake here, for Kierkegaard confers upon the recollection and repetition of doubt, and the teacher's abstraction and negation within it, the highest possible significance.

> The negativity that pervades existence, or rather, the negativity of the existing subject ... has its ground in the subject's synthesis: that he is an existing infinite spirit. The infinite and eternal is the only certainty, but as being in the subject it is in existence; and the first expression for this, is its elusiveness, and this tremendous contradiction, that the eternal becomes, that it comes into being (pp. 75–76).

The philosophical and spiritual significance of this is clear. It is in our negative experiences that the infinite and the eternal come into being, in us, as subjective and inwardly self-conscious individuals. Many people may 'know' objectively of infinity and the eternal, or of God, or of Truth, or whatever, but to know them objectively, merely as knowledge, is an illusion because in 'direct utterance the elusiveness is omitted' (p. 76).

Therefore, and on the other hand, negative thinkers who recognise the necessity of the illusion 'always have one advantage, in that they have something positive, being aware of the negative element in existence' (p. 75). The teacher of the negative is thus master of, yet also servant to, the ambivalence of subjective knowledge. Such a teacher in communicating the truth of this ambivalence remains master and servant in his own subjectivity to that ambivalence, i.e. to its being negative and positive. He is 'constantly in process of becoming . . . [he] constantly reproduces this existential situation in his thoughts, and translates all his thinking into terms of process' (p. 79). Such a teacher has his pedagogy 'in the decisive dialectic of the infinite' (p. 79f) and yet continues to teach. As such, this philosophical teacher 'is the elusiveness that pertains to the infinite in existence' (p. 79).

PHILOSOPHICAL CHARACTER

The philosophy of the teacher as we are presenting it here is not a matter merely of knowing what philosophers have said. It lies elsewhere, in the contradictory and aporetic experiences that teachers have; in the ways that these experiences both mis-recognise and recognise the work that teachers are engaged in; and, perhaps most crucially, in the meaning and significance that can be discovered within this work. There is always a temptation, however, for teachers to seek, and for theorists to provide, prescriptions as to what should be done—if, for example, one is to practise the theory under consideration. This is not the way to approach the kinds of thinking and reasoning that contribute to and constitute the philosophy of the teacher as presented here. Instead, a different question emerges for the teacher: not what should I do, but what do I learn about myself in deciding what to do? In Part I, earlier, we saw the kind of protesting spirit that could live in the equivocation of the broken middle and the failure of nerve of those who could not. We saw the courage required in the face of the overwhelming power of abstraction in modern life to hold to the commitment that our thinking must examine itself. We saw also in Part II the kinds of oppositions that thinking was likely to face in leaving and returning to the Cave, and we saw in the conclusion how Rose argued that it is in such struggles and oppositions, in one's actual work and life, that 'you discover you are a philosopher: it is not something you ever become'; it is 'a passion' (Rose, 1999, p. 42).

The philosophy of the teacher, understood in this way, speaks then of the formation of character gained in working with difficulties and oppositions, and of the significance of the learning therein. In the previous chapter we opposed Miss Marple to Deleuze's knight of faith, arguing that in Marple the transcendental is present in her passing unnoticed whilst noticing everything, and present because its re-presentation in Marple is its condition of possibility and hers. We can expand now upon the knights of faith and resignation as they appear in Kierkegaard's *Fear and Trembling*. As with Miss Marple, it is not the knight of faith himself who is imperceptible. On the contrary, his ordinariness makes him easily recognisable. He looks like 'the tax collector' (Kierkegaard, 1983, p. 39), a book-keeper, a church-goer, a husband, a bourgeois and the local butcher. What is imperceptible in him is the difficult relation between the infinite and the finite. This knight of faith only makes sense in relation to the knight who precedes him, the knight of infinite resignation. This latter, says Kierkegaard, knows the infinite but is resigned to its being impossible in the finite. This is to express the infinite spiritually for it is to know that the truth of the infinite in the finite is negative and as such is true when renounced. The knight of infinite resignation must lose the infinite in the finite in order to gain the infinite in the finite negatively, or spiritually. The ascetic is happy here for there is 'comfort in pain' (p. 45). Thus these knights 'are easily recognisable' (p. 38) for one can see the pain they suffer and the comfort they attain in suffering for the sake of the infinite in the finite.

The knight of faith, on the other hand, has found the infinite in the finite not negatively, in its renunciation, but positively. As such, *contra* the ascetic, the knight of faith gains the finite 'whole and intact' (p. 37). He too is recognisable, but says Kierkegaard (or Johannes de Silentio, Kierkegaard's pseudonym here) 'they who carry the treasure of faith are likely to disappoint for externally they have a striking resemblance to bourgeois philistinism, which infinite resignation, like faith, deeply disdains' (p. 38). The most striking thing about the knight of faith is his lack of distinguishing features. What is not easily recognised here is the infinite in the finite, the sublime in the pedestrian, or how this man of faith has faith without resignation.

Kierkegaard's discussion of the knights in terms of movement, which, as we saw above, is what Deleuze picks up on, contrasts their manner of dancing. The knights of infinite resignation are the ballet dancers who leap and return to earth, but on landing 'are unable to assume the posture immediately, they waver for a moment, and this wavering shows that they are aliens in the world' (p. 41). However, the knight of faith knows finitude to be 'the surest thing of all' (p. 40) and when he lands from his leap he shows himself able 'to come down in such a way that instantaneously [he] seems to stand and to walk, to change the leap into life into walking' (p. 41).[17] This knight does not waver on landing; indeed, there is no distinction to be seen between leaping, landing and walking, or between the infinite and the finite. But this knight of faith is not, as Deleuze would have it, the grass between the paving stones. The movement of this knight of faith is not rhizomatic. Quite the contrary. The roots of the knights are in each other, in the sky as under the ground. The knight of faith and the knight of infinite resignation exist in relation to each other; it is here, in the relation, that the absolute is known and not-known. The knight of faith has found the infinite in the renunciation of resignation and has therein, by virtue of what Kierkegaard calls the absurd, regained what was lost. The point is that it has to be lost in order that faith is found in the loss. If there is no renunciation, then faith is not absurd, and if faith is not absurd, then the infinite does not return, contradictorily, to the finite.

The relation of the knights is the same relation, seen above, of recollection and repetition. The knight of infinite resignation finds peace in suffering through recollection or in reminding himself of the fact that he does not have the eternal. This is infinite movement. The knight of faith finds peace through repetition, or in the movement of knowing the eternal in recollection. Kept separate from each other, the knight of infinite resignation never makes movement his own truth, and the knight of faith never makes truth his own movement. Together, as recollection and repetition, as infinite resignation and faith, they are the movement of truth and the truth of movement, and very different from the idea of movement that Deleuze finds here. When the observer knows what to look for, neither of the knights, nor the truth that encompasses them, is imperceptible. But the observer must not look only for movement, she must also look for the movement of movement, or the relation of learning in truth and truth in learning.

Kierkegaard has made this same argument for the teacher. The transcendent is present but unnoticed in the moment of educational decisiveness between teacher and student. The teacher, here, is the re-presentation of the eternal in its moment of inequality as love. We must not underestimate the challenge, the struggle, and the pain that such re-presentation demands of teachers. Equally, we must not underestimate the philosophical character that they display in realising the truth of such work. If the philosophy of the teacher is to contribute anything to this, it is to help all of us who teach to gain a deeper understanding of the meaning and significance of our struggles: to recognise the transcendent in our own misrecognitions. It is to Kierkegaard now, at the end of our study, that we turn finally for a philosophical, spiritual and religious examination of the character demanded for such struggles. We will make use here of some of his *Upbuilding Discourses* written between 1843 and 1844.

We saw above how doubt for Kierkegaard is the eternal and the finite in recollection and repetition. We saw also the humbling implications of this for the teacher. Knowing that in doubt 'man has a condition he cannot give himself' (1990, p. 137), and further that 'no man can give what he himself has not been given' (p. 156), the teacher finds the essentially negative truth of his work. In Kierkegaard's *Upbuilding Discourses* we find that he extends this humility beyond teaching to the struggle for nothing less than the soul. Because, as we will see, the gift of the soul is determined within the same aporia of recollection and repetition as doubt, the same human characteristics demanded by the latter are, now, also demanded by the former.

With doubt we saw that the teacher must be the occasion of the gift even though it is not hers to give. This can only be worked through or lived out in her own doubting as spiritual difficulty, and known and realised in and as the philosophy of the teacher. She cannot at any time claim to own the gift, for that would be to usurp the gift and assume the title and status of master. Twice within a few pages Kierkegaard emphasises that teachers should honour the gift by giving but should always ensure that they are 'more insignificant than the gift' (p. 147).

Equally, just because the gift is not hers, she cannot simply give up on teaching altogether and become a pious servant with no significance as the occasion or the moment for the student. What Kierkegaard says the teacher needs to do is to struggle with the complexities of the gift and with her part in its being given and received. Thus, he says,

> if you have any truth to offer mankind, reduce the impact of yourself. Nullify yourself, sacrifice yourself when offering your gift lest people take you instead of the gift ... Then you are indeed the giver, but nevertheless more insignificant than the gift, and every good and perfect gift is from above, even though it came through you (p. 151, emphasis removed).

But, the question prompts itself, does one have to believe in God to be this kind of teacher and to experience teaching as being both master and servant? The answer is far from unproblematic. Kierkegaard was not a straightforward believer in God. He questions most strongly what a believer is. For Kierkegaard God is present in all the ways that we do not understand ourselves and the world, that is, in the inequality of the relationship. He has given us the gift of doubt, and God in doubt[18] offers a potentially stronger relationship to God than one of professed belief. The only response he can make to the knights of faith—for example, Abraham—is that they have faith by virtue of the absurd. Indeed, in Kierkegaard's terms, for subjectivity to know itself in doubt is to know itself as the need for God, and further to know that the need for God is the highest perfection.

The view 'that to need God is a human being's highest perfection, does indeed make life more difficult, but it also views life according to its perfection, and in this view a person, through the piecemeal experience of [this need], which is the right understanding with God, comes *to know God*' (p. 321). In these terms there are then many ways that God can be present in the lives of teachers that do not involve being a member of a religion, or requiring church attendance, or even a professed faith. God can be present in all of the ways that a teacher embodies the philosophical struggle for the education of the student. Any teacher who is master so that she may become less than the master is involved in a spiritual struggle and, for Kierkegaard, is working on behalf of a gift that she knows is not hers to give. The teacher here, in Kierkegaard's terms, undergoes a spiritual trial, for in giving the gift that has been given, she will not directly be the master of another. The gift of doubt has a contradictory character; it will 'rob you as it gives' (p. 137) and as such its truth can only be actual negatively.

This whole experience of the negation of the teacher, brought about by her own teaching, reveals the teacher to be both master and servant. In this relationship, with its attendant difficulties and contradictions, Kierkegaard finds what he calls an *upbuilding* education.[19] Such an education is countered by the lives that people lead. Even though 'every human life is planned religiously . . . who troubles himself to think of such things? . . . one has no time . . . one grasps only what lies nearest' (Kierkegaard, 1967, p. 94).

The same commitment to the oppositions and trials of formative work in the material world also apply to the soul. The idea that one should try to gain one's soul begs the more difficult question of whether one is born with or without a soul. If born with a soul, then there is no need to gain it; if born without a soul then it is impossible to gain it, for it cannot be possessed as something external. As with doubt, the soul is not to be found in the temporal except as the inequality of the present transcendent. 'The soul is the contradiction of the temporal and the eternal, and here, therefore, the same thing can be possessed and the same thing gained and at the same time' (Kierkegaard, 1990, p. 163). As doubt could be gained and possessed in recollection and repetition, so the soul can also be gained and possessed in a similar, contradictory way. One gains one's soul in the recollection that one has lacked a soul thus far; and one possesses one's soul in the repetition of this recognition of its absence. Like doubt and the teacher, the soul for Kierkegaard is 'the infinity in the life of the world in its difference from itself' (p. 165). Or, in more detail,

> [The] soul is a self-contradiction between the external and the internal, the temporal and the eternal. It is a self-contradiction, because wanting to express the contradiction within itself is precisely what makes it what it is. Therefore, his soul is in contradiction and is self-contradiction. If it were not in contradiction, it would be lost in the life of the world; if it were not self-contradiction, movement would be impossible. It is to be possessed and gained at the same time; it belongs to the world as its illegitimate possession; it belongs to God as his legitimate possession; it belongs to the person himself as his possession, that is, as a possession that is to be gained. Consequently he gains—if he actually does gain—*his soul from God, away from the world, through himself* (pp. 166–7).

'Through himself' here opens up for us the question of character that was raised at the beginning of this section. The struggle for the soul is the struggle of the eternal in the temporal. It is, we might say, the struggle of the broken middle between truth and being. Have we the philosophical character required to live within the difficulty, to struggle to live in and work for a truth that appears everywhere as a trial of our character? Kierkegaard notes the difficulties that oppose our doing so, and foremost among them is the idea that the meaning of the difficulty is that truth cannot be known. This denial, he says, takes three forms. First, there is the person who becomes 'infatuated with temporality and worldly desires' (p. 187); who seizes 'the certainty of the moment'; 'who danced the dance of pleasure until the end' (ibid.); and who 'vanishes in the life of the world [and] has won the world' (p. 165). Second, there is what Kierkegaard calls 'false doubt'. 'False doubt doubts everything except itself' (p. 137). Such doubt, says Kierkegaard, takes 'arrogant pride in differences' (p. 142). Equality in the one is discarded for the differences, or the heterogeneity of the earthly. Third, we stop thinking altogether: 'if a person's soul comes to a standstill in the monotony of self-concern and self-preoccupation, then he is bordering on soul rot unless the contemplation stirs and moves him' (p. 207).

Kierkegaard also describes stages in this philosophical development and education. In a pathway that resembles Hegel's pathway of doubt or way of despair, Kierkegaard says:

> in the first moment, then, a person is in a position that people later crave as something glorious; he is lost in the life of the world; he possesses the world, that is, he is possessed by it. But in the same moment he is different from the whole world, and he senses a resistance that does not follow the movements of the world's life (p. 165).

At this point, in the disquiet of his separation from the world, he is in doubt. He realises that 'life is uncertain' and is 'gripped by new anxiety' (p. 185).

Faced by this anxiety, he may well respond in one of the ways described above. He may cut his losses and just gain for himself as much as possible whilst he is alive; he may become resigned to difference, forgetting that it fails to recognise its own illusion; or he may give up thinking altogether and get soul rot. In each case, Kierkegaard's warning is the same. Faced by difficulty he becomes *impatient* for some kind of decision that will move him on:

> Impatience can take many forms ... In the beginning, one scarcely recognises it—it is so gentle, so indulgent, so inviting, so encouraging, so wistful, so sympathetic—and when it has exhausted all its arts, it finally becomes loud mouthed, defiant, and wants to explain everything although it never understood a thing (p. 196).

The result? Impatience regarding the loss of the unity with the one establishes itself 'in all its agonising emptiness ... as that cold fire that consumes the soul' (ibid.). 'If unity,' he says, 'does not lie at the base of diversity, similarity at the base of dissimilarity, then everything has disintegrated ... [and] the soul is lost' (p. 193). The child and the youth are a unity with life. But life gets tougher as doubt and uncertainty become more powerful. 'The child is astonished at insignificant things. The adult has laid aside childish things; he has seen the wondrous, but it amazes him no more; there is nothing new under the sun and nothing marvellous in life' (p. 226). The child, says Kierkegaard, has an immediate relation to God but 'when one grows older, it is a long way to heaven, and the noise on earth makes it difficult to hear the voice' (p. 243). Youth has a single voice, the older voice has too many; the older one gets, 'the more complicated the accounting becomes' (p. 246). With age and experience comes doubt and the separation from God, such that 'the wrath of the separation seem[s] to make an understanding impossible' (p. 248).

The way to retrieve joy in heaven and on earth is not through impatience but rather through patience. 'Impatience is always untrue' (p. 216). Patience, however, is seen as the patience to remain with the contradictions, knowing patiently that in the contradiction is the gaining of one's soul. To have patience is, therefore, to grow in patience, and this growth is upbuilding; it is educationally formative of character, for as one grows patient, so one gains one's soul.

> The person who wants to gain his soul in patience knows that his soul does not belong to him, that there is a power from which he must gain it, a power by whom he must gain it, and that he must gain it himself. He never abandons patience, not when he has gained it, since it was indeed patience that he gained, and as soon as he gives up patience he gives up the acquisition again . . . the gain is only in patience' (p. 174).

Patience, he says, is 'joy and sorrow' (p. 189).

And what of the child, the youth and the older person? The child and the youth have no need of patience, their walking is easy, and when patience calls to them, it is of no concern to them for 'at every moment there is a world to win' (p. 195). But suddenly, at some point, and who can tell when it will be, life gets more difficult. Faced with searching now for a meaning to some difficulty in life, perhaps he now questions the glitter and vanity of the easy life; perhaps he now sees through the shallowness of his impatience? He goes on his way again, but this time the walking is much harder and others seem to pass him easily. And 'no one stayed with him for fear of being held back' (ibid.).

But patience—the truth of difficulty and struggle—'does not abandon anyone in distress' (p. 197). It knows 'to use its assistance again in order to understand in all quietness that the most crucial issues are decided slowly, little by little, not in haste and all at once' (p. 199):

> [If] a person knew how to make himself truly what he truly is—nothing— knew how to set the seal of patience on what he had understood—ah, then his life, whether he is the greatest or the lowliest, would even today be a joyful surprise and be filled with blessed wonder and would be that throughout all his days, because there is truly only one eternal object of wonder—that is God—and only one possible hindrance to wonder—and that is a person when he himself wants to be something (p. 226).

Patience is the sign of 'a healthy soul in the temporal' (p. 259). The greater our anxiety, the greater our patience. Such expectancy, Kierkegaard says, 'will reconcile everyone with his neighbour, with his friend, and with his enemy in an understanding of the essential' (p. 265). How? Because we know that what we give is already given, and that what we hope for is already here. Thus Kierkegaard's maxim for serving truth in life is the truly difficult: 'He must increase; but I must decrease' (John,

3, 30).[20] And for the teacher, in the philosophy of the teacher, we can read this as 'learning must increase; but I, *as teacher*, must decrease'.

Herein then is Kierkegaard's upbuilding education, or formation and re-formation of philosophical and spiritual character. Here also is the import of Kierkegaard's philosophy of the teacher; not merely knowledge but the struggle of its being known and not-known, of its certainty and uncertainty. This philosophy of the teacher is wherever one finds the teacher struggling patiently as master to serve the student's own education. Really good teachers know humility, as much as they know mastery, for they understand that however much is achieved in their classrooms by students, the work that is required by teachers is to make themselves unnecessary. So often one finds dedicated teachers humbly stepping back at the moments of greatest educational significance for the student.

Even more difficult, as we noted previously, teachers know that they may never see the fruits of their labours, for the work they have done may only bear fruit many years later. For Kierkegaard this humility in the face of the gift of education, a humility in which teachers recognise they have to be master in order to be servant, is education as God's work, as love's work. Whether teachers are religious in a formal sense or not, the work they do is spiritual work: they are willingly putting themselves forward in the truth of mis-recognition, as teachers, in order that the truth of philosophical experience and education be actual and not suppressed. This is the sacrifice that teachers make: not just to work for others but also to be themselves, to be teachers. This struggle is the teachers' own inner struggle. It is their education about the kinds of persons they are, but it is an education generated by their work with students. Kierkegaard goes as far as to say that a truly spiritual person continually learns through their work that 'the highest is this: that a person is fully convinced that he himself is capable of nothing, nothing at all' (p. 307). To the judgement on Kierkegaard here that such piety is as misplaced as it is impossible, the response must be that this, precisely, is the point! To become nothing in the truth of the occasion of educational significance means that we must also risk being the something that we already are—the teacher! Only in the risk of this work with the student can the teacher realise 'the condition for coming to know himself' (p. 317).

NOTES

1. Kierkegaard re-presents this problematic relationship between the beginning and the end of a system within his own work. The complex relationship between the *Philosophical Fragments* and its *Concluding Unscientific Postscript* is rehearsed by Kierkeggard at the beginning of the later text, raising the question as to whether the *Postscript* is a conclusion, an addendum, and a system. For a discussion of this, see Mulhall, 2001, Part Three.
2. It is for this reason that I speak of Kierkegaard in this chapter rather than refer to his pseudonyms. *Contra* Kierkegaard, we can see the author as the speculative relation of direct and indirect communication. To use only the pseudonyms is to suppress the third partner that Kierkegaard is commending us to recognise.
3. Except perhaps in one sense. A beginning is made with nothing in the life and death struggle as it appears in the *Phenomenology*. Nothing, or death, is determinate in the struggle, and life itself is

only this determinate negation. Nothing *happens*, as it were. The *Science of Logic* also ends with this subjectivity of life.

4. This acts as an argument for McPherson against Wittgenstein's reading of Kierkegaard as private and mentalistic (McPherson, 2001, p. 162).

5. In this ambivalence between Kierkegaard and Hegel, McPherson argues that we, the reader, in seeking to place or identify Kierkegaard's philosophy too abstractly, or too directly, may 're-enact Hegel in our attempts to appropriate or apply, place or dismiss, Kierkegaard himself' (McPherson, 2001, p. 159).

6. Perhaps in some ways this is similar in nature to the concept of influence seen earlier in Buber: to inspire by influence but not by interference.

7. I have argued elsewhere, to the contrary, that the master–slave relation is the whole of Hegel's philosophy; see Tubbs, 2004, Chapter 2. In addition, of course, the structure of the philosophy of the teacher as I have been presenting it grounds its inequality within the master–slave relation.

8. I do not think this is what McPherson intends, arguing as he is for opening the problematic of the inequality of indirect (and direct) communication, but it is the inevitable result of trying to impose the mutual onto a relation of inequality.

9. Johannes de Silentio and Johannes Climacus are two of the pseudonyms employed by Kierkegaard in his writing.

10. In 1841 Kierkegaard was awarded the Magister Artium diploma. This Magister degree corresponded, however, to the PhD in other faculties of the University of Copenhagen, a recognition made in the public announcement of Kierkegaard's success. All those holding such degrees were declared to be Doctors of Philosophy in 1854 when the Magister degree was abolished.

11. The triadic nature of both thinkers was also explored earlier in Chapter 1.

12. A referee pointed out the obviousness of this observation. On the contrary, it is precisely the relation of the teacher as teacher and student that is the substance of the philosophy of the teacher. It may be obvious in an abstract sense, but it is the substance of difficulty in a philosophical sense.

13. Love, here, *contra* McPherson, is not any kind of mutuality. It is the inequality of God and man known as inequality in the relation of inequality.

14. Although it is part of Kierkegaard's argument that such knowledge is not certain at all. See, for example, Kierkegaard, 1968, p. 71f.

15. Kierkegaard notes of Lessing that he prevented any following of disciples, 'fearing to be made ridiculous through repetitioners who reproduce what is said like a prattling echo' (Kierkegaard, 1968, p. 67).

16. As we saw earlier in Chapter 7, it is the same dilemma that Nietzsche's Zarathustra is forced to re-present, eternally, as the teacher of the eternal return of will to power.

17. In *Philosophical Fragments*, Kierkegaard, as Climacus, says of himself 'I have trained myself and am training myself always to be able to dance lightly in the service of thought' (Kierkegaard, 1985, p. 7). He adds, 'all I have is my life, which I promptly stake every time a difficulty appears. Then it is easy to dance, for the thought of death is a good dancing partner, my dancing partner' (p, 8).

18. And, of course, doubt in God.

19. See also Tubbs, 2003c.

20. This forms the title of one of Kierkegaard's *Discourses*; see Kierkegaard, 1990, pp. 275–289.

References

Adorno, T. W. (1973) *Negative Dialectics* (London, Routledge & Kegan Paul).
Adorno, T. W. (1991) *The Culture Industry*, ed. J. Bernstein (London, Routledge).
Adorno, T. W. (1992) Why Philosophy?, in: D. Ingram and J. Simon-Ingram, *Critical Theory: the essential readings* (New York, Paragon House).
Adorno, T. W. (1999) *Walter Benjamin and Theodor W. Adorno, The Complete Correspondence 1928–1940*, ed. H. Lonitz, trans. N. Walker (Cambridge, Polity Press).
Adorno, T. W. (2000) *Metaphysics: concepts and problems* (Cambridge, Polity Press).
Adorno, T. W. (2003) *Can One Live After Auschwitz? A Philosophical Reader*, ed. R Tiedemann (Stanford, Stanford University Press).
Adorno, T. W. and Horkheimer, M. (1979) *Dialectic of Enlightenment* (London, Verso).
Althusser, L. (1984) *Essays on Ideology* (London, Verso).
Anderson, D. (1971) *Simone Weil* (London, SCM Press Ltd.).
Barnett, R. (2000) *Realising the University in an Age of Aupercomplexity* (Buckingham, Open University Press).
Bauman, Z. (1989) *Modernity and the Holocaust* (Cambridge, Polity Press).
Bauman, Z. (1992) *Intimations of Postmodernity* (London, Routledge).
Bearn, G. (2000) The University of Beauty, in: P. Dhillon and P. Standish (eds) *Lyotard: just education* (London, Routledge), pp. 230–258.
Berlin, I. (1999) *The First and the Last* (London, Granta Books).
Benjamin, W. (1985) *The Origin of German Tragic Drama* (London, Verso).
Benjamin, W. (1992) *Illuminations* (London, Fontana Press).
Binder, F. M. (1970) *Education in the History of Western Civilization* (London, Macmillan).
Blake, N., Smeyers, P., Smith, R. and Standish, P. (2000) *Education in and Age of Nihilism* (London, RoutledgeFalmer).
Blake, N., Smeyers, P., Smith, R. and Standish, P. (eds) (2003) *The Blackwell Guide to the Philosophy of Education* (Oxford, Blackwell).
Bottomore, T. and Nisbet, R. (1978) *A History of Sociological Analysis* (London, Heinemann).
Buber, M. (1947) *Between Man and Man* (Glasgow, Collins).
Buber, M. (1967) *On Judaism* (New York, Schocken Books).
Buber, M. (1987) *I and Thou* (New York, Collier Books).
Buber, M. (1997) *Israel and the World, Essays in a Time of Crisis* (USA, Syracuse University Press).
Buber, M. (1998) *The Knowledge of Man: selected essays* (New York, Humanity Books).
Buber, M. (2002) *The Martin Buber Reader: Essential Writings*, ed. A. D. Biemann (New York, Palgrave Macmillan).
Burbules, N. and Hansen, D. (1997) *Teaching and its Predicaments* (Colorado, Westview Press).
Carr, D. (1998) *Education, Knowledge and Truth: Beyond the Postmodern Impasse* (London, Routledge).
Carr, D. (2003) *Making Sense of Education* (London, RoutledgeFalmer).
Climacus, J. (1982) *The Ladder of Divine Ascent* (New Jersey, Paulist Press).
Cohen, J. (2003) *Interrupting Auschwitz* (New York, Continuum).
Comenius, J. A. (1910) *The Great Didactic* (Montana, Kessinger Publishing Company).
Cox O'Rourke, K. (2002) *The Truth of Doubt: an exploration of doubt in Hegel, Kierkegaard and Weil*. Unpublished dissertation, University of Winchester.
Craig, D. (1969) *Hard Times* (Harmondsworth, Penguin).
Cubberley, E. P. (1920) *The History of Education* (London, Constable & Co.).

Deleuze, G. (1983) *Nietzsche and Philosophy* (New York, Columbia University Press).

Deleuze, G. (1994) *Difference and Repetition* (London, The Athlone Press).

Deleuze, G. and Parnet, C. (2002) *Dialogues II* (London, Continuum).

Derrida, J. (1992) *The Gift of Death* (Chicago, University of Chicago Press).

Dhillon, P. A. and Standish, P. (2000) *Lyotard: Just Education* (London, Routledge).

Dickens, C. (1969) *Hard Times* (Harmondsworth, Penguin).

Ellsworth, E. (1997) *Teaching Positions: Difference, Pedagogy and the Power of Address* (Columbia, Teachers College Press).

Evans, K. (1975) *The Development and Structure of the English Educational System* (London, University of London Press).

Farias, V. (1989) *Heidegger and Nazism* (Philadelphia, Temple University Press).

Foucault, M. (1973) *The Birth of the Clinic* (London, Routledge).

Foucault, M. (1977) *Discipline and Punish* (Harmondsworth, Penguin).

Foucault, M. (1980) *Power/Knowledge* (New York, Harvester Wheatsheaf).

Freire, P. (1972) *Pedagogy of the Oppressed* (London, Penguin).

Freire, P. (1995) *Paulo Freire at the Institute* (London, Institute of Education, University of London).

Frost, C. and Bell-Metereau, R. (1998) *Simone Weil: On Politics, Religion and Society* (London, Sage Publications).

Giroux, H. (1992) *Border Crossings: Cultural Workers and the Politics of Education* (New York, Routledge).

Gur-Ze'ev, I. (2003a) *Destroying the Other's Collective Memory* (New York, Peter Lang Publishing Group, Inc.).

Gur-Ze'ev, I. (2003b) *Bildung* and Critical Theory in the Face of Postmodern Education, in: L. Løvlie, K. P. Mortensen and S. E. Nordenbo (eds) *Educating Humanity: Bildung in Postmodernity* (Oxford, Blackwell).

Hansen, D. (2001) *Exploring the Moral Heart of Teaching: towards a teacher's creed* (New York, Teacher's College Press).

Harris, H. S. (1997) Hegel's Correspondence Theory of Truth, in: G. K. Browning (ed) *Hegel's Phenomenology of Spirit: a reappraisal* (Dordrecht, Kluwer Academic Publishers), pp. 1–10.

Hegel, G. W. F. (1956) *The Philosophy of History* (New York, Dover Publications).

Hegel, G. W. F. (1969) *Science of Logic* (London, George Allen & Unwin Ltd.).

Hegel, G. W. F. (1975) *Hegel's Logic* (Oxford, Oxford University Press).

Hegel, G. W. F. (1977) *Phenomenology of Spirit* (Oxford University Press).

Hegel, G. W. F. (1984a) *Lectures on the Philosophy of Religion volume 1: Introduction and The Concept of Religion* (Berkeley, University of California Press).

Hegel, G. W. F. (1984b) *Hegel: The Letters* (Bloomington, Indiana University Press).

Heidegger, M. (1982) *The Basic Problems of Phenomenology* (Bloomington, Indiana University Press).

Heidegger, M. (1992) *Being and Time* (Oxford, Blackwell).

Huxley, A. (1977) *Brave New World* (London, Grafton).

Jarvis, S. (1998) *Adorno: a critical introduction* (Cambridge, Polity Press).

Kant, I. (1990) *Foundations of the Metaphysics of Morals*, trans. Lewis White Beck (New York, Macmillan).

Kant, I. (1991) *Political Writings*, ed. H. Reiss (Cambridge, Cambridge University Press).

Keneally, T. (1983) *Schindler's Ark* (London, Coronet).

Kierkegaard, S. (1967) *The Concept of Dread*, trans. W. Lowrie (Princeton, Princeton University Press).

Kierkegaard, S. (1968) *Concluding Unscientific Postscript*, trans. W. Lowrie (Princeton, Princeton University Press).

Kierkegaard, S. (1983) *Fear and Trembling/Repetition* (Princeton, Princeton University Press).

Kierkegaard, S. (1985) *Philosophical Fragments/Johannes Climacus* (Princeton, Princeton University Press).

Kierkegaard, S. (1989) *The Concept of Irony* (Princeton, Princeton University Press).

Kierkegaard, S. (1990) *Eighteen Upbuilding Discourses* (Princeton, Princeton University Press).

Kohli, W. (1995) *Critical Conversations in Philosophy of Education* (New York, Routledge).

Kojève, A. (1969) *Introduction to the Reading of Hegel* (Ithaca, Cornell University Press).

Krell, D. F. (1993) *Martin Heidegger: Basic Writings* (London, Routledge).

Lawton, D. (1992) *Education and Politics in the 1990s* (London, The Falmer Press).

Locke, J. (1975) *An Essay Concerning Human Understanding* (Oxford, Clarendon Press).

Luther, M. (1989) *Martin Luther's Basic Theological Writings*, ed. T. F. Lull (Minneapolis, Fortress Press).

Lyotard, J.-F. (1984) *The Postmodern Condition: A Report on Knowledge* (Manchester, Manchester University Press).

Lyotard, J.-F. (1992) *The Postmodern Explained to Children* (London, Turnaround).

Massumi, B. (1998) 'Deleuze', in: S. Critchley and W. R. Schroeder (eds) *A Companion to Continental Philosophy* (Oxford, Blackwell).

Mackenzie (1909) *Hegel's Educational Theory and Practice* (London, Swann Sonnenschein).

McLaren, P. (1997) *Revolutionary Multiculturalism* (Oxford, Westview Press).

McPherson, I. (2001) Kierkegaard as an Educational Thinker: Communication Through and Across Ways of Being, *Journal of Philosophy of Education*, 35.2, pp. 157–174.

Miles, S. (1986) *Simone Weil, an Anthology* (London, Virago Press Ltd.).

Monroe, P. (1905) *A Text-Book in the History of Education* (New York, Macmillan).

Montaigne, M. (1958) *Essays* (Harmondsworth, Penguin).

Montessori, M. (1964) *The Montessori Method* (New York, Schocken Books).

Montessori, M. (1965) *Dr. Montessori's Own Handbook* (New York, Schocken Books).

Mulhall, S. (2001) *Inheritance and Originality* (Oxford, Clarendon Press).

Murphy, D. (1988) *Martin Buber's Philosophy of Education* (Blackrock, Irish Academic Press).

Murphy, D. (1995) Comenius: a critical re-assessment of his life and work (Blackrock, Irish Academic Press).

Neill, A. S. (1962) *Summerhill* (London, Pelican Books).

Nietzsche, F. (1968) *Basic Writings of Nietzsche* (New York, The Modern Library).

Nietzsche, F. (1979) *Ecce Homo* (London, Penguin).

Nietzsche, F. (1982) *The Portable Nietzsche*, trans. W. Kaufmann (New York, The Viking Press).

Nietzsche, F. (1983) *Untimely Meditations*, trans. R. J. Hollingdale (Cambridge, Cambridge University Press).

Noddings, N. (2003) *Caring: a feminine approach to ethics and moral education* (Berkeley, University of California).

Oppenheim, M. (1985) *What does Revelation Mean for the Modern Jew? Rosenzweig, Buber, Fackenheim* (New York, The Edwin Mellen Press).

Parker, S. (1997) *Reflective teaching in the Postmodern World* (Buckingham, Open University Press).

Pestalozzi, J. H. (1966) *How Gertrude Teaches Her Children* (London, Quantum Reprints).

Pike, A. (2004) *The Search for Truth: either/or . . . or truth*. Unpublished dissertation, University of Winchester.

Plato (1956) *Protagoras and Meno* (Harmondsworth, Penguin).

Plato (1969) *The Last Days of Socrates* (Harmondsworth, Penguin).

Plato (1987) *Theaetetus* (Harmondsworth, Penguin).

Plato (1992) *The Republic* (London, Dent).

Peters, M. (2002) *Heidegger, Education, and Modernity* (Lanham, Rowman & Littlefield Publishers).

Popper, K. (1962) *The Open Society and its Enemies, Volume 1 Plato* (London, Routledge).

Pring, R. (1984) *Personal and Social Education in the Curriculum* (London, Hodder & Staughton).

Quintilian (1921) *Institutio Oratoria Volume 1* (London, Heinemann).

Ramaekers, S. (2001) Teaching to Lie and Obey: Nietzsche on Education, *Journal of Philosophy of Education*, 35.2, pp. 255–268.

Rogers, C. R. (1969) *Freedom to Learn* (Columbus, Charles E. Merrill Publishing Company).

Rose, G. (1978) *The Melancholy Science: an introduction to the work of Theodor W. Adorno* Basingstoke, Macmillan.

Rose, G. (1981) *Hegel Contra Sociology* (London, Athlone).

Rose, G. (1984) *Dialectic of Nihilism* (Oxford, Blackwell).

Rose, G. (1992) *The Broken Middle* (Oxford, Blackwell).

Rose, G. (1993) *Judaism and Modernity* (Oxford, Blackwell).

Rose, G. (1995) *Loves Work* (London, Chatto & Windus).

Rose, G. (1996) *Mourning Becomes the Law* (Cambridge, Cambridge University Press).

Rose, G. (1998) Walter Benjamin—out of the sources of modern Judaism, in: L. Marcus and L. Nead (eds) *The Actuality of Walter Benjamin* (London, Lawrence & Wishart).

Rose, G. (1999) *Paradiso* (London, Menard Press).

Rousseau, J. J. (1973) *The Social Contract and Discourses* (London, Dent).

Rousseau, J. J. (1993) *Emile* (London, Dent).

Schön, D. A. (1987) *Educating the Reflective Practitioner* (California, Jossey-Bass Publishers).

Silver, P. and Silver, H. (1974) *The Education of the Poor* (London, RKP).

Smith, A. (1958) *The Wealth of Nations, Volume Two* (London, Dent).

Sylvester, D. W. (1974) *Robert Lowe and Education* (Cambridge, Cambridge University Press).

Tubbs, N. (1996) Hegel's Educational Theory and Practice, *British Journal of Educational Studies*, 44.2, pp. 181–199.

Tubbs, N. (1997) *Contradiction of Enlightenment: Hegel and the broken middle* (Aldershot, Ashgate).

Tubbs, N. (2003a) The Concept of Teachability, *Educational Theory*, 53.1, pp. 75–90.

Tubbs, N. (2003b) Return of the Teacher, *Educational Philosophy and Theory*, 35.1, pp. 71–88.

Tubbs, N. (2003c) For and Of the Truth: 'upbuilding' higher education in Church Colleges, *Journal of Philosophy of Education*, 37.1, pp. 53–69.

Tubbs, N. (2004) *Philosophy's Higher Education* (Dordrecht, Kluwer).

Tubbs, N. and Grimes, J. (2001) What is Education Studies?, *Educational Studies*, 27.1, pp. 3–15.

Usher, R. and Edwards, R. (1994) *Postmodernism and Education* (London, Routledge).

Vanderstraeten, R. and Biesta, G. J. J. (2001) How is education possible? Preliminary investigations for a theory of education, *Educational Philosophy and Theory*, 33.1, pp. 7–21.

Weil, S. (1977) *Waiting On God* (London, Fount Classics).

Weil, S. (1987) *Gravity and Grace* (London, Routledge).

Weil, S. (1988) *Oppression and Liberty* (London, Routledge & Kegan Paul).

Weil, S. (1995) *The Need For Roots* (London, Routledge).

Williams, R. R. (1997) *Hegel's Ethics of Recognition* (Berkeley, University of California Press).

Wolin, R. (1993) *The Heidegger Controversy* (London, The MIT Press).

Index

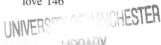
UNIVERSITY OF WINCHESTER
LIBRARY

UNIVERSITY OF MANCHESTER
LIBRARY